7/7

AFTER
THE DANCE

To
HENNIE SWART
for generous help and candid insights

AFTER THE DANCE

Travels in a democratic South Africa

DAVID ROBBINS

JONATHAN BALL PUBLISHERS

Johannesburg & Cape Town

Published in 2004 in trade paperback by
JONATHAN BALL PUBLISHERS (PTY) LTD
P O Box 33977
Jeppestown
2043

ISBN 1 86842 193 7

Cover design by Michiel Botha
Cover image: Gallo Images
Typesetting and reproduction of text by Alinea Studio, Cape Town
Printed and bound by CTP Book Printers, Duminy Street, Parow, Cape

Contents

PROLOGUE
1   From the outside   3

PART ONE
2   The corridor   25
3   Beyond the mall   42
4   Heading west   71

PART TWO
5   In the desert   85
6   Finding the past   104
7   Sacred sites   122

PART THREE
8   Old homeland   141
9   Girl at the river   161
10 Dividing the spoils   184

PART FOUR
11 The merger   209
12 In between   225
13 No longer fishing   247

EPILOGUE
14 Ending in mist   267

PROLOGUE

Maputo

So here it was, the African pattern. First the struggle, then the euphoria of the freedom dance, then the collapse into grandiose caricature and chaos. And after that, the pale new dawn, the promise and sometimes the reality of ascent.

1
From the outside

ON MY first day in Maputo the clouds grew dark and it began to rain. Although people said this was the first rain of the season, the city seemed already used to clouds and damp. The buildings of the central business district stood in stained and unpainted tiers, rising from the leaden waters of the estuary. The buildings were multi-storeyed, essentially modern in feel, but they had from a distance a somewhat decrepit look that was intensified as the rain began afresh to streak their tall sides. These were the first glimpses I got of the city from the balcony of my hotel room. I saw also a white church below me with bushes and lank weeds growing in those places of the silver-painted roof where the drainage had failed; and beyond the church, the solid shape of a colonial-style structure with wide steps and columns adorning its grandiose front.

When the first strong shower had subsided I walked in the streets, going to see a woman named Dr Maria Tumbi. Potholes were full to overflowing and the mounds of rubbish in the side streets had been thoroughly doused. I stepped over brown rivulets of slime, and over several two-dimensional rats squashed flat by passing tyres, part mummified, but still with their eyes staring and their long tails intact. The rubbish heaps stank in the humid air. I walked in Avenida Ho Chi Min, then cut up a side street to Avenida 24 de Julho and later to Avenida Eduardo Mondlane. These main streets were crowded with traffic and pavement stalls. The sign-writing was in Portuguese; but the noise and colour, even on that grey day, was spontaneously African.

It seemed strange, all at once, that I should begin my travels through a democratic South Africa in a foreign country. Yet it was as inevitable. During the 1980s, when I had first begun to travel in South Africa, there was little thought of a continental context except in so far as that context constituted a threat to white domination. Even in the early

3

1990s, as South Africa prepared for its first democratic embrace and the borders became demilitarised and easier to traverse, there was little appreciation of the rest of Africa – except as the source of worrying numbers of illegal immigrants. Now, though, as the century had turned and economic imperatives had replaced those of national defence, the need to look in from the outside, for a few moments at least, seemed important. South Africa had already begun to dominate the southern region of the continent. As significantly, regional trends were making an impact inside South Africa. The intellectual isolation was receding as the physical isolation broke down. That is why, looking into Maputo plate-glass shop fronts, my reflection caught in the downtown throng did not seem too strange. South Africa was at last, in the words of John Donne, a part of the main.

Maria Tumbi said: 'Yes, there are outward signs of a new prosperity in Mozambique, in Maputo especially. Yes, there are advantages to be had in a new relationship with South Africa, via the so-called Maputo Corridor. But this is not an easy issue, trying to develop an impoverished country by giving emphasis to foreign investment. We'll have to devise real and effective ways of getting the investments to filter down directly into our poverty reduction programmes.'

Her eyes seemed slightly enlarged behind her spectacles. She was a small woman, very neat, very precise, regarding me from across the table in a boardroom dominated by several potted palm trees and the rattle of a well-used air conditioner. She wore, I noticed, a delicate crucifix at her throat.

Maria spoke – she had mentioned that her doctorate was in economics – of the damage to the country that colonialism had wrought – even though it had also brought Catholicism. Then she spoke with some nostalgia of the Marxist period in Mozambique.

'It made us proud to be Mozambican, and we had a collective sense of belonging,' she said in her quiet way. 'Then there was this move to capitalism and large foreign investments. People got very excited. The emphasis shifted to individuals. People cared only about themselves. Some of us said that this was simply a new form of colonialism. Whatever you care to call it, we have definitely lost something in the recent economic process.'

'What is it that you've lost?' I asked.

She looked at me with her slightly enlarged eyes. 'It was something spiritual, some sense of community that capitalism tends to destroy.'

Outside in the street it had once more begun to rain. On the wall of a building against which I sought shelter I saw the Mozambican coat of arms. In its design was depicted an agricultural implement, an automatic rifle, a book – all brought together before a rising sun. Such idealism and hope, I thought, expressed by a people who had been more or less colonised for 500 years. For centuries the Portuguese had extracted and exported Mozambican gold, ivory and slaves. Even into the 20th century, slaves were being shipped to the New World and to other Portuguese colonies in Africa. Throughout the second third of that century Portuguese settlers were encouraged to emigrate to Mozambique where they were given land and labour. Lorenço Marques (since independence called Maputo) began to look like a tropical Lisbon with swarthy Europeans and fair-skinned South Africans mingling on the palm-fringed beaches and street cafés in places that now reeked of decomposing rubble. By the early 1960s, the final guerrilla war against the Portuguese had begun. But it would take another decade and a half for independence to be achieved – in 1975 – and a new Marxist African state under the presidency of Samora Machel to be born. But the country was plunged into almost immediate civil war, with South Africa playing a major but dubious role. At last peace had come when the ruling party abandoned its Marxist philosophies and ended one-party rule, thereby paving the way for the increasing investments – not least from Australia, Japan, Britain and other European countries, and also of course from South Africa – that had characterised the 1990s and that were giving Dr Tumbi some cause for concern.

Back at the hotel I received a message from a South African I had been advised to contact while in Maputo: 'a remarkable businesswoman' named Diana. 'Catch the ferry to Catembe in time for twelve noon tomorrow,' Diana said. 'I'll meet you then.'

CATEMBE WAS clearly visible on the southern side of the Maputo estuary as a grey stretch of low-lying land studded with buildings and clusters of trees. The staff at my hotel showed me the position of the pier on the map, and I drove down through crowded streets that after-noon to make sure I would be able to find it in the morning. The har-bour lay spread out along the waterfront to the west of the pier; to the east stood the open sea. The sea-front road – Avenida da Marginal – went on for kilometres beside the palm trees and beaches which, prior to independence, had attracted hundreds of thousands of South African holiday-makers each year. After independence, of course, this flow had dwindled to nothing. Now it was beginning again. All along the beach-front stood new developments still in the building. South African money was pouring in. One South African explained what spectacular returns he would get on his investment, adding, however, that he needed to 'go back home every now and then for a bit of normality'. He smiled knowingly as he explained: 'It's very black here, as you can imagine.'

Black enough on the extensive beach front, as I drove slowly along it, wondering if Diana would display a similar arrogance. Young men in unbuttoned shirts sold fish fresh from the sea. Other people cooked on open fires, the smoke drifting between the palm trees. The old rondavel resorts of the colonial era, quite close to the new Holiday Inn, were empty now, thatch collapsing, walls crumbling, and soon to be cleared to make way for another bright brush stroke of the new. The Holiday Inn itself attempted a mediaeval Portuguese flavour through heavily beamed ceilings, archways, tiles. Nouveau colonial with guests to match, dipping their toes into the edge of the blackness of this African resort. Meanwhile, in the roadway, a few ragged beggars mingled with a crowd of crows. One of the beggars staggered grotesquely on crutches, and I wondered if he had stood on a land mine during the years of civil war. As if in mockery of this, here was a limping crow, a wing spread and its beak open as it floundered forward.

The sea was calm against the shore, the sky a rain-laden grey; and on the landward side of the road I noticed a row of lavishly flowering trees that had spread a carpet of pale pink petals on the pavements below. And later on I saw the property boom continue: lavish beach-front houses, security fences, electric gates, evidence of closed-circuit televi-sion cameras, and of course those ubiquitous satellite dishes staring so steadfastly in another direction.

Outside a large restaurant called the Costa del Sol, Mozambicans from the country were selling polished carvings and musical instruments under the palms. They began at one stage to make a strange percussive music. Other people sold beers and cool drinks out of polystyrene cool-boxes. On the beach beyond, seine nets had been spread out, figures moving among them, boats pulled onto the sand, women waiting with baskets and plastic buckets. Further out, people waded in the sea or walked on the sand banks which the ebbing tide revealed. The sense came to me of a people at peace, preoccupied with their work, laughing and chattering together, drinking languidly and leaving their empty tins and bottles among the lines of debris washed onto the higher reaches of the sand.

It came to me quite strongly, also, the idea of a colonial and post-colonial pattern in Africa of which Mozambique was a prime example. First there was the struggle, varying in intensity and length according to the colonial masters as well as the level of settler involvement. In both Anglophone and Francophone West Africa, for example, no settler populations had been established to bedevil the urge for independence. In most countries in the central, eastern and southern regions, however, the situation had not been as simple. The struggles had been long and bitter, particularly in the Portuguese territories, and independence hard-won. Then there was the phenomenon of the post-independence collapse. Most colonial economies were geared to the provision of raw materials. Therefore their wellbeing was dependent on commodity prices controlled by demand rather than supply. The Francophone countries, still linked to the French franc, fared better than the rest. Elsewhere, economies staggered close to collapse. The state, with its ability to borrow on the international market and its access to donor funding, became the only viable option for individual and group economic interests. Coups d'état became the order of the day. The scent of civil war was everywhere. Dictators and saviours arose who often did little more than continue to torture their people in order most fabulously and grotesquely to enrich themselves. Corruption and incompetence added their own unique flavours, and ultimately many millions of African people tasted the bile of their national descent into political and economic perdition.

So here it was, the African pattern. First the struggle, then the euphoria of the freedom dance, then the collapse into grandiose caricature and chaos. And after that, the pale new dawn, the promise and sometimes the reality of ascent. This last phase in the African pattern seemed to come in many guises: economic structural adjustment, debt relief, multi-party democracy, abandonment of socialist experiments, free enterprise, new partnerships with the developed world, neo-colonialism, regional development endeavours, and also the growing resolve of another generation of Africans to live their lives in peace and prosperity. It was some inkling of this that I caught among the people going about their business under the gently waving Maputo palms.

At the northern end of Maputo's long beaches, the road changed from tarmac to rutted sand, and on the seaward side there appeared large sand banks filled with coarse vegetation and drifts of black-looking rubble. Tiny houses and shacks of grass and cardboard appeared. Stagnant water lay in ponds, and sometimes the vegetation had succumbed to an excess of salt, with only blackened stumps remaining. The faces of the people who lived at this end of the city looked out at me unsmiling as I drove.

I STROLLED out of my hotel in the afternoon to take a closer look at the big white church and colonial-style building I had seen from my balcony. In front of the church lay an extensive square on several levels, empty save for a few youths who called 'hey, amigo' in my direction. I guessed the church had been built in the 1930s. The tall spire reached upwards in steps, with large louvres on four sides near the top, a stopped clock, and tall sequences of stained-glass squares adorning the facade. Many of the squares had been broken, and in some places the glass seemed to have been ripped out, including the lead surrounds. Beer bottles lay on the church steps, and an unkempt dog was eating something among the narrow buttresses. A youth sped by on roller skates. The church needed paint, needed repair, and that was not so surprising in a country emerging from the rigours of civil war and the doctrinaire atheism of Marxism. But I thought fleetingly of the delicate crucifix at the throat of Maria Tumbi as well, providing as it did the comfort of anomaly.

The colonial-style building turned out to have something to do with the Maputo municipality. It stood, an imposing grey presence, at the top of rigid rows of steps. At the colonnaded entrance I passed a few guards, one of them sitting on a plastic chair with a sub-machine-gun across his knees. They returned my greeting affably enough. Inside I found myself in a large entrance hall dominated by a handsome staircase curving upstairs. The entrance was empty save for a few large models of Lorenço Marques, one depicting the settlement as long ago as 1883. Here were houses set down in orderly rows between the bush and the sea, with a palisaded military fort to one side. Another model, undated, showed a railway marshalling yard and ships at a long straight quay. This would have been the culmination of President Paul Kruger's railway that in 1895 linked the landlocked Transvaal Republic to the sea.

But the building itself reclaimed my attention. An intricate chandelier hung from the ceiling, and the stairs were of marble. The brass fittings on each step to keep the carpet in place still existed, but the carpet was no more. On the landing, a stained-glass window depicted a small sailing vessel riding a boisterous sea.

'Vasco da Gama's ship. He came in 1498,' said a stout perspiring man I had discovered in an office downstairs. I had asked if he knew when the building had been erected. He said, dabbing at his face with a white handkerchief, that he thought it had been around 1947. And here in one corner of the stained-glass window depicting Da Gama's ship was a date that confirmed this vintage.

It seemed almost startlingly recent for so solid a construction. Had there been no inkling, then in the early post-war years, of what might happen during the second half of the 20th century? 'You may come upstairs,' the man said in an amiable voice.

So we continued to the first floor and entered a large room, extending the width of the building itself, with prominent undraped windows although some were still fitted with curtain rods, and a superb moulded ceiling. 'This must have been a ballroom,' I remarked; 'can you imagine the dances?'

'The hall is never used,' the stout man said. He took my arm and led me into an antechamber near the stairs. 'See. Here is all the furniture stored.'

It stood piled up against the walls: upholstered chairs with ornately carved backs, and scores of narrow server tables in a similar style. Everything was smothered in dust, and the upholstery was dirty. And the thought persisted of taffeta and satin and the bare shoulders of women, and men in black attire, perhaps even clicking their heels, and the orchestra over there probably, playing waltzes and old quadrilles. But when the colonial power had lost its will to govern, then another dance began. The streets had rung with Marxist slogans, and the power of the colonial had melted away. But there was no sign of waste in this grandiose building, so illustrative of colonial pomposity, yet so untouched. Perhaps the carpets and the curtains had been recycled, but the furniture had not been broken and the building itself had survived unscathed. Even the models of the early settlements were still intact. The overarching sense was not of any apocalypse, but rather the way the passing of time increasingly magnified the irrelevance of all the building stood for.

My stout guide presently excused himself, and I made my way downstairs to look once more at the models of the earlier times. I was stooping forward to examine the detail of the railway and harbour, thinking of Kruger's exit after the first phase of the Anglo-Boer War had been lost, when someone coughed politely behind me.

'I am apologising for disturbing you,' said a smiling, deferential security guard who carried his cap in his hands.

'You aren't at all,' I said.

'But I must ask what you are doing.'

'I'm looking at these models.'

'But I have to give permission.'

'There's a man in that office over there. He said I was most welcome. He even took me upstairs.'

'I know that,' the guard said, stepping confidentially closer. 'But he is only administration. I am security. I have to know why you are here. I have to ask you that.'

'Well, I was curious to see inside. That's really the only reason.'

The guard would have said more, but I bade him farewell and walked out into a renewed drizzle before he could get any closer to actually demanding a small gratuity.

ALTHOUGH DIANE had suggested that I catch the small ferry, I arrived at the end of the pier just in time to see this battered vessel cast off and set its nose rather sluggishly towards Catembe on the farther shore. It seemed overburdened with passengers and luggage, however, with the gunwales not far above the breeze-ruffled surface of the water. So I was content to travel more sedately on the larger boat. It bore the name *Vitoria*, and by means of a winched ramp an assortment of vehicles could be driven onto the rusting deck. Pedestrians embarked also, including a legless man in a wheelchair and a young boy leading with a bright blue cord a constantly bleating kid. Small motorbikes bounced on amid clouds of their own exhausts. A hooter sounded from the bridge, and the ramp was winched up. Someone leaped across at the last moment amid a brief barrage of rebuke. The breeze plucked at the open shirts of slouching young men in dark glasses. Someone shouted out peanuts for sale, and the big diesel engines vibrated through the steel of the deck as we began our 15-minute passage to Catembe.

Some sunlight dazzled on the surface of the sea upon which a few gaff-rigged fishing boats stood in silhouette. But the clouds were still piled up over Maputo. As the distance between *Vitoria* and the shore increased, so the extent of the city centre became more apparent. The dirty buildings crowded down towards the estuary along a front of several kilometres. I spotted the spire of the white church next to my hotel. At the water's edge I clearly saw the long straight quay, as I had seen in the model, with evidence of the railway beyond. I saw trucks moving slowly along the rails. I saw cranes turning above a ship. For ten years the railway from Pretoria had remained closed. South Africa and Mozambique had been virtually at war. South Africa had certainly supported the non-Marxist rebels as they disrupted the struggling new nation through the 1980s. And when Samora Machel was killed in an air crash on the South African side of the border, everyone immediately suspected the South Africans.

The young boy had tied his goat to a metal stake and disappeared. After a while, the bleating stopped, and the small white animal stood exhausted, head lowered. I could see it panting in a rapid rhythm; and for a second it looked up at me with pale eyes glazed with disorientation. Then it bleated once, softly, and lay down among a rusted steel

11

cable on the vibrating deck. In another place, a swarthy Portuguese man was rearranging building material in the back of a spruce new twin-cab, while a young woman sat in front, her head in one hand as she tried to read a book. The breeze blew cool on the faces of the passengers, and for a few moments they were still.

The entire city now spread out like a panorama behind the V of the ferry's wake. This jagged urban skyline was the start (or the end) of a development corridor that bore the city's name. It pressed west, by road and rail, across the border into South Africa. The old barriers were down. Enemies had become partners; the waste of war replaced by joint ventures. In its ultimate manifestation this corridor, I had heard, would press further even than the industrial smoke of Gauteng. It would cross more international borders, its course charted by considerations of economic development rather than national sovereignty, and finally end at another port, this time on Namibia's gaunt Atlantic coast. Could it be that an age of southern African rationality had dawned?

The throb of the engines died and the ferry drifted in towards Catembe. A newer jetty had replaced an old which stood rotting and half-submerged close by. The broken hulls of fishing boats lay among rocks and tidal debris. The hooter sounded as the winch let down the metal ramp. Passengers surged forward, some of them jumping ashore before the ramp had reached the edge of the jetty.

Catembe was a cheerful jumble of commerce and transportation. The goat that had travelled with the ferry (I recognised the bright blue cord) was being hoisted onto the roof of a dilapidated minibus. What terrors lay ahead? I remembered that look of glazed bewilderment in its foolish goat's eyes, that sense of utter helplessness in the face of its own experience. They tied the animal on either side to the roof rack. It fell in a gawky tangle of legs as the vehicle lurched forward. It struggled up and fell again. I stood watching from under the trees growing next to the roadway where I waited for Diane.

SHE ARRIVED just after twelve, driving a pickup truck with two large dogs standing on the back. She removed dark glasses to greet me, revealing faded blue eyes and skin turned to fragile paper by long exposure to the glare of the tropical sun. She wore jeans and a sleeveless blouse. I judged her to be in her middle forties. 'The easiest will be to take you home. There's nowhere else really where one can sit and talk.' Her accent was English South African, still quite polished; and her manner was easy.

We drove through the jumble of the Catembe ferry area and then headed east along an emptier dirt road. Between the road and the sea stood a row of dwellings, most of them extravagant in design and all of them in ruin. Walls stood crumbling without roofs. Everything movable had long ago been ripped out. Facades were profoundly cracked and blackened by mould. Women with fires burning in shallow buckets moved noiselessly in and out of doorless doorways or picked their way through piles of broken bricks and plaster overgrown with many generations of weeds.

'These used to be South African holiday homes,' Diane said, 'before the war. But they'll be redeveloped now – and sooner rather than later, I think. It's absolutely prime property, of course.' She stopped a little further on to show me a house she herself had redeveloped. The front veranda gave access directly onto the beach, and beyond the wide waters of the estuary I saw the skyline of Maputo. I saw evidence of a burglar alarm system. Diane addressed a man working in the garden in basic Portuguese. I asked how long she had lived in Maputo. Since 1995, she replied.

At the entrance to her property – we had turned into a driveway blocked by a heavy gate – she pointed out next door a particularly lavish double-storeyed house in poor repair, but not in complete ruin.

'That's what I'm after,' she said, pressing the pickup's hooter in a few staccato bursts. 'Four bedrooms *en suite* and an indoor Jacuzzi. That's more my style. At the moment I'm haggling over the price. Meanwhile, I live in a shack.'

A guard came running to open the gate. He saluted as we drove through. The gate clanged shut behind us and the dogs, one mostly bull terrier, the other more or less Alsatian, waited to be lifted off the back of the truck.

Diane's house was no palace, but it was hardly a shack. The ceilings were low and some of the cornices were coming away from the walls, but the view from the sitting room where we settled was of Maputo across the water. Bare light bulbs hung down and a circular table top adorned with plastic lace had been fitted to an old wrought-iron sewing-machine stand, still complete with treadle. A black woman brought in a tea tray and Diane answered the telephone. Once more she spoke Portuguese, but I guessed this time it was not to an employee. She simpered slightly, playfully perhaps, as if she might be talking to a man. She seemed quite blowzy then, standing with her hand on a hip thrust out. She was more blonde than she had at first appeared, more gone to seed. Yet her face still showed some beauty – and some strength besides.

'So, what exactly,' she said when the telephone call had been completed and she was pouring tea, 'is it that you want from me?'

I explained that I was interested in Maputo and its new relationship with South Africa, and that she had been recommended to me. 'I'm particularly interested in the so-called Maputo Corridor,' I added.

'I only have personal anecdotal stuff. But I've got strong views on everything,' she said, looking directly at me with lights of slight mockery in her eyes. 'For example, you'll probably be disappointed to hear that Mozambique is riddled with corruption. The Mozambicans are lovely people. They're soft and gentle, they're fun-loving, with none of the arrogance of South African blacks. But they are all thieves.'

We smiled at each other. I realised she was testing me, trying to find out where I stood. I said nothing. In the truck earlier, she had mentioned the inconvenience of the ferry and the possibility of the building of a bridge across the estuary. I had asked if it was not possible to drive round. Of course it was, she said, but it took four hours and there were bandits along the road.

Now she said: 'Do you realise that it costs only about three hundred US dollars to have someone killed here?'

'How awful,' I said. 'Whatever made you come?'

'I'm originally from Durban.'

'I believe so.'

She sat regarding me for a moment. Then she changed her position on the chair slightly and began to talk.

'An old family, mine, old Durban money. I did all the right things: posh school, varsity, society wedding to a man as wealthy as my father. A carefree life. Then my husband died. It was a shock. But I went on living in luxury on the Berea. But the crime got totally out of hand. In 1994 alone, they got into my house three times. They stole my gun. I was too scared to go out at night. Then my husband's car got stolen out of the garage where it was being stored. Then mine disappeared out of a shopping mall. They even stole the hire car I used while the insurance was being sorted out. I had to get out. I came up here on an impulse. This dirty, filthy place. No, don't get me wrong. I saw the potential.'

She told me how she had come directly to Catembe because accommodation – the remains of a cottage belonging to an acquaintance from Durban – had been available. 'And I'm still here,' she said, gesturing around her.

'What I did first was to set up fifteen grocery and hardware stores that also sold fuel from drums. I trained all my own staff. The venture was immediately lucrative. I then set up my staff in their own businesses. I said to my staff, if you can pay me for the stock, I'll give you the building. I must say it has worked very well. I had no defaulters. And now I run a wholesale business that supplies my retail chain.'

She had other projects up her sleeve as well, some of them ambitious. A shopping centre, a big hotel, a prawn dam, camping sites. 'But I've gone through hassles like you can't believe,' she said, sounding very South African, and I had a fanciful glimpse of her in lavish summer dresses and wide-brimmed hats (she was tall enough to wear them) in the marquees at Greyville Racecourse for the Durban July.

'I brought millions of US dollars out of South Africa. I was determined to establish myself in Mozambique. The place was being billed as southern Africa's new economic giant. But the fine print said something else entirely. The fine print is all about middle-management officials, streetwise people who can speak English but are without influence, offering to show potential investors the correct channels but instead leading them deliberately into dead ends that cost plenty in bribes and gifts and all the rest of it.

'With my own projects, I never really got past city hall. Councillors seek kickbacks at every stage, otherwise the project gets shelved. When I realised how the system worked I wrote a long letter to the prime minister, outlining the corruption. Two weeks later I was called in to see some or other high-ranking national official. All he said was that I had to work through the local authority. He advised me to make an appointment to see the mayor. A day or two later I was contacted by the mayor's secretary. At our interview the mayor raged at me for going above his head. So I said: well, let's get on with my projects. I want to invest. I want to add to Mozambique's prosperity. So then the corruption began in earnest. One councillor said: give us 45 per cent of the projected annual profits and pay us in advance one week from now. I refused. I'm afraid I got terribly angry. So the councillors said: but have you really got any money? If you had money, you'd drive a Mercedes Benz. You live in a funny manner. Where's your jewellery? I told them I'd driven more Mercs than they'd had hot dinners, and I said to the mayor: get your pack of jackals off my back, otherwise I'm going to the prime minister again. If necessary, I'll go all the way to the president.'

Her cheeks had flushed slightly. She laughed quite gaily, but with an undertone of cynicism. 'All this has gone on for several years. Some of the councillors got axed, but there's still one left who thinks he owns Catembe. He cannot believe there won't be kickbacks from this silly South African bitch. But I've told them: I will pay nothing but the gazetted fees for the right to invest in their country. I'm prepared to build a new market and a sports field and a clinic as part of the project package, but I'll not pay anything, however small, into the pocket of any councillor or official. Now I hear that two of my projects might soon be approved.'

She laughed again. 'They run around at the top level all over the world looking for investment, and then on the ground this happens!'

She stood up to pour a second cup of tea, calling to the kitchen for more hot water. The woman came and went in silence. Diane glanced at me. 'But all this is beside the point. You wanted to talk about the Maputo Corridor.'

So we turned our attention to that. The major investments coming in on both sides of the border. Essentially, Diane said, the corridor idea had to do with building links between the two countries. So of course transportation – especially the road – loomed large in this perception. The railway had been reopened, but the road had been specially built. The corridor and the smart new road had in fact become synonymous.

'The journey, before, was horrific. Up to five hours from the border at Komatipoort to Maputo, depending on the season and whether the road had been graded that year. Now the new toll road cuts off all the corners – of course, it's tarred, with decent verges and so on – and reduces the travel time to around forty-five minutes. What a pleasure. You can go for an afternoon's shopping in South Africa. Komatipoort is full of signs in Portuguese. Or you can have a weekend in Nelspruit. Go to the new Riverside Mall. The shops there are always looking for assistants who can speak Portuguese. Without the dollars coming from Mozambique, the mall wouldn't stay open.

'Yes, the impact on South Africa has been huge. The crime rate in Nelspruit has certainly risen. There've even been one or two Mozambican vehicles hijacked between Malelane and Nelspruit, I've heard. Easy pickings from the wallets of weekend shoppers.'

We spoke for over two hours, then she said abruptly: 'Let me take you back to the ferry. I've got people to see.'

On the way, as we drove past the long-ruined holiday homes of the South African wealthy, she said: 'It's been hard, but I have really needed this experience. Here in Mozambique, I've learned self-reliance; I've come of age, as they say. I've done things for myself, and I'm a better person for it. I've also learned that there's real suffering in this world. I never really understood that before. Initially, I had a lot of problems, being a woman. Now nearly everyone asks me for advice.'

I asked her about the suffering.

'So many people are so poor. Especially women and children. It's no wonder so many are thieves. But it's the quality of the suffering,' – she drew her features into an expression of pity and distaste – 'the powerlessness, the awful patience ...'

At the head of the jetty, we shook hands as I thanked her for her time. Her grip was surprisingly pliant. Then she drove off into the crowds milling about the stalls and mud-splattered buses pulled up under the spreading trees.

I ATE an early breakfast the following morning with a tough-looking Portuguese with a completely bald head, an unabashed moustache, and quantities of hard intelligence in his eyes. His name was Paulo. He had been born in Mozambique of a Portuguese mother and Greek father and, apart from a stint at a Brazilian university, had lived all his life in his native country.

He said: 'The Corridor is made up, first, of large anchor projects and then of linkage programmes that attempt to grow related smaller projects around them. A good example of an anchor project is Mozal – that's the big aluminium-smelting plant just outside Maputo. Then the linkage programme comprises the development of the surrounding free trade zone which is expected to attract at least 200 small-to-medium manufacturing and service industries.' But he told me these things mechanically, as if his real interest lay elsewhere.

We sat on the terrace of the hotel under an overcast sky. The table cloths fluttered in a breeze not strong enough to dissipate the aroma of coffee coming from the machine on the counter. Paulo said he was pleased to meet a South African who didn't pretend to know more than everyone else in southern Africa. He looked at me keenly to see how I took this mildly jocular criticism.

He said: 'White South Africans are very First World and often very arrogant. But they tend to show great ignorance of Africa. It's the result of that old barbed-wire mentality, I suppose. They're eternally suspicious of their neighbours. Yes, of course, South Africa is powerful. But what too many South African businessmen simply don't understand is that without regionalisation, their country won't survive. They're wasting huge opportunities right under their noses. I'm talking about white businessmen. The black empowerment companies are more adventurous. It's black South Africans who are becoming regional thinkers. But only some of them.'

So his real interest, I discovered in this way, lay in talking to me about the concept of southern African regionalism. The idea of development corridors (a visionary South African invention, Paulo called it) was only the beginning. Beneath the corridors must grow a complex network of cross-investment and economic reciprocities. That was the way forward for southern Africa.

'But look what's actually happening,' he said energetically. 'People are crossing the border in increasing numbers. Mozambicans go to shop in Mpumalanga. South Africans are coming here on holiday again – and to do business. But the border post is hopelessly congested. The South

African border officials say: why don't the Mozambicans spend their money in their own country? And Mozambicans talk uneasily of South Africa as a neo-colonial danger. All this is ludicrous. There needs to be a massive awareness campaign. I say: open the corridor and do it right now!'

I told him that I would be driving to South Africa later that day. Could I expect delays at the border post?

He shrugged his shoulders. 'It's the middle of the week. It won't be too bad. Weekends and holidays are the time. Sometimes you've got several kilometres of queueing vehicles on either side. If all this money has been spent on the corridor, why restrict people's movements with visas and permits and all the rest of it?'

He leaned towards me, his eyes bright with enthusiasm, his moustache seeming to bristle. 'You know what I'm working for? I'm working for a powerful southern Africa where my kids will be able to drive around a region without border posts, or at least without visas.'

I said this would be a difficult concept for South Africans of all hues to accept. I said that xenophobia had become an open preoccupation in many places. I said that since the 1960s, when the country had withdrawn from the commonwealth and begun to listen to the chants of freedom from the north, South Africans had closed the curtains against the world. They had become inured to isolation, and they thought of Africa mainly in terms of the threats it seemed to pose. Under these conditions, the new freedoms and possibilities that had become available since 1994 seemed hardly real.

'Don't give me explanations,' Paulo retorted, 'give me remedies. How are we supposed to convince South Africans – these First World snobs, yes? – that regionalisation is the surest ticket to survival and prosperity?'

THE DRIVE out of Maputo took some time. It was not so much that the roads were in disrepair – although in places they were – as that the city seemed almost frenetically busy, the streets for kilometres at a time thick with traffic and pedestrians. One arterial road had coils of razor wire reinforcing the fence running along the island between the streams of traffic – presumably to prevent people from haphazardly crossing the road. Informal traders also made the roadways narrower than they actually were. In the suburbs, cement-block houses with stones holding down the roofs stretched away between patches of sugar cane and banana trees; but even here the traffic was heavy.

It was only when I passed a big board which told me that I had now begun to travel on the N4 toll road to Ressano Garcia that my pace quickened somewhat. But the city dragged on; and at the end of it, the giant aluminium plant called Mozal stretched out for several kilometres. The buildings were constructed out of expanses of silver sheeting with blue-green trim. Small eruptions of steam issued from a few chimneys. Otherwise the place seemed clean-looking, very modern and stark. The building of it, so Paulo had told me, had provided work to 10 000. Now, with the plant in operation, the workforce had shrunk to 600. But I had heard the rationale: it would be the secondary programmes developed around this huge anchor that would ultimately describe its significance.

So there stood Mozal, a multi-national investment worth billions of US dollars; and in the foreground a single file of women carrying bundles of wood on their heads. More contrasts a moment later: a heavy lorry filled with large-diameter steel pipes turning onto the main road towards Maputo, while turning in the other direction was a hand cart loaded high with grass and reeds (rural building materials) pushed by a pair of barefooted young men.

The biggest contrast was between town and country. The thriving streets of Maputo gave way quickly, even dramatically, to the primitive sights of the bush country through which the corridor road so effortlessly swept. Here was stark visual evidence of the poverty that had overtaken Mozambique through nearly thirty years of war. Ragged patches of hand-tilled land. Women toiling with hoes. Piles of vegetation burning sometimes, pale smoke spiralling above the low thorn trees. Abodes made of grass with bits of plastic and cardboard to improve their weatherproof qualities, built so low, some of them, that access could be got only by crawling. Naked children with big bellies by the roadside. An abjectness pervading the settlements.

And the voices emerging from my memory. Maria Tumbi: 'We'll have to devise ways of getting the investments to filter down directly into our poverty reduction programmes.' And Paulo, the tough-looking

Portuguese who had little patience with South Africans: 'You must understand that in Mozambique we're dealing with a government that came to power in a revolutionary context. As a consequence, our development thinking is often confused. We hang uneasily between the two systems: socialism and capitalism. More and more, though, people are learning that poverty will only diminish in a sustainable way through investment, and investment at the proper scale will only occur through regionalisation and cross-border initiatives. Our biggest allies in this should be the South African capitalists. We all remember –' (his eyes had glinted sarcastically) ' – how South Africa helped to save us from Marxism. But they're now too busy thinking about Europe and Taiwan and Australia to take hold of the opportunities right here under their noses.'

The corridor road had been built and was still administered by a consortium called Trans-African Concessions, a name that kept in a corner of one's attention the idea of a distant destination on the Namibian coast. The name was constantly before one in its abbreviated form – Trac – which adorned the signage around the toll plaza and also the overalls of the men and women on bicycles employed to patrol the road and pick up any roadside litter.

The country became more hilly as I approached the border. There were also a few signs of habitation. Here was a ruined brick abode, no doubt the remains of a Portuguese farmstead; and here a rest-stop for lorries; and then the road descended through cuttings into Ressano Garcia itself. Hovel houses stood by the roadside, goats scavenged among rubble, a few people trudged the verges of the road, and the countryside seemed denuded. Even at the border post there was a sense of ruin and waste. Portuguese buildings disintegrating. The whole scene – people and structures and the landscape itself – released a sense of being long ago exhausted.

I queued for no more than ten minutes, then I was through.

PART ONE

Komatipoort, Nelspruit, Escarpment

A beggar asks for money. You give him bread. He takes it and eats,
but he is not satisfied. He wants money because money gives him power.
It is probably the same with the Afrikaner now. I think the intense interest
in money and business success since 1994 is one manifestation of
our post-traumatic stress.

2
The corridor

THE SOUTH Africa that I encountered beyond the armed soldiers and barbed-wire fences of the border post could not have been more different from the apparent stagnation and poverty of rural Mozambique.

The positioning of the border post on one side of a narrow valley gave little room for informal trading, yet on the South African side the various business activities fairly hummed. Food and drink and Mozambican money by the wad, and even overnight accommodation and the services of sex workers could be got at the roadside or in prefabricated shacks built at precarious angles on the sloping ground beyond.

More striking differences became apparent later. After a few kilometres I turned off the corridor road and travelled south. I had responded spontaneously to a sign which promised to direct me to the memorial of Samora Machel, and in this way I found myself driving through lush sugar cane plantations irrigated with arching water from the sprinkler systems on sophisticated commercial farms. Entrances to the driveways leading to graceful farm houses glimpsed among a deepness of trees were sometimes smothered in brilliant bougainvillea. Paulo's voice returned to me again: 'For Mozambicans, South Africa is absolutely First World.' I passed one place where big machines were ripping out the trees of the bush. There were fires on the land as more space was cleared for sugar cane or bananas. Here was slash and burn on a gigantic scale compared to the ragged hand-cleared patches under the hoes of Mozambican women. Here, people worked in fields of young cane in yellow waterproofs and Wellingtons under the spray of the sprinklers. Water lay in silver curves defined by the furrows of contour ploughing, and the workers looked drenched. The pickup trucks of the farmers and farm managers stood shiny to one side.

Further on, I came to the sugar mill. For some time as I approached

I could see a great plume of effluent billowing into the sky, like smoke from a crashed aircraft. Then I saw the chimneys and then the black mill itself. A heavy sweetness pervaded all the air around. That presidential aircraft in 1986, crashing into a South African hillside one night, 80 kilometres off course from Maputo airport. Then another directional sign turned me east again, and I could see I was driving through an old 'homeland' and directly towards the high hills of the Lebombo range.

But before the turn, a town called Kamaqhekeza, a settlement in what had been one of the remoter pieces of the self-governing Kangwane, itself a result of South Africa's erstwhile preoccupation with separate development. Of course, the old homeland area was still full of people and vehicles and bustle, as was Kamaqhekeza. But there was now the unmistakable sense of economic purpose and possibility beyond the preoccupations with stark survival as in the past. Crowds of children were just leaving a large newly-built school; the girls in black gymslips, the boys in grey trousers and white shirts. An informal market thrived on the sandy square where the minibuses stopped; and spread out along the roadside were various shops: a supermarket, clothing and furniture and hardware outlets, and a Cash Build store with pickup trucks loading materials in a yard. The sight of shiny new corrugated iron enlivened a view of the town from a distance. Building seemed to be a major activity. I noticed also a row of public telephones, a wheel-balancing business and 'five-star barber cuts' as I passed through.

The road climbed into hills and the plain spread out on one side, dotted with homesteads and, again, the glinting of new galvanised roofing. I seemed to ascend from one hilltop to another in a series of steps, each one as peopled as the one before, with the air cool under the low grey sky. I passed a pair of soldiers walking on a pathway a little distance from the road, automatic weapons slung on their shoulders. I guessed I was less than five kilometres from the border. Then I came into another settlement, called Mbuzini, and here was the final turn onto a narrow concrete way that dipped through a small valley and then went steeply up the hillside beyond. I could see where the concrete roadway ended: a wound of red earth in the grey-green hill. The sight of the wound evoked an involuntary tension in me. I thought of the aircraft ploughing into earth, the sound of tearing metal, the instantaneous death.

From the brick-paved parking area I looked up at the monument. It comprised a concrete plinth set into the red earth; and mounted vertically on top of the plinth a collection of pipes 15 to 20 centimetres in diameter and about four metres high. I climbed the steep bank and stood on the plinth and looked down at cattle grazing peacefully all along the fateful hillside. I could hear the sounds of children in the settlement far away.

And then I heard the sound of the gentle breeze in the pipes. It blew down the hillside, rustling the grass and low mountain bushes, and then it passed over the open tops of the pipes to produce a soft but deliberate moaning. Each pipe had been tuned to a different pitch, and the effect was a mournful chorus of sounds that grew more compelling as the velocity of the breeze increased.

Set flat into the plinth was a plaque containing a list of 35 names headed by Samora Moises Machel, and containing a Santos, a Lobo, a de Sousa, a Khan, a Falteiri, a Kartmychev and Choulipov, and a Viegas. Behind the pipes, in an open concrete depository with a floor of boulders, lay pieces of the wreckage. A torn and twisted part of the fuselage was there, as well as a complete jet engine, badly dented but still intact. I noticed a large lizard slithering among the maze of pipes.

Then I heard the sound of a distant vehicle.

I turned to look back along the length of the narrow concrete way as it wound through the little valley below me. A car drove slowly up to mine and a man got out. I could see clearly enough, even from that distance, that he was black. He was looking up at me, so I waved. He returned the greeting and ascended the path towards the monument. The whole landscape seemed empty, save for the two of us, and a few lowing cattle in the grass of the hillside. The man was young, perhaps in his late twenties, and neatly dressed in jacket and tie. He stepped – with a slight hesitancy, I thought – onto the plinth and stood regarding me from a position among the murmuring pipes.

'This is an interesting monument,' I commented, to open some sort of intercourse.

He nodded. 'Am I intruding?'

'Not at all,' I said. 'Are you the caretaker?'

'No, no. I'm from the supermarket down there,' he explained, gesturing vaguely across the valley. 'My name is Mpumelelo.'

We shook hands. He looked around him, seeming slightly at a loss. 'All this human life,' he said, as if it genuinely pained him. 'Lost. So quickly.' He snapped his fingers.

In a moment he spoke again. 'Thirty-five people were killed. And there are 35 pipes. It is like the voices of the dead,' he added, inclining his head to listen to the moaning of the monument.

I walked up past the vault containing the lizard and those bits of aircraft left over from the crash, and onto a higher level. Mpumelelo accompanied me, saying: 'I was at the official opening. The hill was full of people. Read here on this plaque.'

The inscription was in Portuguese and English. It said: *The aeroplane carrying President Samora Moises Machel of the Republic of Mozambique and 34 of his compatriots and colleagues crashed here in Mbuzini, in unexpected circumstances, on 19 October 1986.*

'You see,' he said, pointing at the words. 'Unexpected circumstances. People thought the South Africans had made the aeroplane crash. For a long time we all believed it. But no longer.'

'What changed your mind?'

'I have read of these matters. Such a thing could not have been possible, even with the hatred of the South Africans. That is what many people who are not South African have said. It is wise, I think, to believe them.'

I looked directly into the face of my companion for the first time. I saw an obvious candour and intelligence there. I imagined him sitting in his country shop, scouring week-old newspapers to read the reports of what might or might not have caused the crash. He was concerned with setting the record straight. But deeper down in his expression I saw a simple sense of pride, as of ownership. He was showing me a precious possession.

'Read here,' he said.

Another inscription: *Throughout the day we shall mourn with you a mighty soldier, a courageous son, a noble statesman. We must believe that his death will strengthen our resolve to be finally free ... Our struggle has always*

been linked and we shall be victorious together. This was the message of con-
dolence from Nelson Rolehlahla Mandela, while still imprisoned, to
President Machel's widow, Graca Machel.

Mpumelelo said: 'And now they are married. There is always love
everywhere.'

I looked away across the valley. The breeze was stiffening and the
moaning of the pipes seemed to rise into a despairing and protracted
cry. A few drops of rain coming over the hills from Mozambique blew
into my face.

I asked Mpumelelo why he came to the monument.

'I come quite often,' he said. 'I like to think when I am here. Everything is so difficult and it is also easy. There is this tragedy, and then
there is this love. There is always tragedy and love. And yet there are
also enemies. And I think: why is it so easy to have enemies? I cannot
find the answer. But I hear the pipes, and I think the answer must be in
there, if I can one day understand.'

He left me suddenly. I saw his jacket flapping in the wind as he
walked to his car. I watched the car turn and slowly descend into the
little valley and up the other side. I stood within the voices of the pipes,
gripped by Mpumelelo's artless and yet profoundly poetic vision of the
brutalities and the miracles of the world we shared. The rain came in an
obscuring mist to that lonely and sombre place.

THAT EVENING I had dinner at the Restauranta Tamberina in
Komatipoort's main street. The rain had passed, leaving the land hot
and expectant for more. So I sat outside, seeking a fresher flow of air,
and the big subtropical flowers in the darkened garden seemed to open
wider so they could breathe. The candles swooped and wavered sometimes, and their reflection was repeated in wine glasses and the gleam
of cutlery on white linen. The heat and the candles brought a languid-
ness to the spirit, almost a cessation of mind. In contradiction, the
heavy scent of the flowers seemed like a faint echo of the sweetness
of the sugar mill that spurred and coaxed old images to life. Like a
memory drug, those wide-open flowers. At first the sugar mill and the
sight of smoke as from a crashed aircraft somewhere; and then
Mpumelelo that afternoon and the sadness of the pipes. It struck me as

astonishing that he took some form of sustenance from them, that he went there to think, or perhaps simply to clear his mind. Or to contemplate the proximity of tragedies and love and enemies and once again tragedies in that endless circuitry of what it means to be human.

Was I astonished simply because Mpumelelo appeared to stand so firmly outside the stereotypes of what should interest young black men? Perhaps he was a poet. My food was brought by slender white hands. I ate, listening to voices from neighbouring tables, some in Portuguese, others in Afrikaans. I leaned back in the languid darkness and inhaled the heady scent of flowers.

Other young black men came to mind. A fearsome march and their sticks and spears like a shuddering forest above their heads. The phalanx of chests, some of them naked and gleaming with sweat. In downtown Johannesburg one morning, taking a call from a friend who had immigrated to Australia. She asked me what was the background noise she could hear. I told her that from the window I could see 20 000 Zulus marching down the street, marching 30 deep and leaving no room for even a mouse to pass in the opposite direction. I said facetiously: 'Come home, Mary, how can you leave us now?' My friend said that she had just fetched her children from Kindies. That was Australian for pre-primary school, she explained. Her voice sounded thin and distant. She asked me what was happening now. I said that the marchers were massing around the library, waiting for their leaders to address them. When the shooting started, my friend said, 'Oh, Christ!' and rang off. The marchers lay flat on their stomachs, at first not knowing where the shots came from. Later they crowded behind street furniture and low walls in the library gardens and stared up in attitudes reminiscent of blindness at the general direction of the firing. Snipers concealed in the tall buildings on the other side of the gardens, I read later. Voices began to shout through loud-hailers, attempting to rally the prone marchers. Police reinforcements arrived in a howl of sirens, the doors of their vans left gaping. But they too took cover. When finally the crowd dispersed, we counted those bodies in the gutters and in the gardens that did not move. The young men stepped silently over them on their long way home. There was such a desolation to be got from looking upon this scene and counting in this way a small part of the price that was paid for South Africa's democracy dance. My friend in Australia never telephoned again.

THERE IS a vantage point above the flat plain that clearly positions Komatipoort in its specific corner of the country. With the Mozambican border only a few hundred metres behind, one looks down at the confluence of the Crocodile and Nkomati rivers. The former comes out of the west, defining the southernmost boundary between the province of Mpumalanga and the Kruger National Park; the latter from the southwest from its source in Swaziland. The town of Komatipoort, characterised mainly by painted iron roofs and the suggestion of a modest central grid, lies in the V made by the rivers as they converge. But the place is hardly visible as it sprawls among trees and dense bush.

Even down the main street, the big-leaved trees provided a dense canopy over one pavement. In the shade stood taxis, doors rolled open, music from within thumping out into the heat-charged air. Women sold fresh produce from wooden stalls covered with cardboard and ragged hessian. Heavily laden minibuses, often with trailers hitched behind, drove out of town and onto the corridor road, heading either for the border and Maputo, or turning west towards Johannesburg. Luxury buses, large windows showing rows of tourists, eased between this traffic, heading for the Park where they would see glimpses of the natural wilderness that Africa once was. The buses entered at Crocodile Bridge, a dozen kilometres from the town. From there the Park stretched 350 kilometres to Pafuri Gate in the north, forming a natural buffer zone between Mozambique and the north-eastern regions of South Africa. Nevertheless, to escape the brutalities of their civil war, thousands of Mozambicans had walked across the park, braving security forces by day and predatory animals by night. Park officials had often found the barefoot spoor of these desperate refugees; and sometimes they had found only their remains.

In a coffee shop clearly aimed at the tourist market – whole rooms of the old house were given over to the display of curios – I chatted to a woman with short blonde hair who had lived in this part of the country all her life. She served me tea in an area where thousands of macadamia nuts had been set into the concrete of the floor. I admired this decoration, and the woman smiled. She seemed very reserved. Later she thawed, and sketched for me some of the realities of life in Komatipoort.

In previous times, she said, there used to be two customs-clearing houses coping with the passage of goods across the border; now there were 25. There was a two-kilometre-long runway just out of town, used by the South African air force during the war, but now the authorities had blocked it with tons of gravel to prevent its illegal use by smugglers. The woman told me she had grown up in Malelane, a village 45 kilometres west along the corridor road, and her family had regularly holidayed in Lorenço Marques. But the war stopped all that: the transborder railway closed completely for ten years; road traffic was virtually non-existent. Now, the upgrading of the road had changed the situation once more. The border post was too small, congested every evening, but especially over weekends, by Maputo people rushing back to beat the six o'clock closing. The woman had been back into Mozambique only once after the war, but she no longer wanted to go. The poverty had been too extreme. Everything alive in Mozambique – chickens and animals – got eaten long before it was fully grown. Even these days. There were now nine thriving butcheries in Komatipoort, and all the customers were Mozambican. Many people crossed the border simply to have a good and affordable meal. All the bed-and-breakfasts were doing brisk business. From one of them, the woman said, you could look down at the Crocodile River, and sometimes you could see the animals coming to drink. Elephants, the other day; the first time for several months. And always you could see the crocodiles.

She accompanied me onto the veranda of the coffee shop when I was ready to leave. Across the road stood the Restauranta Tamberina, its blue walls covered with murals painted in a colourful naive style: chickens, baskets of fruit, crayfish. Such plenty so close to the gate of a country plagued by poverty and famine.

A MAN NAMED Karel agreed to talk to me in the municipal offices. He was an amiable man with fair hair and enormous upper arms. Indeed, he was generally muscular; yet there was about his demeanour that gentleness and slight puzzlement not uncommon in large and powerful men.

The border opened again in 1992, he said in Afrikaans, but it wasn't safe. The safest times were between nine in the morning and two pm. Otherwise you were in danger of being robbed or even killed by bandits. But Karel and his friends (a slightly crooked smile accompanied this admission) had gone in for the fishing, taking seven to eight hours to cover 250 kilometres to their favourite spot on the coast not too far from the border with KwaZulu-Natal. But conditions had gradually improved. The corridor road, the N4, was completed in 2000. That's when the traffic really began to increase. Today, there were three trains a week between the two countries, and an average of 8 000 vehicles a day crossed the border, going in both directions.

'But the border facility is too small to carry all that traffic,' Karel said. 'The whole approach road needs widening and the facility must be enlarged. Then there's the question of moving all those entrepreneurs – the money exchangers, the eating places, the sex workers, the overnight accommodation ...'

They were being moved to the airport, Karel told me, where heaps of gravel had already been thrown onto the runways. That was where all the lorries would go, because that was where the clearing houses were being sited.

He folded his muscular arms across his chest and looked at me in his vaguely puzzled way, yet pleasantly enough. A desk littered with files and trays of papers lay between us. I asked him how long he had been in Komatipoort.

'Since 1988,' he replied. 'Ja, the war was still going on then. We could hear the fighting sometimes, and at night we saw the tracers.'

Had the flow of Mozambican refugees stopped?

He shrugged his shoulders. 'I'm not so sure we've ever had refugees here. What is certain is that the black people, the Shangaans, see the border as artificial, a white invention, and they ignore it. There's not a big military presence here any more. Therefore people are walking over the border all the time, in both directions. Most of the farm workers in the district are Mozambican. Mozambicans are taking the South African first-time home-owner subsidies and building houses here. Is there xenophobia? I don't know. They're all family here. The trouble starts when the Mozambicans go west. There have been killings on the trains.

And of course the real xenophobia is in Gauteng. All these foreigners taking the local jobs ...'

Could Karel tell the difference between Shangaans who were Mozambicans and those who were South Africans?

Karel said: 'I can hear the Portuguese accent.'

I raised my eyebrows.

Karel laughed. 'I know Angola quite well. I got used to the Portuguese accent there.'

'You've lived in Angola?'

'I was there a lot in the army. I was a paratrooper in Angola.'

Then I saw his mind making the switch from impersonal to personal admission. I saw a mild recklessness appear in his eyes. 'I was fighting a war about what I don't know,' he said in English. 'What was it for? Now they're all our friends.' He lifted his shoulders – the huge upper arms flexing inside the short sleeves of his shirt – and chuckled in his slightly bewildered but amiable way.

I WENT TO see the airport with the heaps of gravel on the runway. At the entrance directly off the corridor road, a large sign proclaimed it to be the Komatipoort Commercial Freight Clearing Facility. The old military installation was being civil-engineered to accommodate its new use. Already, a long row of timber prefabs housed various customs-clearing agencies. Then there were some caravans with Coca Cola signs, and a few containers with the doors flung open and serving purposes that I could not determine. The surface was churned up by earth-moving machines. But I was able to drive to the far end of the collection of makeshift accommodation where I found a police station and a dilapidated military aeroplane standing in the bush beyond a sturdy fence. Pieces of the tail assembly had been broken out, and it looked as if in other places – under the wings and in the exposed engines – the aircraft had been raided for spares. A few groups of men stood watching as I turned my car and drove back into town.

Outside a lawyer's office, I encountered a young man in khaki with a gun strapped to his hip. He wore boots and short trousers from which deeply tanned thighs protruded. He began to talk on his cell phone. Then the lawyer – I had arranged an interview with him – emerged from the office to talk with him. Later I asked the lawyer, a man named Engelbrecht, about the armed man. 'No, not a farmer. He works for a security company. Farmers still have weapons, obviously, but they no longer wear them.'

Engelbrecht was a small man with small oval spectacles. He some-times glanced at me over the upper rims. But above all he was a rapid talker. He presupposed my questions and gave me 30 minutes of answers in a single monologue. It was like listening to a legal summa-tion that I did not interrupt.

He said that we were living in uncertain times, but that they were not without opportunity. He seemed to have something to do with the local combined commerce and tourism association. The Maputo Corridor initiative had promised much, but for the past while nothing had happened. The difficulties were with the border post, the long waits at peak times, and especially with the expenses involved – visa fees and vehicle permits – in using the N4 corridor road to attract tourists. As a result, the town had not prospered as expected. The whole initiative was surrounded by bureaucratic tangles and downright chaos. Corruption was widespread. People were bribing soldiers and crossing the border at will. The same was happening on the border with Swaziland to the south. Many problems were simply falling between the various depart-ments and authorities. Theft from the goods trains was widespread; and small-time smugglers used the passenger trains to move liquor from South Africa to Mozambique. It was true that commercial turnover in groceries and medicine in Komatipoort had risen 40 per cent, but so had rates and taxes. Portuguese Mozambicans were buying properties in and around Komatipoort. Mozal employees were living here and commuting on a daily basis. It was simply a safer and more pleasant environment for the expatriate Mozal families.

Despite the problems, though, there had been what he called 'a defi-nite cultural shift'. For obvious reasons, he said, this had been a South African right-wing area. After all, there had been a war going on over the hill, and communism had been so close. But the new political dis-pensation had been acknowledged by whites; and there was a general acceptance that black and white were here together and would have to work together – forever.

He glanced pointedly at me to make sure I had caught the import of that word.

The extremism of the old white right had been dimmed, he went on. People were now being dictated to by the economic demands – and possibilities – of the region. The realities were that they were living in the middle of some of the richest farmland in South Africa. Sugar cane and bananas; plentiful water; plentiful labour from Mozambique, although now there were problems from the Department of Labour. The possibilities were something different. The idea of working together now needed to be put into practice. How to cope practically with extensive land claims from black people – that was one of the burning issues. The black people involved in the biggest land claim had been removed first from the Kruger National Park early in the 20th century. They had been settled on the now extraordinarily lush land south of the Crocodile River – until the policy of separate development had moved them once again into that much more arid land that had been allocated to the old homeland of Kangwane. Now they wanted their share of the lush farmland once again. Understandably, these claims had created considerable tension within the white farming community.

Engelbrecht glanced at me over his small oval spectacles. He stopped speaking. I thanked him for his time. He gave me the telephone number of someone in Malelane who could tell me more about the land claim.

'Enjoy the rest of your stay,' he said, extending his hand.

I sat inside the cool interior of the Restauranta Tamberina for lunch. Outside, the temperature soared, as did the humidity. Even when the rain had come that morning, in fitful showers or brief drizzles, there was little respite from the heat. A few tourists came into the Tamberina for lunch, mopping their faces with large khaki handkerchiefs. They spoke German and English. One of the men wore a khaki waistcoat full of small zipped pockets and loops designed to carry cartridges. Of course, the loops were empty. They spoke to a South African – no doubt, their guide – about a confrontation they had witnessed between warthogs and elephants, about the huge ears of the elephants seeming to be thrust forward and enlarged as the irritated trumpeting began and the sand of the roadway was churned to a brief red cloud drifting against the denseness of the wall of bush into which the warthogs had nimbly disappeared. They drank beer and tackled large steaks and chips while they continued to mop their faces.

But my thoughts turned in different directions. The sense I had, above all, was of the softness and vagueness of the international border. The intermingling of the two countries, the blurring at the edges. I thought about the commerce between the two sides, legal and illegal, the smugglers and the heaps of gravel on the runway, and the nine butcheries and the houses being bought on the South African side by expatriates working in Mozambique. All this interdependence. A farmer had told me: 'We've never had a problem with labour here, even during the war. They came and went as they liked, or according to our needs. While others were dying on the electric fence further north, or were being eaten by lions in the Park, our labour always got through.'

That was my initial sense: this softness and the arbitrary blanket of control. Then there was the profound change on the South African side. People seemed to be taking seriously the Maputo Corridor as a regional development initiative. But it needed to be made easier for people to move through the border posts. Why all this nonsense about visas when the imperative, implied by the corridor road, seemed to be towards a greater interchange? The tough Portuguese man with whom I had breakfasted in Maputo had talked about melding the whole southern African region into one economic unit. Meanwhile, the South African Department of Labour was trying to control an uncontrollable situation. Who belonged where? It was the same on the northern borders between South Africa and Zimbabwe. Trying to expel foreign workers. Who was foreign? Black Mozambicans were sufficiently connected in eastern Mpumalanga to avail themselves of South African housing subsidies, and then walk across the border to their friends and relations on the other side. Clearly enough, one sees the two layers of interchange, the official and the informal. They did not correspond. Yet they had in common one thing: it was above all the transactions that mattered – the commodities and the money – at both levels. The butcheries and the smuggling. The hijacking and theft on one side, and the transformation of Mpumalanga into South Africa's boom province on the other. Take a look at the shopping centre on the outskirts of Nelspruit. 'Go to the new Riverside Mall,' Diana Harvey had suggested. 'Without the dollars coming from Mozambique, the mall wouldn't stay open.'

It was time to do just that. While I paid my bill, I heard the Germans explaining how some predators went straight for the rectum of their prey, exploiting first this vulnerable part in their quest to rip the animal to pieces.

I JOURNEYED west towards Nelspruit along the corridor road, soon driving into light rain that was sometimes caught in shafts of sunlight slanting across the lavish land. Mist rolled in damp clouds, making the country soft, and the light remained soft even when the spears of sun stabbed through. Lush sugar cane, with the irrigation sprinklers fed from the Crocodile competing with the rain; banana trees, some held up with poles to take the weight of bunches invisible inside blue plastic bags protecting against the greediness of birds. Everywhere, the sense was of husbandry and plenty. This was the land that black farmers wished to claim. Even when the crops gave way to bush, with fat cattle coming through the thicket into long grass, the sense of plenty remained. The road lay straight and easy before me, extending forward over the undulations of the fecund country. The road shone wetly, and lorries heading for Mozambique passed in a tumult of white spray.

At Malelane, a small village midway between Komatipoort and Nelspruit, I was met by groups of placard-holding school children standing by the roadside protesting high crime levels. The children were largely black but I noticed also a few fair-haired participants. *Bring back life sentences for criminals*, proclaimed one of their posters. *Let children grow in safety*, said another. A few police vehicles, and some from the military, stood about – no doubt to ensure an orderly protest, uninterrupted and protected. I wondered if the hijacking of Portuguese shopping parties on their way to Nelspruit, or even the fear of hijackings, had helped to precipitate the protest. Or was it a more general motivation? After all, crime was post-apartheid South Africa's great anxiety.

But my business in Malelane returned my mind to the subject of the land claims, and the potential tussle that might ensue over that wet and productive landscape through which I had just driven.

'Not a tussle, definitely not. This is what we are trying to avoid,' a young Afrikaner told me enthusiastically.

The lawyer Engelbrecht, glancing at me over his small oval spectacles, had given me the details of someone I should speak to in Malelane. I had made the call. Now this enthusiastic young Afrikaner was showing me a map: Kruger Park stretching north; the Crocodile River flowing west to east, the land to the south of it, the road on which I had travelled. This Eden, he said. A successful land claim could seriously damage productivity. 'Let's be honest about this.' Yet to exclude the black claimants would be equally detrimental.

The young Afrikaner was enjoying the opportunity to lay the plans before new eyes. There was a possibility that the claimants could be given land further south, he said, but that was not the solution. The claimants should be brought into the heart of Eden, otherwise there would always be resentment. Black and white should work together for the economic benefit of both. He gave me a document headed *The Greater Tenbosch Land Claim*. Its purpose was to report on 'the outcome of discussions and agreements in preparation for negotiations between the stakeholders in the ... claim'.

Negotiations were already under way. The land claim was being used as a development tool. There were government targets relating to the percentages of commercial agricultural land that should be in black hands by 2020. 'Let's exceed those targets immediately. Let's bring the black farmers in and work towards increased productivity and profits. Let's do it together. We're talking about a R2-billion development programme, extending irrigation, putting in the necessary infrastructure, including agricultural villages, and building the skills and capacity to ensure the continuance of the economy of the district.' Working together to build a sustainable future. Making money together.

The young Afrikaner's eyes sparked with enthusiasm as he told me of their contact with 'the Malaysians' and other potential backers. 'This is one of the largest land claims in the country (150 000 hectares and 7 000 beneficiaries),' he said, 'and we are using it to underpin one of the largest agricultural development programmes. Black and white working together. That's the future.'

The enthusiasm stayed with me as I continued my short journey to

Nelspruit. I could not shake it off, as if the whole idea had settled on me as some sort of burden. The ingenuity and boldness of the plan had the texture of a new idealism. The transformation of vision seemed too good to be true. Was there no pain anywhere from the past; was there no doubt concerning the future? I remembered the friendly ex-paratrooper in Komatipoort shrugging his shoulders and chuckling in his slightly bewildered way. I was fighting a war about what I don't know, he had told me. Now they're all our friends. Making money together, not war.

About twenty-five kilometres from Malelane, the road crossed the Crocodile and ascended into the Krokodilpoort, which marked the end of the irrigated farmland. I stopped and looked back the way I had come. A vista of great fertility and green spread out along the plain. The young Afrikaner had told me that precisely this view would forever cause discontent. Every time black people came through the poort and saw those lavish white farms with the irrigation water in hundreds of arcs above the crops they would feel disgruntled – unless, through the Tenbosch Land Claim, they were installed as equal partners. And plenty of black people used the road each day. There were 600 000 people living in the Nkomasi area (through which I had travelled to visit the Michel memorial) of the old Kangwane homeland alone.

The road through the Krokodilpoort turned quite sharply sometimes, and gradients steepened. Down to the left wound the river and the railway with a goods train grinding up from Maputo. The hills beyond were high and close, characterised by a series a bald brown slabs of rock seeming to bolster the sides. I stopped again to watch the train. I could hear it clacking on the rails below. The sight of it turned my thoughts back to Maputo, all the way back to Maria Tumbi and her regret at the passing of Mozambique's age of socialism and communal belief. Slowly, the train disappeared.

The country grew hilly. To the north, at one point, I glimpsed extensive settlement in another of the pieces of Kangwane, a dense expanse of housing still looking like a rural slum, the air above it sullied with smoke. Then Nelspruit began. Jacaranda trees, wide pavements, barefoot boys on bicycles, traffic lights, a few neon signs showing in the early evening gloom near the town centre, the streets wet with a renewed drizzle.

At the wailing pipes on the hillside where the aircraft had crashed, the young man Mpumelelo had stood with me talking of the tragedies and the love of human experience. I did not know why I thought of him then, in the evening streets of Nelspruit, except that he was no longer simply a manager of a country grocery store. He came to me now, irreversibly and unshackled, as the poet of the crash, as a counter-argument to the fizz of the new economics, as a bearer of deeper verities. I remembered how a few drops of rain, then, had blown over the hill from Mozambique and into our faces. It was drizzling again now, in Nelspruit. Perhaps that was what brought him so vividly to me again: the cool of the rain on my face.

3
Beyond the mall

THE SPRAWLING Riverside Mall lay a few kilometres north of Nelspruit's town centre and to the right of the multi-lane road going up to White River. The parking area occupied the space of several rugby fields. The mall itself was filled with artificial light and piped music. It had that slightly muffled feel of such commercial places everywhere, where the footsteps and voices of the shoppers are audible but somewhat belittled by the sheer size of the space around them.

A pleasant young man named Mohamed Abdool responded to the query which I directed to the enquiries counter in a big department store. 'Yes, of course we can change US dollars for you. Mozambican currency? I'm not sure. I'll ask one of my bosses. But didn't you see the money exchanger as you drove into town? That's where everyone goes.'

I also discovered a *bureau de change* a little deeper into the mall. It is true that I heard Portuguese spoken sometimes, but mostly I heard Afrikaans. Certainly, at Surfers' World, the boards and goggles must have been bought by Mozambicans starved of such luxuries in Maputo. And Tribal Trax, its window filled with African artefacts, including a gathering of tall carved giraffes, was geared to tourists who passed through Nelspruit on their way to the Kruger National Park. For the rest, though, the local market was by no means forgotten.

A shiny apple-green Harley Davidson motorbike with wide handle-bars stood on display, no doubt the prize for some or other competition. C Sharp Music sold guitars and electronic keyboards. A travel agency advertised skiing holidays in Switzerland and Austria. Some of the hairdressers had Afrikaans names, as with a book shop filled with religious publications, almost all of them in Afrikaans. And an electronic machine displayed information on places indicated on a touch-sensitive map of southern Africa. A small black boy was standing on tiptoe to manipulate the machine. I asked him where he came from. He pressed on Swaziland and looked up at me. When I asked which part of Swaziland, he mumbled a reply and asked for R5. I walked on.

At one of the intersections inside the mall I went down a short passage and looked through the glass of a back entrance. Dense trees and hills showed above a collection of hardly completed buildings dominated by a large and windowless dome. Prefabricated site offices were still standing amid building material. The buildings were big dust-coloured edifices rising just beyond more parking space behind the mall. The dome, in particular, drew the attention. It must have been the equivalent height of eight to ten storeys at least.

I went into a stationers' to look at the local newspapers. A song in the country-and-western style came plaintively to me through loudspeakers set into the ceiling:

I've lived a life of sin
In this world I'm living in ...
Across the bridge, there's no more sorrow;
Across the bridge, there's no more pain.
The sun will shine, across the river;
And you'll never be unhappy again.

I asked the woman at the till about the big buildings just completed at the back of the Riverside Mall. 'The funny ones, you mean? The big beehive? Oh, that's the Mpumalanga government,' she said in her Afrikaans accent.

The Afrikaners. They seemed slightly out of focus to me. In a Nelspruit restaurant the previous evening I had listened to a television crew from England, clever young people out to do an insert on embattled Afrikanerdom, by the sound of it, discussing in detail their sequence of shots: the snarling dogs at the electric fence, cut to the farmer's holster (which, disappointingly, had been empty), cut to the chains and locks, then to the interior of the sheds where the fruit and vegetables were being packed and where the interview would take place. The glib knowledge of South Africa's paranoias and the searching for stereotypes – this bearded boer, the dogs – to bolster their perception of the facts.

43

But, above all, the supercilious vantage point, the confidence of A levels and English provincial universities and the ticket back to London.

But here in the Riverside Mall, a subtler reality. Where were the stereotypes? The big-bellied men, holsters at the hip and combs in socks, shoulders squared with aggression. Not here. Here were people going about their business: getting their hair done, doing the weekly grocery shopping, buying hooks for that fishing expedition, drinking coffee, parenting their children, reading newspapers. I tried to engage the eyes of some of them. They walked past me with indifference, some serious, some laughing together, some glancing my way, some even nodding briefly because my attention of them seemed to demand this acknowledgement in return. One elderly woman smiled. She walked with a stick. She looked at me steadily, her eyes filled with beauty and determination. 'This passage,' she said, indicating the length of the mall, 'is so long.'

I heard the buzz and bleeping of an electronic games arcade. Boys with intent faces stared into the various screens. I heard Afrikaans spoken. I heard Portuguese. I heard Swazi. Then I heard again that country-and-western song about the crossing of the bridge. It sounded like an allegory for some kind of conversion: the bridge of faith and then the rewards on the other side. But suddenly I heard it in relation to the Afrikaners. I stood watching them pass. A small girl, clutching her mother's hand and trotting to keep up, wore a T-shirt with the words *Lam van God* printed on the back. Suddenly I knew there had to be an abyss, this deep river to be got across.

I thought of their profoundly rural roots, their isolation, their pre-Enlightenment faith, the families seated about the big Dutch Bibles, the chosen people searching for their promised land, fighting to attain it, fighting to retain it, and being smashed into defeat in 1902, the rural base destroyed, and the distresses of urbanisation that followed. All through this humiliation and the social restructuring that followed, the Afrikaner carried his faith, this belief that God would bring victory in the end. It came in 1948. Church and State fused with a potent residue of bitterness – and the Afrikaner knew that he was saved. Gratitude turned to arrogance and the building of those massive defences known as apartheid and later separate development. Meanwhile, some good times came to Afrikanerdom. Politically they were secure, and

44

becoming more so with each election that was fought. The 1960s and 1970s were characterised by rapid growth and increasing wealth for a people once caught in severe economic travail. Big Afrikaner business came into its own. This general good fortune led in turn to the partial secularisation of Afrikaner society. Faith in a protecting God was not needed quite so much. And, besides, the State was impervious – even to international condemnation. So the State blustered on, too often ignoring the signs as the signs turned ominous, and black faces pressed against the windows of privilege and political power. The 1980s brought the enemy smashing through the windows as violence and repression grew. When was it that Afrikaners realised that their much-vaunted State and military would soon be forced to negotiate? Was it in 1984, when the townships began to boil? Or in 1987, when a big military offensive into Angola ended in failure and hasty withdrawal? With a receding church and a staggering State no longer able to assert control over the entire country, much less in the southern African region, Afrikaners in reality faced a profound abyss. How could they get across, and at what cost? Where, indeed, was the bridge? This was how so many Afrikaners – but by no means all – approached their country's first great dance with democracy.

In defeat, in fear, in resignation, they found themselves pressing onto the bridge and rushing across it. For some, it must have been like death. Yet they were across the river almost before they knew it. Sometimes they waved old flags at rugby matches. A few plotted revenge. But usually, they went on with their lives. At what cost though? Engelbrecht, the Komatipoort lawyer, had spoken about a definite cultural shift with conservative Afrikaner farmers accepting that black and white were here together and would have to work together – forever. People were now being dictated to by the economic demands and opportunities of life across the river. But the question remained: at what inner cost? Should one be tempted to rewrite the last lines of the country-and-western song?

The sun won't shine, across the river;
And we'll never be happy again.

For many, no doubt, this was true. There was a sense of political emasculation and shame among the younger men sometimes. Yet there was

45

an even surer sense of engagement. The Afrikaners had nowhere else to go. They stayed, tasting the aftermath of the dance.

On an impulse, clasped by curiosity and those idle pleasures of chance, I returned to the religious book shop further along the mall. I had seen a volume in English entitled *Daybreak with God* which provided passages of scripture for each morning throughout the year. I looked up the day's date. I read.

Behold, like the clay in the potter's hand, so are you in my hand, O house of Israel. Jeremiah 18:6. And another: *The wall of Jerusalem also is broken down. Nehemiah 1:3.* The old defences of Afrikaner church and Afrikaner state had undoubtedly been breached. Yet from somewhere within Afrikaner society a small voice had begun with the years to get louder in its insistence that all was not lost.

NEXT TO the Riverside Mall stood the Nelspruit casino, called Emnotweni. In fact, one could pass from one to the other without going outside. Unless one needed the air. Then the overflowing car park presaged the crowd of gamblers inside. Their faces were illumined by the lights of machines; and their shoes passed noiselessly over expanses of carpeting. The one-armed bandits – there were 298 of them – made their particular music, that tuneless composition of buzz and bell and the metallic rattle of the payout. More ordinary music blared out across an army of intent heads, interrupted only by a smooth male voice doing his best to encourage the gamblers to part with their money. But there was always the chance that it (their money) would multiply and return. Another chip, another chance, another muttered disappointment. The music was endless and the voice said there would be special lucky draws this Sunday, and here was one now. Machine number so and so. Who was playing it? Puce and green-lit faces turned to look.

In one part of the casino, an entire row of slot machines were operated by black women with cloths wound in the traditional manner about their heads. The coins disappeared and perhaps the desperation grew. In other places white women did the same thing. People had dressed up for their night out. They sipped drinks. They watched the endless games of roulette and blackjack. They passed up the wide carpeted steps into a restaurant called Livingstone's which offered good views of the gambling. Here at one of the tables was a middle-aged white couple, and a little distance beyond them, a Coloured family. A few black youths slouched half-asleep against the soft upholstery of a long settee. The white couple drank brandies in regular succession. Their broad faces seemed expressionless, the eyes small and uncertain and constantly shifting. When their food arrived, the man tucked his serviette in at his throat. The woman stooped her head to eat, straightening only to listen to the slow machine-gun rattle of a jackpot won. 'That's lucky,' she said in Afrikaans. 'Yes, lucky,' the man replied with some bitterness. Where, I wondered, would these people have been 15 years before? They were now explorers like Livingstone. Venturing into the unknown of Africa and sin.

The waitresses came and went through a pair of service doors. Once, I saw a petite blonde waitress slap the backside of one of her black counterparts as they passed into the kitchen. Almost immediately she scampered through the other door, laughing and writhing away from the black girl in close pursuit. Later, I saw black and white staff (perhaps it was this same pair) embrace as one of them went off duty. It seemed a moving gesture almost, so unaffected and free, and made even more so by comparison with the plastic gaudiness and single-minded obsessions that abounded in that place.

I TOOK THE road north to White River, and thence to Sabie, one overcast morning. I thought I might go all the way to Pilgrim's Rest, that gold rush town from a previous era, and then descend into a crowded old homeland area (near Bushbuckridge and adjacent to the western boundary of the Kruger Park) to see a man who grew tomatoes there.

After passing the Riverside Mall, the road ascended in a series of curves that took me floating further into mist. Moisture gathered on the windscreen as the finest of drizzles; and the roadside trees looked ghostly and pale. This was timber country, although bananas were cultivated on the flatter places. The plantations stood in straight rows and close together so the trees were forced to grow tall and straight and useful as mining timbers. Between each row, long narrow avenues appeared as one drove, a swift succession of these vistas revealing sky and light at their distant ends.

The higher I went, the brighter became the light, as if I might break through at any moment. Indeed, for a while, a suggestion of pale sunlight filled the air and the view of the wet road ahead improved as it tunnelled through the dark plantations. Once I glimpsed the view from the escarpment slopes: trees sweeping away to vistas of distant lowveld down there so far below the road. But the sun was disappearing. Its momentary light gave shape to the lumpy canopy formed by the close-planted trees only for a second or two, then the golden haze had been swallowed once more. The world settled into a grey indistinctness; and the tarmac of the roadway steamed in places sometimes.

In a clearing not far from Sabie, and surrounded by bare earth, stood a sawmill: enormous piles of debarked poles, pyramids of sawdust, tractors churning up the mud, shreds of steam leaking from pipes mounted on the roofs of factory-style buildings. Men in overalls and wellingtons worked in the yard. They seemed to be dragging chains.

Yet it had been gold that first put Sabie on the map. Indeed, gold had brought great but fleeting fame to the whole area. The first great rush centred upon Pilgrim's Rest in 1873. Prospectors poured in from all over the world, watched by isolated and bemused Afrikaner farmers of the old Transvaal Republic. A second rush centred on Barberton in 1883 and finally Sabie in 1890. The names surrounding these early mining centres provided more clues: Revolver Creek and Eureka and Joe's Luck around Barberton; Battery Creek near Sabie; and Mac Mac Pools and Falls on the way to Pilgrim's Rest. Gold was most plentiful in the streams and rivers as they tumbled over the escarpment from highveld to lowveld, scouring through the reefs containing the precious metal. The mountainous country through which I drove had once rung to the chip and scrape of thousands of prospectors' shovels, working the waterways in a frenzy of hope and avarice. All too soon, though, the massive finds on the Witwatersrand (in 1886) had drawn most of them away. Although gold mining went on until well into the second third of the 20th century, the farmers of the Transvaal Republic on the escarpment and down in the lowveld were left in relative peace. In 1892, the railway from Lorenço Marques arrived on a farm called Nelspruit, being finally connected to Pretoria in the other direction a few years later. But in less than six years the turmoil of war was upon them. The farmers and their sons rose up to fight the British. As the Transvaal Republic faced defeat in Pretoria, its government retreated along the railway, operating out of Nelspruit for a while, before their President, Paul Kruger, boarded a train to Lorenço Marques, a fugitive who would never return.

At Pilgrim's Rest, a friendly young black man named Sidney took us (a small group of tourists) down to the river and showed us how the early prospectors had searched for gold. First, we looked around a reconstruction of a mining camp, primitive huts and tents serving the various purposes necessary for those rough and ready times. There were some French tourists with a predilection for making wisecracks. Sidney simply smiled while he gave us some of the background. The town had been connected to the outside world by stagecoach. Hold-ups were not infrequent, presaging the hijackings of today, someone suggested. There had been four women prospectors working independently in this particular camp. Each claim measured six by six meters. Now Sidney was balancing himself on stones jutting from the water of the stream. We crowded round as he washed the pan. He showed us the contents, pointing to one tiny speck of gold. One of the Frenchmen said facetiously to Sidney: 'Are you going to take it home, or put it back for tomorrow?' Sidney laughed. He told me later that he enjoyed working in tourism, but that he was studying to become an archivist. 'The old things are very interesting.'

Pilgrim's Rest, the town, consisted of little more than a main street which began in the 'upper' town and ended in the 'lower'. Jacaranda trees had spilled their blossoms in circular blue carpets all over town. The buildings lining the street were constructed of wooden frames and iron cladding. Their quaintness had been carefully preserved for the tourists. Luxury buses parked in rows, and the tourists strolled in the main street, going in and out of the buildings which were now museums, restaurants, and shops filled with curios from all over sub-equatorial Africa. It was an impressive tourism triumvirate that Mpumalanga boasted: the animals of the Kruger National Park down in the lowveld; the history of early gold mining in South Africa; and the natural wonders of the Blyde River Canyon. And of course in all these places, tourists were provided with the opportunity of being in touch with things African. The pots, the carved animals, the fabrics, the slightly dusty smell of grass mats and baskets and the attractive earthiness of the trinkets. Pilgrim's Rest was particularly well-endowed with the flavour of Africa – not only in the curio shops as I wandered through them, but outside under the trees as well, where freelance crafters (many of them women with babies on their backs) peddled their wares.

In one of the museums I found early photographs of mining operations and read that the alluvial activities had lasted only seven years, and that thereafter mining companies had taken to the hills. Nearly thirty mines had been successfully operated around Pilgrim's Rest before the deposits were exhausted. The scars of some of these activities disfigured the high green hillside that dominated the view from a tearoom veranda where I sat among a group of chattering tourists for a while.

LATER ON that day, I drove down into the lowveld once more, then turned north onto the crowded road to Bushbuckridge. This was an old homeland road. It passed through a combination of the old Kangwane and some scraps of the old Lebowa, a region now administered in part by Mpumalanga, and in part by South Africa's most northerly province, Limpopo. From my perspective as I drove, it hardly mattered who administered – except that the question had several years before become vexed, with most people seeking to maintain the traditional, and closer, connection to Nelspruit. Their demonstrations had turned to rioting, and for some time armoured vehicles had patrolled the area.

It struck me as remarkable that all this humanity – this crass physical manifestation of what had once been called separate development – was wedged so obviously between the Kruger Park in the east and the wonders of the escarpment in the west. This was South Africa's most lucrative tourism region; and here, in the middle of it, lay a strip of congested rural under-development. The hillsides were covered with housing, and children and bicycles and animals and smoking taxis choked the road. What did the tourists make of it? Perhaps it was part of the romance of being in Africa. And their air-conditioned buses did stop sometimes at roadside stalls to enable people to make a few purchases or to take videos of children dancing for their next meal – or perhaps for their next music tape or T-shirt.

How long would it take to erase these scars of the old South Africa? Perhaps they never would be erased. A representative of the World Bank (it was Jan Vermeulen, the tomato grower, who told me this) had once admitted that the best way to develop such places was to build big roads directly to the cities. Let urbanisation take a hand. There was no way that local resources could sustain the hundreds of thousands of people living there. These areas had been designed as dormitories for the families of labour required on the farms and in the towns and cities. Dormitories they would long remain.

Bushbuckridge sprawled across the top of elevated country as an area of dense settlement, plentiful mango and avocado trees surrounding cement-block abodes, vehicles on bricks, people hanging about the roadside stalls waiting for the occasional motorist to stop. But it was only when I turned off the main tarred road that the full flavour of this homeland reality came to me. It had the taste of desperados and struggle. In many respects, the big roads to the cities had already been opened. The old restrictions on movement had been abolished. Migrancy as an economic option had therefore increased since 1994, not decreased. And poverty was in many cases overlaid, rather than neatly eradicated, by new resources. I passed through a small settlement called Dwaasloop (literally translated from Afrikaans as Fool's Walk) that contained at least two big furniture stores. Colourful hoardings advertised the wares available at these stores, the lounge and bedroom suites, the shiny kitchen cabinets and appliances. Also advertised was the national lottery and the very latest in cellular telephones. Then I noticed the cellular masts. This old homeland, on the simple rationale of supplying demand, was better served with cellular facilities than many sizeable towns. Certainly better than Hoedspruit, the nearest town in the centre of white farmland some 50 kilometres to the north.

A taxi went tearing past. Its doors were held on with wire; its bodywork was rusted and everywhere extensively dented. Nearly all the windows were long gone, the openings covered over with plastic ripped and flapping in the rush of movement. The taxi, even this still-mobile wreck, was in the service of the big road out. Transportation became a fundamental economic driver. The maze of tracks and small dirt roads of the homeland fed into the system of regional roads, the regional roads

aimed at the towns, like Nelspruit, where these roads joined the high-
ways. I thought of the corridor road, built all the way from Maputo to
Gauteng. It had been designed to stimulate economic development
along its length. It also served perfectly the purpose to which the World
Bank man had somewhat cynically alluded. Urbanisation. But not so
much the desperate stampede. It came rather in the form of voluntary
migrancy (by both men and women, I had heard) with a base and a
family retained in the homeland.

I SAW THE long shade structures, like greenhouses, in which the
tomatoes grew. They stood in neat rows on ascending ground to the left
of the road; and I bounced along a tributary track towards them. Jan
Vermeulen, middle-aged but fit-looking in a short-sleeved shirt, came
out to greet me. His handshake was firm. He held my gaze for a frac-
tion longer than necessary, as if searching for my real motive in driving
all the way out there to see him. I told him I had been to Pilgrim's Rest.
So the tomatoes were, in a roundabout way, on my way back to Nelspruit.

The tomatoes were grown in 16 units, each measuring a quarter
hectare under metal structures clad in green shade cloth. The plants
were fed and watered via an automatic drip feed arrangement, the solutions being mixed and pumped from a centrally controlled system. The
tomato operation was run by a consortium of 16 women, each woman
operating one unit and employing four additional women workers. That
meant 80 women benefited. Annual output averaged about forty tons
of tomatoes per unit. At R2 000 a ton, this meant a gross income of
R80 000 per consortium member. Each woman was responsible for paying her own labour, servicing the original loan, covering other opera-
tional costs, and paying a set percentage into a stabilisation fund. Jan
told me these basic facts as we walked around the project, going into a
few of the greenhouse units, chatting to some of the women, and looking at the central pumping system. He told me too that none of the
consortium members had yet developed the managerial capacity to take
responsibility for the overall project. The Land Bank and other institutions with money in the project had therefore contracted with him, Jan
Vermeulen, to serve as general manager.

We went into one of the buildings to chat. A few women sat at desks, tapping computers. Their greetings were friendly, their handshakes generous. Two of the women wore doeks wound around their heads, and I had a momentary vision of an entire row of slot machines operated by black women with similar headgear, and how rapidly the coins had disappeared. One of the women provided milk and sugar for the tea that Jan had set about making.

We then settled in his office where we would not be disturbed. He sat on a straight-backed chair in front of the single window. Throughout our conversation, therefore, I saw him without detail, lit as he was from behind by this vivid rectangle of lowveld bush and a portion of one of the shade-cloth structures filled with ripening tomatoes. The sky was a vivid blue – I had driven out of the rain and clouds as I descended from Pilgrim's Rest – and the afternoon smouldered in a combination of heat and humidity.

We talked in a desultory way at first, Jan telling me of some of the problems he had encountered with the tomato consortium. There was the difficulty that the members had, for example, in trying to come to terms with the conditions and time period of the original loan. The time period in particular: it seemed to stretch far beyond their conventional view of time. Then there was the problem of the women taking ownership. They behaved, always, as if they were employees. That was why they had started bewitching each other out of jealousy; and also why there was evidence of consortium members stealing from the project – which meant that they were stealing from themselves. Finally, there was the problem of outside criticism. He told the story of the American Peace Corps volunteer with whom he had become friendly, and then who had attacked him in a Hoedspruit shop one day about the wages paid to the women workers on the project. But when those wages were compared with the going rates on white farms in the Hoedspruit area, there didn't seem to be an argument. And, anyway, the wages were paid by the consortium members, although admittedly under his guidance. But the Peace Corps volunteer's outrage had not been dimmed. Jan Vermeulen, the exploiter of black women. His face was indistinct against the glaring background. But I saw him bare his teeth in a slightly grim smile.

I asked him to tell me how he came to be involved in growing tomatoes in an old homeland.

He told me his story. He had been a successful member of the corporate world in Johannesburg. He drove the latest luxury cars and lived
high above the general sprawl of the city in Northcliff. But he had
become sickened by constantly chasing the materialist dream in a country where a large percentage of people had access to little but a seemingly inescapable poverty. He got involved in a fellowship on the West
Rand; the fellowship became pro-sanctions against South Africa in the
1980s; and some of them became involved in struggle politics. But he
needed to do more. He therefore gave up his opulent lifestyle and came
to Bushbuckridge to help with the development of income-generating
activities. Although not a Christian, he based himself at a mission of the
Church of the Nazarene. At first he worked very closely with a big
university, but the relationship had soured. He ended up in debt. Then
he developed a system of bulk buying for small poultry farmers, while
at the same time assisting with technical and business skills. The result
was the establishment of a cooperative that worked exceptionally well
before it was hijacked by local politicians. Within a few months, R46 000
had disappeared and the cooperative fell apart. Then he got involved in
the Business Service Centre that had been established in Bushbuckridge
(and in numerous other places throughout South Africa) in recent years.
That was when the tomato project had been developed. Now he seemed
disillusioned with the Business Service Centre, and he was certainly
critical of the tomato project. Why was it, he said, that so many of our
beautiful ideas weren't working?

We talked about socialism and capitalism. He shrugged his shoulders.

'I don't think we know which way to turn,' he said. 'Socialism is too
expensive. Capitalism presupposes that everyone wants to be an entre-
preneur. Nothing could be further from the truth. So the idea of free
enterprise and creative economic solutions quickly degenerates into
consumerism. Air-conditioned four-by-fours and designer labels and a
thirst for bright lights. Not many people are interested in building
businesses, only in blowing the profits. I think we had a major opportunity when we changed governments. But too many of the new leaders

have succumbed to greed. At the same time,' he added, 'maybe there were some really good ideas, some potential solutions, that got thrown out when we changed direction in 1994.'

He sat looking at me for some time. Again he shrugged his shoulders, and I thought it was a slightly reckless gesture. I peered through the glare of the window at his eyes, but could make out no detail, except that their gaze remained fixed on my face.

'Actually, I'm at a low ebb,' he confided. 'I had this dream that my contribution would make a difference. But it hasn't. I'm no longer inspired. I'm not even being creative any longer. You know what was difficult for me when I gave up my career? Disentangling myself from the bonds and insurance premiums and all the complex ties of my city existence. But I managed it. Now I'm back where I started. I haven't been paid for months, and I know that nobody's going to look after me. I'm on my own. The bonds and insurance policies and credit cards are on their way back.

'The white Hoedspruit farming community has rejected me completely. So have the university liberals. I feel much more accepted by black people. I have a black wife, a Shangaan, and we've just had a child.'

I thought he would leave it there, his statement made. I shifted my position in my chair, a prelude to rising. He leaned forward suddenly. His eyes came into a detailed focus, and I thought I glimpsed a great store of disillusionment there, and sadness also. I imagined him behind the wheel of the latest luxury car as he steered it through electric gates that closed protectively behind him. But here he was with the lowveld bush of his adopted home visible through the window at his back, and this pain of displacement in his heart.

He said: 'But, deeply, I'm not accepted by black people either. There's no real hostility. They smile and they joke. It's just that I can do nothing about the one most basic reality of my life. I'm white.'

THERE HAD been sustained unhappiness and pain in the approach to South Africa's great dance with democracy in 1994. For many, the pain had begun when white people first stepped onto southern African shores. Other people might identify other beginning points. Like the coming to power of the National Party in 1948 and the beginning of

55

organised repression against the aspirations of black South Africans. Or 1960, the year of the anti-pass campaign and the Sharpeville tragedy. Or 1976, when Soweto exploded. Or 1977 when Steve Biko was murdered by security police. Or 1984, when the final insurrection began. Or the states of emergency that followed. Or the struggling for power between the major black constituencies. Or the brutality of the early 1990s when the course towards the dance was still being set. Even to the bombs, the murders and massacres, and the killing in the streets of which the Library Gardens debacle (when my friend from Australia had telephoned) was but an example. Pain and danger everywhere.

And then the great hush, that breathlessness of expectation as the dance began. The cessation of crime for several days. The queues at the polling stations. The sense of triumph, not at the inevitable result, but at the means. Substantially free and fair. No violence. And so began the parties and the midnight music taking hold as the country danced – literally – for joy. South Africans held their heads at a particular angle. People were even tempted, albeit momentarily, to listen to the rainbow-nation hype.

But now it was time to understand the cost. I had already thought of what it must have been like for Afrikaners. That political emasculation. That attempt to come to terms with life on the far side of the abyss. But for black people also, I thought as my stay in Nelspruit lengthened, there had been a remarkably similar cost. I remembered the Mozambican economist, Maria Tumbi, looking at me through her thick spectacles. It was something spiritual that we lost, she had said, some sense of community that capitalism tended to destroy. The emphasis had shifted to individuals. People cared only about themselves. And hadn't Jan Vermeulen said the same thing when he talked about consumerism? That – consumerism – was what mattered now. It was like another sort of gold rush. It was like a smothering of the old ideologies. They had served their purpose, those beliefs that grew for Afrikaners from the concept of being God's chosen people and of the profound importance of the fight against communism; and those beliefs that grew for black people out of the whole socialist-religious package that had first given rise to the Freedom Charter and had remained the popular credo throughout the years of open confrontation and struggle.

So for the first time in the history of South Africa, large numbers of previous opponents began to rush in the same direction. The wall of Jerusalem was breaking down, for black and white alike, and a new set of imperatives was being born.

This idea of new imperatives seemed to me to be Musi Skosana's view. He was a friendly man, neatly dressed in bright shirt and tie, and his handshake was firm. He was a senior person in an organisation called the Mpumalanga Investment Initiative. And he talked to me one morning in his Nelspruit office.

We began by drinking coffee and discussing the Maputo Corridor. The primary idea had been to reinstate the transportation links. This had been done. The second phase had been deliberately to attract investment into the corridor area, all the way from Gauteng to Maputo itself. This had brought some development, but it had been happening at 'a sluggish level'. The third phase was to have been a linkage programme that would stimulate small and medium enterprises along the corridor by using poverty alleviation funding from various state departments. But this had failed to take off. Musi talked about a change of emphasis. The arrival of new politicians had meant new development agendas. Numerous attempts to get the new leadership to 'buy into' the Corridor concept had yielded little enthusiasm. And anyway, the 'spatial development initiatives' especially designed for accelerated development in under-developed parts of the country (the Maputo Corridor was one of at least half a dozen SDIs) seemed to have fallen out of favour – provincially and nationally. There were also suspicions that had grown up concerning its cross-border character.

'But the Corridor fire is still burning,' said Musi in his cheerful way. 'It is really, now, all about recognising under-utilised development possibilities and exploiting them. But we need more flexible officials capable of dealing with development in whatever guise. At the moment, I'm afraid, they're simply not seeing the importance of the Corridor as a development tool.'

But it was in the realm of more general economic and ideological issues that Musi seemed to be particularly convincing.

'We are all now essentially capitalists,' he said. 'And on one level it's logical. The whole of Africa has traditionally been based in the marketplace. Yet there's been this other influence as well. In the struggle we

57

always spoke socialism and communism. The ANC certainly modelled itself around socialism; and for many of us the struggle was socialism fighting against capitalism. But it hasn't worked out that way. Events in Eastern Europe have made an impact. So has the realisation that the new South African state cannot afford development on its own. It can hardly even afford a reasonable safety net of welfare. The biggest shift in our thinking – but it's by no means universal – has therefore been the realisation that the private sector must be let in. We have to exploit every win-win situation we can find. You speak of traditional enemies now working together. Yes, all over the province are examples of Africans working with Afrikaners. Both sides of the old divide have been released into a new world. My view is that it's a formidable partnership. We need a whole array of supporting mechanisms to allow such partnerships to move onto higher financial levels. If we can achieve such support, then let me tell you: the best is yet to come.'

THE HANDSOME young Afrikaner named Nico sat looking at me across the study in his fashionable Nelspruit home. There was a zebra skin on the floor and a laptop computer on the desk. Marula trees and large paving stones adorned that corner of the garden outside the study's sliding doors.

'These days,' he said, 'I speak only to people who are positive. Of course, there are negative perceptions. They're everywhere. You know the sort of thing: the crime, the bad government, the fear of collapse, the colossal Afro-pessimism, the endless talk about setting up in Australia or Canada. But I haven't got time for any of that now. I'm too busy. The new spirit is for everyone. It's not limited to the Afrikaner. There are English colonial people in Swaziland who are catching it. And many Africans are now looking beyond the racial and political stereotypes to new partnerships.'

He stepped into the garden to put out his cigarette, carefully burying the stub between the paving stones. 'My wife will kill me if I leave my fag ends lying about.'

I was visiting him because he had been instrumental in the formulation of a new development model that was considered to be an advance on the spatial development initiatives like the Maputo Corridor. The new model was once again based on a geographic continuity, and once again it crossed international borders, but the development process was different. Large top-down investments were replaced by a multiplicity of local community involvements, bottom-up planning and increased private-sector buy-in. This was the jargon he used as he described the model. He called it a Tourism and Biodiversity Corridor. The prototype TBC with which he was involved began around Barberton, swept south through Swaziland, and ended in northern Natal.

Nico owned land around Barberton. He wanted to use it for tourism. Instead of proceeding on his own, he began negotiations with other parties, most notably the provincial Parks Board and some black communities in control of communal land. The result was a considerable tract of land with multiple tourism uses like traditional villages, the preservation of gold-mining sites, the highlighting of some of the oldest rock formations on earth, the erection of luxury tourist facilities. The next step was making a strong road link with Swaziland. The Chamber of Business got involved, using R20-million poverty relief funding from the state, and R40-million from the private sector (several large forestry companies) to upgrade the tortuous mountain road from Barberton to Piggs Peak. To stimulate local economic development, it was decided to pave the road with bricks. Brick factories were established around Barberton, creating significant numbers of jobs. In these ways, everyone was involved right from the start, and people began to understand such terminology as 'community involvement' and 'economic sustainability' and 'private public partnerships'.

'Put another way,' Nico said, 'the TBC constitutes a convergence of different interests, institutions, resources from different quarters. This is why it works.'

I asked why he had become so actively involved in administering the project as a whole.

'Self-interest,' he said promptly. 'I own some of the land. Self-interest is the best possible motive for involvement in the whole. It's also rewarding to be involved in the bigger picture. We live in very exciting times. Afrikaners can get involved. Everyone can. There are new freedoms for everyone. There are huge economic opportunities now that apartheid has gone. In this new environment, schemes will stand or fall only on economics. There's another personal factor at work here for me. As an Afrikaner, I have a duty to myself and my children to make it work. This is the way we can entrench ourselves and help to protect the country – our home, after all – from any typically African post-Uhuru crash.'

So this was the thinking that sustained what Nico had called 'the new spirit'. It had to do with economic success. It had to do with opportunity. But above all it had to do with new perceptions. He told me that the provincial logo which depicted a sun close to a horizon was being reinterpreted. 'It's always been seen by Afrikaners as a setting sun. Now the question being asked is: is it setting or rising?'

The new spirit also had to do with democracy and a balancing of the power of the state. Nico told me, as an example of this balancing process, that a delegation from the TBC had already successfully visited the Swaziland roads department. No Mpumalanga or national South African officials had been involved.

'There's a growing realisation,' Nico said, 'that things can happen without state approval. Of course, good government at the provincial level is important; but they'll get left behind by events. What is interesting is how some of the officials and politicians are dealing with this. They're going with the flow. They want to be seen to be a part of the avant garde. In other quarters, though, there is disgruntlement and suspicion.'

When it was time for me to leave, Nico accompanied me to my car. At the entrance to his house stood a collection of exquisite earthenware pots. When I admired them, his reply seemed to me to be characteristic.

'We decided, when we got married, to have around us only those things that we really wanted, otherwise to do without. We wanted nothing second-best. So the pots are from Crete, which we have visited. The people we bought from can trace their family as potters all the way back to 2000 BC. That's astonishing,' he added. 'And it makes you realise: we have such a short history. But this can be turned into an advantage. The opportunity for shaping the next phase of our history is a huge incentive.'

'THE FACT of the matter,' Mark Ngwenyama told me, 'is that there are individual Afrikaners who are genuinely seeking transformation. They are some of the forerunners of the African renaissance. But there are others who are trying to exploit the current situation. The question,' he said with a slow smile, 'is how do you tell the difference?'

I had driven down to Barberton to speak with Mark and have a look at the stock exchange that had been built at the height of the gold rush. In fact, Barberton had boasted two stock exchanges before the ascendancy of Johannesburg changed the economic axis of the country. I found the building easily enough, but only the arched facade remained from the original. And I found Ngwenyama at the constituency office of the African National Congress. A young man working at a computer in the office indicated silently where I should go. His T-shirt bore the slogan: *End racism – Give us our land now*. Ngwenyama himself was young, having been born in Soweto in the early 1970s, and then coming to the old Kangwane homeland as a young adult to help to organise ANC support for the general elections in 1994. He took me into an empty room where we could talk.

'In the long run, you can't teach an old dog new tricks,' he said, stroking his neatly trimmed beard. 'So I'm not saying I trust Afrikaners. I'm saying we need to be sure that our systems and partnerships are designed to limit exploitation and opportunism. And I'm not talking only about Afrikaners or whites. Our own people too. The Reconstruction and Development Programme was corrupted by our own people. We may as well have held workshops in thuggery and white-collar crime. We have got to such a point now that some of us are saying: we are failing our people. This is not a racial issue. We are all in this corruption and exploitation mess together: black and white, politicians and ordinary citizens.'

Later in our conversation, he took up this theme once again. 'There is a growing distrust of development programmes,' he said. 'Talk to our constituents about the Maputo Corridor and you'll discover that it's been too widely rejected already for it ever to succeed. The problem? Politicians want to control the process – that's paramount for them – rather than wanting to nurture the development potential. Yes, that's what it means. Control before development. Control means influence. It also means an opportunity for personal enrichment.

'Now you want to speak about the TBC and Nico. Yes, the TBC is working better than the Maputo Corridor. Why? Because of the bottom-up approach. Good leaders get good responses, but one rotten potato spoils the whole bag. The mayor of Barberton is just such a good leader. He created a platform for the community. At first there was interest, then the community started to talk. People vented their anger and frustrations. Then came the ideas and plans. This was genuine community involvement. Nico's approach has been crucial. He has guided the business partners. He has said to them: we won't be moving anywhere without community participation and a system of accountability. This is what keeps business honest and makes partnerships possible.'

He went out at this point, staying away for a few moments, and when he returned he carried two cups of tea. He sugared and stirred in silence. I sensed his thoughtfulness lying in him as a burden.

'You know, the big contradiction between before 1994 and after 1994 was our view of capitalism. People do see, in their moments of introspection, that capitalism – big sharks eating small sharks – might not be the right way to develop the country. But then they get hooked into the excitement of money and self-gain, and they do a lot of propaganda to justify what is happening because their appetite for the smaller sharks is not yet satisfied.

'The conditions in South Africa when democracy started meant that many of our politicians and government officials became corrupt. We have failed to understand that the people on the ground should be leading the country, not the politicians. This is what is encouraging about the TBC. It is returning development to a more logical modus operandi. The TBC approach says there must be high levels of public accountability. There must be public whistle-blowers. There must be a sense of morality and patriotism. This is what the mayor of Barberton is helping to achieve with the TBC.'

I asked the mayor's name and whether it would be possible for me to see him.

'Richard Lekela,' Mark replied. 'It will be easy for you to see him. He works in Nelspruit. He is, in fact, a government official in the health department. His office is in the new buildings. You know those ones behind the shopping mall.'

Later on, as we chatted more generally about the country, he said: 'My wish is for people who are truly dedicated. I know they're not easy to find. We hear a lot of talk about the lost generation. They emerged from the struggle without much education and were quickly obsolete. Too many of them are now rapists, hijackers, crooks. They're unemployed and operate like packs of hyenas. But their younger brothers and sisters are something different. Cell phones, yes. Living in flats in Jo'burg's northern suburbs with smart cars in the basement, yes. Racially mixed friends, and white or Indian girlfriends, yes. Going overseas, yes, of course. They're the new generation. They're okay. Those are the people we need. So how do we stimulate dedication underneath all that consumer excitement?'

He was smiling at me, stroking his neatly trimmed beard; and it suddenly struck me that it took some courage for him to speak in this way. When the loose political slogans, invariably based on generalisations and stereotypes, were abandoned, all that remained was an often unsightly reality. Mark's smile seemed to be saying: accept my view of this reality as all I have to offer right now.

ON SUNDAY morning in Nelspruit, with nothing better to do, I went to take a closer look at the Mpumalanga government buildings that had risen beyond the car park at the rear of the Riverside Mall. Large red-brick office blocks of four or five storeys were dominated by the huge dome construction that had first attracted my attention through the glass of a rear exit to the mall. It looked like a representation of a bee-hive hut or perhaps even a representation of an ancient corbelled structure of some sort. This was the home, as I had found out, of the Mpumalanga legislature, while the office blocks housed the multifarious administrative functions of the province.

I had heard from a man staying in my bed-and-breakfast that Nelspruit had a surfeit of office space, thousands of square metres of empty offices in the town centre now that the Provincial Administration had moved into its own home. And someone else had mentioned a budget of R600-million for the construction of this new home. Hundreds of offices behind the long rows of windows: all those civil servants. I remembered the description (by Musi Skosana) of inflexible officials incapable of recognising the value of the Maputo Corridor as a development tool. And of course I remembered also the mayor of Barberton, Richard Lekela, by Mark's reckoning a visionary man. These details helped to impress a few faint features into the side of the monolithic edifice rearing before me.

It being Sunday, the gate was barred, so I drove round the perimeter on a road between the offices and the Riverside car park. In this way I came to what looked like the main entrance to the large domed legislature building. I parked my car against the curb and walked 150 metres across a sweep of brick paving to the entrance. The beehive dome soared away above me towards its apex. It was connected to a more conventional building by a series of passages piled one on top of the other above a grand entrance made of glass. Along the base of the dome had been mounted a series of glass cases filled with rows of glass containers holding a quite remarkable array of different coloured soils. I moved closer to read the labels. The samples were from all over the country. But I had no time to discover more.

A security guard with a sub-machine-gun dangling from his shoulder emerged from a side door across the paving and immediately called out to me. I called out a greeting in return. I asked if he would let me have a brief glimpse inside the chamber, perhaps from the public gallery. But my request seemed to anger him

'No, no, definitely not!' he shouted. He was rapidly approaching. 'In fact, even where you are now – where you are standing – you are not allowed to be,' he said as he stopped before me, staring at me with a belligerent expression.

'But surely this is public space. Here, on the paving.'

'Definitely it is not,' he said sternly. His eyes were bloodshot.

'But surely, then, there should be a fence and a gate up there at the road.'

With a jerk of the barrel of his gun he indicated that I should leave.

I apologised, but with some irritable sarcasm colouring my response, for having unwittingly trespassed on his domain.

'Go,' he said.

I returned across the wide expanse of paving to my car. I looked back at him over the roof of the vehicle. He had not moved. I waved a farewell to which he did not respond.

IN THE morning I returned, presenting myself this time at the gate to the blocks of offices directly behind the mall. Another guard took down my details in a painstaking hand. Who was I wanting to see? Mr Lekela in Health. Then he asked me to open my boot. I did so. We parted on good terms. But just before he lifted the boom, he presented me with an advertising booklet from a furniture store. I remembered the prominence of these stores in that desolate homeland place called Dwaasloop as I drove on my way to see Jan Vermeulen and the tomatoes. Here were the same lounge and bedroom suites, and all those tempting appliances from electric kettles and toasters to television sets. The salesperson's name (Redford) and his telephone numbers were stamped in purple ink on the front cover. I asked the guard if he was Redford, or was he advertising for a friend? The guard provided me with a boyish but unabashed grin. 'Big discounts,' he said. I grinned in return and drove through.

THE MAYOR of Barberton, Richard Lekela, said: 'It's an interesting comparison: Bushbuckridge with Barberton. Of course, Bushbuckridge is old homeland. There are several hundreds of thousands of people in that rural slum. Barberton is smaller. Most of the people live in town, about 30 000 of them, with the remainder on the farms and on some community land. Nevertheless, we have our problems. Mining is in serious decline. There have been retrenchments in forestry. We have our share of poverty. So when I was elected, we saw the need to refocus our economic aims. We were aware of the rise of tourism. In fact, Nico – the Chamber of Business – had come up with the TBC initiative before I was elected. We saw the value immediately. We particularly liked the cross-border initiative. So we are pursuing the whole plan with speed.'

He was a lean man, both physically and intellectually, with no fat or sluggishness anywhere to be seen. He had a small goatee beard, sharp features, and constantly smiling eyes. We sat together in an empty conference room, not at the table but in two easier chairs in a corner. He had a habit of tapping me on the arm or prodding my thigh from time to time when he wished to emphasise a point. It struck me as we spoke that here was a part of the South African future: his ability to combine a careful seriousness with an unquestionable enthusiasm. He sat before me in a blue-and-white-striped shirt and slightly gaudy tie.

He told me about the various aspects of the TBC. The Mountainland Game Reserve, already fenced and comprising community land, Parks Board land, and privately owned white farmland (including Nico's piece). The road to Bulembu and Piggs Peak in Swaziland, the brick-making, the buy-in from the big forestry companies. And now the negotiations with the Swazis to upgrade the road on their side of the border, thus extending the TBC right through Swaziland and into northern Natal.

'My role is to run the facilitating committee, to maintain provincial and national links, and to ensure the involvement of the communities in the whole project. Of course, the people are very enthusiastic so far. They see an opportunity to make money.

'The way we in local government see it is that we can strengthen our links with civil society. In this way, we can begin to create a balance between political and civil power. That's how development will take place, with large inputs from business and from communities. We must never forget what the late Minister of Foreign Affairs, Alfred Nzo, said. That the pace of development won't be determined by people who are empowered, but by the weakest and slowest. Of course, the private sector is the fastest and strongest. My role is to bring the weakest and the strongest together into civil society power structures. Like the TBC, yes,' he said, prodding my forearm. 'That's the way forward.'

He sat back in his chair for a moment, regarding me with a thoughtful expression. 'But there are problems with people's perceptions,' he said. 'A frequent complaint from the weakest and slowest is that development takes too long. I always respond in the same way. I say to them: yes, but can you afford for it to be any quicker? They are amazed because they think development comes from the outside. And I say to them: Yes, of course, the government can help in this way or that. So can the private sector. But your development is your own affair. You have to make the decisions.

'And so the process of education starts. I've got a whole programme. I hold large meetings, and we go through all the provisions of the Municipal Systems Act. Determining the standards of services, participatory budgeting, everything. And then I ask my question again: inside this budgetary context, what sort of development can you afford? This

process of empowerment doesn't undermine political power, it comple-
ments it. It strengthens the power of civil society for real participatory
democracy – and for real participatory development like the TBC.

'Viva, civil society!' he said with a sudden rich laugh, his finger once
more tapping intimately against my forearm.

As I drove from the government offices – I was obliged to open my
boot again – I had to explain to Redford's agent, that candidly smiling
security guard, that I would be needing no furniture or appliances in
the foreseeable future. Not even some nice chairs and a table with free
umbrella for the garden.

I SOUGHT respite from the avalanche of words. On the surface, this
avalanche had indicated surprising co-operation and partnerships. There
was the sense of adventure that had so often characterised the post-
apartheid era. Everything was new; everything was rapid (Richard
Lekela had told me how he was pursuing a plan 'with speed'); and there
seemed to be great quantities of sincerity and faith. But underneath all
this, it was difficult to tell what uncertainty or pain might still be fes-
tering. The sense was finally of great fluidity, of new attitudes not yet
solidified into belief, of tentative gestures, intimate yet probing, much
like Richard's habit of tapping my forearm or jabbing my thigh. Yet I
sought respite. Perhaps I needed space for my own perceptions to settle.
So I ate a leisurely lunch alone and drove slowly and aimlessly about the
suburbs of Nelspruit.

The most striking element of the town was its lavish vegetation.
Some of the streets were lined with jacaranda; and within many suburban gardens I saw mahogany and huge African fig, olive and marula,
fever trees and other acacias, and flamboyants and banks of blazing
flowers from poinsettias to aloes. The overall impression was of lowveld
fecundity and generous growth, interspersed with glimpses of lawn and
water; and not infrequently the looping flight of hornbills with their
prominent beaks and extravagant crests. The sight of all these things
spoke of restfulness and ease.

Such were the sensations evoked by a Dutch Reformed Church at
which I paused. Restfulness and ease. Psalm 84 verse 11. *One day in His
company is better than 1 000*. These words were inscribed on a stone in the

front wall of the building. *Built March 1968 Enlarged 1975.* These dates almost perfectly described the height of Afrikaner economic wellbeing. They had been 20 years in political power and seven years into the life of the Republic when the church was built; and only a year after the enlargement did events in Soweto begin to suggest that their rule might not last forever.

I stood in the shadow of the church, looking up at its tower, but being engaged for the most part by the surrounding trees. The deepness of their shade. The strength of their branches. Only they, and the birds in them, had not changed. How rapid, by contrast, were the shifts in the affairs of humanity as they searched for the illusive comforts of permanence.

I remembered other dates, other stances. The non-negotiable of the old Republics – no (racial) equality in church and state – had been brought forward as a fundamental for the Dutch Reformed Church as it moved proudly into the position of state church after 1948. Then, in the wake of the 1960 massacre at Sharpeville, the Cottesloe Consultation took place when South African churches tried to find a common response to recent events. They failed. While many churches had already realised the profound racial injustices then being perpetrated in the country, the Dutch Reformed Church could find no fault with apartheid. In 1974, the same situation pertained, and a major church report of that year spent some time attempting a theological justification of prevailing government policies. After the Soweto uprisings of 1976 (and Biko's death the following year), the Dutch Reformed Church expressed regret over the violence, pledging support for its victims, and urging its members to follow the teachings of Christ in loving one's neighbour. But no mention was made of the links between apartheid and what had happened.

Then, in 1982, the World Alliance of Reformed Churches declared apartheid to be a sin and a heresy.

Only in 1984 did the Dutch Reformed Church respond, and then it did so defiantly. Yet two years later, in a new document entitled *Church and Society*, apartheid was at last rejected as an ideology, and its application was described as a mistake. A path of gradual reform – as was already happening via the tricameral constitution by that time – was advocated as the solution. Even in 1990, the Dutch Reformed Church was saying that although apartheid should be condemned as sin on biblical grounds, various people believed that it had made some positive developmental contributions.

Later that afternoon I met the dominee of the church, a gentle middle-aged man in an open-necked shirt. He came to me as I stood under the trees. We chatted for a while about the beauty of Nelspruit's gardens and trees, and then we began to talk about the changes in the Dutch Reformed Church and also in the hearts and minds of Afrikaners since 1994.

He said in a voice that carried with it the authority of careful thought: 'A *bedelaar*, a beggar, he comes and asks for money. You give him bread. He takes it and eats, but he is not satisfied. He wants money because money gives him power. It is probably the same with the Afrikaner now. Money has become the surrogate for religion. Perhaps it is the new religion. I think the intense interest in money and business success since 1994 is one manifestation of our post-traumatic stress.

'Our religion,' he went on, 'has always been our safeguard, bolstering our sense of national identity. But it no longer exists as a safeguard in this sense – because the links between church and state have been sundered. Money is the obvious alternative.

'There is another strand to consider. The people who benefited from apartheid also paid a price. The ideology that gave us our power also weakened us. Our religion was too unforgiving. It inhibited our creativity and freedoms. But with the severing of church and state, people's imaginations have been unshackled. Overnight, we've become a nation of entrepreneurs. The same process has also paved the way for a sort of religious post-modernism. Everything is being challenged. The power and authority of the Bible itself. The new credo is: so long as you're happy, everything is fine. But this in its turn leads to fear and uncertainty. There's also some bitterness. Young men, now approaching middle age, risked their lives in Angola and Mozambique. We fought for nothing, they say; and now look at all the abortions and prostitution and pornography and child sex, not to mention all the casinos and the lottery. What has happened to the power of the church?

'You'd think that all this would lead to a decline in church attendance.'

He shook his head. 'There must be something in religion because people keep on coming. The point, I think, is that the church has changed. Being cut loose from the state means that the issues with which the church is concerned can now become much more personalised. It's more about finding comfort in the Lord, and how we can help and support others, and a lot less about keeping Afrikanerdom strong. In a truly liberating way, we can begin by saying that the Bible is the word of God for everyone, and that real comfort can be found for individual people, regardless of who or what they are. Of course, this includes the Afrikaner capitalist when he realises that there are still some things that money cannot buy.'

We smiled comfortably together. He regarded me for a moment, his eyes thoughtful, as if deciding in which direction to proceed. Then he said: 'We are talking about change. Let me tell you about one of the biggest influences in my own personal life. I was for some time in the eighties an army chaplain on the Angolan border. When I asked the young soldiers why they were there, at first they would answer that they were fighting to keep out the red danger, to uphold our Christian values. And of course I agreed with them. But then in the effects of the terrorists they killed they sometimes found Bibles. I will never forget the first time I became aware of this. The soldiers called me to come and look. The godless communists lying there with Bibles. A New Testament with bloodied pages. Could it be that some of them, like ourselves, were Christians? I cannot tell you how disturbed I became, thinking of these things.'

He gazed away between the trees to where a small community of hadedas rose from the grass with those penetrating cries of laughter mixed with pain.

4
Heading west

IN THE morning I left Nelspruit and drove west on the corridor road. The country was hilly and deeply wooded, and the road was like a switchback through it. It was easy driving, and the promise was of ascent, of surmounting the escarpment at its most dramatic (indeed, where the historic railway descended), and of gaining the great plateau beyond. Yet my thoughts lingered behind me. Before I left Nelspruit that morning I had talked with a man who for five years had been closely involved with the Maputo Corridor. In fact, we breakfasted together in the Brazilian Coffee Shop with its tables spilling out onto the tiled walkway of the Riverside Mall.

The man's name was Arkwright, and he told me about some of the achievements of the corridor project before the government had lost interest. 'My estimate,' he said, 'is that eighty billion rand has been invested in the past five years in the corridor area. That's no more than thirty per cent of what the region can accept before environmental degradation becomes a problem.'

I asked if he could explain the government's loss of interest.

He shrugged his shoulders. 'I think there are several reasons. First, they see the corridor as a typical spatial development initiative, which was supposed to be a quick top-down intervention to stimulate development. But what they fail to see is any special relationship with Mozambique, or that a long-term collaborative relationship between the two countries had been painstakingly developed out of the relationships forged during the war. They also fail to see that local economic development initiatives need to be deliberately stimulated. Nearly thirty towns had been earmarked for special attention, but all financial support has been withdrawn.

'Second, there has been a change of key political and administrative personnel. The current Mpumalanga premier, for example, hasn't been anywhere near the border for over two years. And third, the idea of cross-border co-operation and regionalisation appears to be viewed with considerable suspicion these days, not least by the military.'

But most of all, my conversation with Arkwright reminded me of where my journey had begun. It had taken him five years to establish fruitful relationships in Mozambique, he told me. I remembered the cluttered streets of Maputo, the faces I had encountered there: the thick lenses of Maria Tumbi's spectacles; and Diane the South African expatriate on the other side of the bay with her ambitious business plans; and Paulo the tough-looking Portuguese who had little patience with South Africans. From those initial encounters, the corridor road had taken me into South Africa, and to my encounter with the poet of the crash, and now directly towards the escarpment at that point where the Maputo railway snaked down against the cliffs.

But first, a factory called Godwana with mountains of stacked timber ready to be pulped and rolled into paper. Smoke belched from chimneys; superstructures were decorated with persistent spurts of steam and lit by harsh yellow floodlights turned on even in broad daylight. On every side, the dark green plantations stretched up and over the hillsides to the horizons. Later, the plantations thinned, and even the citrus orchards dwindled away. I drove with a harshness of mountains above me.

When it was planned, the railway from Pretoria to Delagoa Bay had one overriding purpose: to provide Paul Kruger's Transvaal Republic with an outlet to the sea that was not controlled by the British. Work started at the coast in March 1887, and had traversed the 88 kilometres to the border at Komatipoort by 1891. The cost in lives was high, hundreds of men succumbing each year to malaria and other lowveld hazards. There was, according to popular legend, a corpse under every sleeper – but the work went on. In December of 1891, Malelane (where now a land claim was incorporated into a development initiative) had been reached; and by the following April the line was facing the challenge of Krokodilpoort. But much greater challenges lay ahead. Early in 1894 work started on the engineering work necessary to lift the line from Waterval Onder to Waterval Boven more than 200 metres above. The work included the digging of a 200-metre tunnel, a one-kilometre approach cutting through solid rock, and four kilometres of rack railway (later replaced by a realignment offering easier gradients). Thereafter, the line had forged across the highveld, ultimately to meet with the railway from Pretoria at a place called Balmoral. The Transvaal's outlet to the sea was complete, and officially opened in 1895.

In Waterval Onder, where I stopped for a while, stood the simple cottage in which Paul Kruger had lived in July and August of 1900. *Here*, explained a plaque, *he daily conferred on the war with State Secretary FW Reitz and the executive committee. At the beginning of September he left for Nelspruit and from there to Europe. This was therefore the President's last official residence.* Kruger had worked hard to achieve the railway, this British-free outlet to the sea, only to lose it all so soon. There is something pitiful in the picture of Kruger using this symbol of Boer independence to flee the juggernaut of British power. At first he tarried in Machadodorp, on top of the escarpment, but it was too cold there for the ailing old man, and so his train went down to the cottage below.

The cottage was now a museum, with each of the rooms devoted to a particular period of his life. Room one dealt with his birth and childhood, including his experiences as a 15-year-old boy on the Great Trek, and early political career. Room two was devoted to his four terms as president. And in room three, the subject was the personal catastrophe of the Anglo-Boer War. His country was smashed. He himself had fled like a refugee. Here was a photograph of him outside his private railway carriage at Nelspruit. And then the bleakest picture of all. A silhouetted Kruger at the rail of the *Gelderland*, the vessel that took him up the east coast of Africa, through Suez, to Europe. He sojourned first in Holland, then in France, and finally in Switzerland where he died in 1904. The photograph is taken from behind him, and his head seems to be thrust forward in pain as the vessel steams out of Delagoa Bay on water now regularly traversed by ferries to and from Catembe.

The caretaker of the Kruger cottage was a tall and serious black man. He sat in a small room at the far end of the front veranda, making model furniture and elaborate pen and pencil holders to sell to tourists. He listened to township jive playing softly from a portable radio. The cottage was surrounded by tall trees filled with the singing of many different kinds of birds; and the pathway between the trees had been swept meticulously into chevron patterns in the sand.

A train went drumming and screeching down the railway beyond the trees. This outlet to the sea for a landlocked Boer republic. This escape route for a bowed and defeated president. This conduit for holiday-makers to the long Lorenço Marques beaches. More than 250 000 a year in the 1960s and early 1970s. And then the cessation of traffic while the guns blazed and the antagonisms festered. And now the corridor was opened and the port of Maputo was being revitalised. Before the war, the port had been handling 14 million tons of cargo a year, a figure that had dwindled to less than a million. And now the figure was up to four million and rising still. The train clattered faintly on the joints in the rails and then receded out of earshot on its way to the sea. One reality overlaying another. Migrant workers from Bushbuckridge and Mozambique in evidence all along the path of the defeated Kruger. Same route; same railway; different direction and reality.

I drove up to Waterval Boven, glimpsing as I climbed the old railway tunnel not far below the current alignment hewn into the cliffs of the escarpment. I sat on the veranda of the Shamrock Country Arms in a slightly chill evening. Some drizzle, some mist, a glimpse earlier of silent rails shining under lights and a directional sign for the Rack Rail B & B; and Arkwright confessing to me that he was leaving his corridor job. Because, he said, all the main anchor projects were now in place, and also because there was no longer any support from the government. The absence of policy clarity troubled him. Yet he admitted that this was giving rise to a mood of doing things privately, like the Malelane agricultural development programme being worked out between white farmers and black claimants, or like the Tourism Biodiversity Corridor happening around Barberton and all the way into Swaziland and beyond. Private opportunities for finding new partners and for making money. A rising enthusiasm for capitalism, the new power, the new religion.

But there was also something else, he said, something deeper and more sinister. He had been accused, suddenly and shockingly, of being part of a conspiracy against the national president. He had been visited

74

by National Intelligence. He was, after all, a white Zimbabwean. He had worked as a town planner for the Zimbabwe government. Then he worked in private practice in South Africa's old Transkei homeland. And after that he had joined the Development Bank who seconded him to the Maputo Corridor project. He had worked out of Nelspruit for five years. But a major problem, he believed, was that he had served in the Rhodesian army as a young man. The record was part of his history and impossible to erase. In any case, it seemed that they wanted him out. He had obliged by resigning. He had also destroyed most of his corridor documents: letters, reports, budgets, concept documents. Had he, I asked, done this in anger or in fear? He smiled at the question, saying he could not recall his emotions at the time but that they had definitely not been flavoured with fear, and giving no indication of his real feelings now.

My thoughts turned in more general directions. As they did so, I suddenly realised that the corridor reality, overlaying so many earlier preoccupations, was itself already being overlaid. The conflicting views, the contrasting words and ideas, the ferment of new worlds growing up to cover the old, and not so old, and even the most recent. This perpetual flow of new over old appeared as the only constant worth considering, especially when trying to find points of focus in a country, a region, a continent so profoundly in flux.

The garden of the Shamrock was lit by a few lights set low and shining up into foliage; and by this illumination I saw a mantis walk sedately along the underside of a long fleshy leaf with serrated edges. It mattered nothing to the insect that it was upside down. It even found time to stop and pray for a moment while carelessly defying the idea of gravity.

THE MORNING was all mist and raucous hadeda birds and rows of railway houses looking quite attractive in the softness of the day. The foliage of Boven dripped, generously wet; and at the station I saw a big black locomotive adorned with steam. The carriages behind the locomotive lay against the gravel platform, and many of the doors stood open. A pleasant woman with auburn hair, bright earrings and a clipboard sold me a ticket to Belfast, a town some thirty-five kilometres further west on the highveld plateau. This was a special train operated by the Oosterlijn Steam Company, a group of steam preservation volunteers who also took tourists down the spectacular pass to Waterval Onder and back on certain weekends. The *oosterlijn* (eastern line) was in the last decade of the 19th century the great hope for the Transvaal Republic. Unlike those lines forging over the South African veld towards the Witwatersrand gold fields, from Cape Town (via Kimberley), Port Elizabeth (via Bloemfontein) and Durban, the eastern line was a Republican creation, a proud achievement that had nothing to do with those ubiquitous and irritating British.

On the platform, a short piece of the rack railway had been preserved to serve as a monument to the men who had died in the construction of the eastern line. How many hundreds or thousands? It was not known. And their sacrifice seemed remote from the jollity on the station now. People climbing aboard with picnic baskets; a fat man already drinking a beer from the bottle; a collection of people with cameras paying attention to the shining locomotive with its polished copper piping and painted wheels. And all those hurried footsteps crunching on the gravel of the platform as the whistle blew and the doors slammed in a salvo that rattled along the length of the train.

I sat on blue leather seating and looked out of a window with the old railways emblem, a springbok's head, sandblasted onto the glass. I could smell the locomotive as it drew us from the station. The wheels clattered slowly on points. We were in a cutting of damp rock, and when that changed to embankment I saw green and stony hillsides, a mountain stream with cattle on the banks, other cattle running in fright from the locomotive as it gathered some speed and took us with screeching wheels into one curve after another.

On the seat opposite mine sat an elderly woman who asked whether I spoke English or Afrikaans. She gave me a *vetkoek* filled with mince from her picnic basket – 'I can see you've brought no breakfast,' she said – and told me she loved to go on the train. It reminded her of the old times. She had grown up on a farm just east of Nelspruit, she said.

In one place, with the train going slowly, I saw a swathe of new green shoots awash against the black of last winter's fires. And then a siding, a metal-fenced pen for the loading of animals, a rusting nameplate showing altitude and the distance to Pretoria. Cars at a level crossing waited in a renewed drizzle. Children stood on the strands of a nearby fence, waving with handkerchiefs as we passed.

The elderly woman returned her attention to me. 'Karino,' she said, 'that's where the farm was. Just east of Nelspruit on the road to Krokodilpoort. When my father first got there, he had no chair. So he cut down a tree and used a piece of the trunk to sit on.' Her face brightened in amusement, and she watched to see whether I had enjoyed the story. 'I went to school in White River. I took the bus on the terrible roads. But all our produce went out by train. I always helped my mother with the waybills. All afternoon I helped, and then I used to do my homework on the bus in the morning.' Again her face showed some mild amusement. Her memories seemed to have been compressed, especially for the telling, into a series of humorous anecdotes.

'There was a huge tin of quinine tablets for us, I remember, and the black workers. Bilharzia was also a problem. At school, there were plenty of Portuguese children. Then I went to high school up here in Belfast. I took music and played in the school orchestra. Oh, I must tell you about a school concert we had in 1940. I was 15. My parents had travelled up to hear me play. At the end we played *God Save the King*. My father jumped up and shouted: "Stop, stop! My child will never play that tune." I was so ashamed. But feelings were running very high at that time.'

The whole carriage was filled with chatter. People were eating and drinking and smiling as the train ground up through the last of the escarpment hills. The train staff all wore fluorescent waistcoats with *Oosterlijn* printed in silver across their backs. They spoke in Afrikaans to one another. I thought again of the achievement of the original railway, the political significance and the one-upmanship over the powerful British. Was there still a sense of pride, I wondered? Especially now, perhaps, in the new political reality.

'When I was about eight or ten,' the elderly women said, 'we went to Lorenço Marques on holiday. We camped on Palamo Beach. It was the first time I had seen the sea. We also went to the harbour and watched them loading or unloading coal. The blacks ran with baskets full of coal on and off the ship. The Portuguese were there with whips. I watched in absolute horror. It was 1933 or 1934, I think. It was one of my first racial experiences. Then I read *Uncle Tom's Cabin*. So you learn. You see on our farm there was a church school for the children of the labourers. My father was a humane man from Cape Colony ...'

I walked – to stretch my legs, as I said to the elderly women – from coach to coach along the moving train. Everyone greeted me. I saw the auburn-haired woman with bright earrings sitting beside a man with a weathered face in repose beneath a faded blue peaked cap. She was light and vivacious. The man was her antithesis. He said in a quite ponderous way that his African thesis was very simple.

'Productivity will have to improve if the continent is going to amount to anything.' And from there he was able to proceed to his next definitive statement: 'The only real solution is recolonisation by some non-African interest.'

Did he think that regional efforts like the corridor, for example, might help?

He glanced at me in surprise. 'What corridor? It's fizzled out,' he said. 'They put up the toll plazas. They charge big tolls to finance the road to Maputo. In so doing, they do major damage to tourism here, on the old trains. All our protests are ignored. Then they lose interest. The corridor's stone dead.'

At Machadodorp (a small town named after Major Joachim Machado, the Portuguese engineer who had laid out the route of the eastern line), the train stood in the station for several minutes. The station building had burned down, and everything of value had been stripped off the blackened carcass. On the platform slouched a group of obviously poor white people. A trio of ugly young men with shaven heads kept pushing each other towards the train and sniggering through the gaps in their teeth. The women had rounded shoulders and short necks; they stared at things with vacant looks of ignorance and acceptance. And a few red-headed children stood by a pile of boxes and stuffed carrier bags and suitcases all secured with pieces of string. A shrill whistle sounded; and the wheels of the locomotive spun on wet rails as it carried us into open country once again.

In one of the carriages I got into conversation with a huge man with only one leg. He said his name was Gerhard Fraser. His leg had become poisoned after an accident. But he did not want to talk about that. He

78

invited me to sit down, wanting to know if I was a steam enthusiast. Where was I from? Did I have my family with me? He was a lonely man, and I sat with him for a while. In fact, I continued an earlier train of thought, placing it before him as a proposition. Was there still a sense of pride, of Afrikaner pride, in wearing the fluorescent waistcoat with *Oosterlijn* printed in silver across the back, in recreating a proud achievement in their history, in saying to their new world: look, we have had our triumphs?

'I'm not convinced,' Gerhard said. 'Don't expect any sense of history from people. They don't even know that the connection between Boven and Onder was once the only rack rail system in Africa. They're more interested in watching television and buying Lotto tickets than in any Afrikaner pride.'

Later, he said: 'I heard you talking about the corridor. Well, it took off like a Boeing, but then it flopped. We don't see anything happening. All we see are towns dying. Machadodorp is very ill. Waterval Onder is a disgrace. I can't think of anything that's happened. Except of course the road. It's a beautiful road. And Nelspruit is booming because of all the business from Mozambique. You know what people say around here? That Mandela had the corridor road developed so he could get more easily to see his lady.'

The train travelled faster now that the hills had subsided and the plateau stretched out as treeless vistas on every side. We passed a large industrial plant full of pipes and conveyor belts and mounds of grey sand. Something to do with steel processing, Gerhard said. And then for the last five kilometres to Belfast, the corridor road appeared on the left of the railway, the tarmac wet and dark, the traffic speeding past.

Gerhard and I had begun to talk about the classic post-independence model in Africa. First the struggle; then the euphoria of the freedom dance; then the collapse into caricature and chaos; and only after that, the pale new dawn, the promise and sometimes the reality of ascent. Would it be like that for South Africa?

Gerhard nodded. 'Almost certainly, but the dip after the freedom dance will be nowhere near as severe as it's been elsewhere. Perhaps we've already gone through it. Actually it was a miracle, in 1994. We're certainly far better off than we were in the 1980s. I have a lot of hope.

But we need to understand one thing. If we don't have open politics then we're dead. To try to suppress politics is to create huge trouble. Everyone, from the government to all the opposition and extremist groupings, must understand that. I see a big future, but there'll always be a lot of tension and squabbling.'

The train rolled into Belfast station. Doors swung open. Gerhard reached for his crutches. We shook hands. I noticed the elderly women who had played *God Save the King* at the school concert here. We waved goodbye. And there was the vivacious woman with her sparkling gypsy earrings and auburn hair, clipboard in hand, talking to people who wished to board the train. I looked once more at this train from the past, the carriages shining wet with rain, the doors standing untidily open, the locomotive already uncoupled and steaming away to take on water. Then I turned and went on my way.

I DROVE on the corridor road as it swept over the undulations of the country towards South Africa's industrial and commercial heartland, now called Gauteng. Beyond Gauteng, it had been planned for the road to continue into Botswana and across the Kalahari desert to end in a harbour town somewhere on the Namibian coast, a truly trans-African road. Perhaps it would happen, but perhaps not – certainly not if, as seemed to be the case, the government had lost its appetite for regionalisation.

Meanwhile, I thought of the Kalahari with some anticipation now. But I thought most of all of the places I had come from, the taste and complexity of them, and the various levels of reality they had offered to my gaze. The detail swirled in my mind. Yet a theme recurred. I had thought at first that it might have to do with softening borders and regionalisation, but this had been smothered by something more pressing. The real theme of my experiences had to do with the new materialism of the post-apartheid age, of people being released into opportunities hitherto concealed by the strictures of ideology and the false expectations of their faith. The view across the detail was therefore of this materialist rationality, the thrill of panning for gold, the adventures and hopes that came with partnership. Yet there was something else besides. I saw again, as I drove through the grey day, the perplexity of the poet of the crash. His sense of pain and then of love. But above all, I remembered his consciousness of the moaning of the pipes and how the sound was transmuted for him into the voices of the dead, even into the voice of humanity's collective past, that raw stuff of history and poetry alike. I wondered if he would also agree that both history and poetry were a little like the building of a railway through dangerous country, filled with difficulties but also with small and costly triumphs.

Huge pylons marched out in straight lines from the power stations built all over the eastern highveld places through which I drove, the cables between the pylons looping in shallow arcs. Black whydah birds with long tails struggled from point to point in the grass by the roadside. In the early dusk of the overcast afternoon, the power stations stood festooned with lights. They looked like ships out there on the rolling grassland where the coal was mined. And the big road – dual carriageway by now – swept forward like a dark and diminishing brush stroke across the dun canvas of the land. It seemed unstoppable, drawing me to another destination, even towards the deserts lying baked and open on the other side of the continent.

PART TWO

Kalahari, Schmidtsdrift, Wildebeest Kuil

Giving people back their land is not the full solution. Also, there is something about funding that makes it difficult for people to take responsibility. And the combination of the land and the funding is also feeding that sense that they are special, that someone can always be found who is willing to pay. I am convinced that this is helping to stunt fulfilment. It's certainly slowing down the Bushman's assimilation into mainstream South Africa.

5
In the desert

THE BORDER post between South Africa and Namibia at Rietfontein was characterised by a water tank set on top of a steel construction that reared high into the uncaring blue of the desert sky. Below, the usual official buildings were clustered around the wide gravel road as it swept from one country to the other; and on one side, protected by security fencing, stood a tight group of houses for the officials and policemen who worked there. It was a place of great desolation. It seemed imprisoned in hostility, surrounded as it was by undulating ochre earth baked concrete-hard and littered with millions of dark stones and scattered grey bushes never higher than a metre in height. The day on which my companion and I drove the few kilometres from the border post to Rietfontein town, a fierce wind raged across the country and, according to a radio report that morning, the temperature in the Kalahari would soar to 46 degrees.

The town was as imprisoned as the border post. It lay against the earth, this little collection of buildings, while the wind stretched the palm trees and rattled through the loose sheets of roofing iron. Few people had ventured out in the midday heat. Dust raced along the roadways, and even the goats sought respite in what shade could be found. We drove through slowly, turning off only to look at an old church built on slightly elevated ground.

From the vantage point of the bare churchyard, Rietfontein looked dismal and derelict, and the desert stretched out on every side. Behind the church, a chain from the free-standing bell swung in the wind. Over the years, the chain had worn a deep gouge into plaster and bricks, and its constant clashing was the only sound. Apart, that is, from the roaring of the wind as it ripped through a spindly gathering of palm trees close by. Beneath the palms, some undergrowth grew greenly in the otherwise dun expanse of sand and stones, and we guessed this damp patch to be the source of the settlement's name.

The church itself was locked, but my companion found a young girl from a nearby building who was able to give us access. The interior felt cool and protected. It took only a glance, though, to see that the church had fallen into disrepair. Walls were marked with damp, timber was pulling away from surrounding masonry, and numerous windows had been broken. Untidy rows of chairs occupied the floor, and incongruous light fittings from the early 1960s hung from the ceiling. On the stage pale blue steps led to a pulpit. But the painted plaster was badly chipped, and what looked like a small sacred icon had been repaired with bandages of sticky tape now yellowed with age. In the vestry, the ceiling had begun to collapse, the handles had gone from the doors, and all around the base of the walls the plaster, loosened by rising damp, was crumbling away to raw brickwork underneath. Services were held elsewhere, the young girl had told my companion; the old church was used for other gatherings. A pre-paid electricity meter had been wired to the vestry wall.

My main interest lay in the plaques that adorned the wall behind the pulpit. It seemed to me the plaques were new and all of the same vintage. Nevertheless, they outlined the story of the church. It had been established by Rhenish missionaries in 1885. Sixty years later (in 1946) the isolated congregation of Rietfontein threw in its lot with the Sending Kerk, missionary arm of the Dutch Reformed Church. Then on 14 April 1994 the Sending Kerk changed its name to the Vereenigde Gereformeerde Kerk. There were no more plaques. Indeed, they had been so arranged that no more could be fitted. It was as if the story was now complete. A biblical text from the Book of Hebrews had been inscribed in the centre of the wall. My companion translated from the Afrikaans. *Think of your forefathers who have passed on to you the word of God. Take note of the way they lived.*

There was a sense in the church that the past had become more important than the present or the future. Perhaps that was the nature of churches generally; but here the acknowledgement of the past seemed to have been elevated to an active denial of the future. The general dilapidation and neglect enhanced this mood. Largely, though, the mood depended on the date of the final plaque and the lack of space for any additions. April 1994. The actual day, the 14th, was less than two weeks before the date of the start of the country's first democratic elections, an event that had taken place amid a 'national euphoria'. I remembered these exact words used by one historian. But almost certainly this mood had not reached the polling queues in Rietfontein. I tried to imagine the Coloured inhabitants waiting in the wind to make their crosses. Or perhaps there had been no queues here. What was there to be euphoric about in a place like Rietfontein? The previous change in the affairs of the church, in 1946, must have been crushing enough. Two years later the National Party had come to power and the Dutch Reformed Church had been elevated to the status (although never officially declared) of state church. And less than five years after that, the names of all Coloureds had been expunged from the national voters' roll. Had 1994 signified to the people of Rietfontein simply that the self-interest of whites would be replaced by the self-interest of their successors in the corridors of power? The atmosphere in the church suggested subtly that this was the case.

We drove through the blasted town, seeing only dust and a few trees with branches stretched out like streamers in the wind. On the outskirts stood a general dealer's store with a shattered pediment and badly wounded walls. One part of the building had served as an abode, but now stood roofless, and a sea of mud on one of the floors had cracked in the perpetual heat into thousands of jigsaw puzzle pieces. The shop was still in use, trading in fresh produce and videos. A price list on one wall was painted as hanging from a witch's broom. The witch herself had a black hat, a menacing nose and chin, and curling toes on her buckled shoes. My companion took photographs while he smoked a cigarette. A few children appeared out of the dust to pose for him. They picked up his cigarette end when he discarded it. Then the town was behind us, and the road went into flat country edged with red Kalahari dunes.

We came to a settlement called Noubos, and later another called Kleinmeer. In the latter, the heat was intense. A distant pan threw up huge columns of pale dust. Closer at hand, rubble bowled along the unpaved streets, and back-yard windmills raced. A man in a vest and hat who was working on his car told how birds in Kleinmeer would

sometimes shelter in the shadow of people, their fear of humans overcome by the torture of direct sunlight. Some of the houses had satellite
dishes attached to their walls. The man in the hat grinned and said that
sometimes on the television they saw *lelike dinge* – ugly things. We conjectured on the strangeness of having this window on a world that was
utterly unattainable. Did the television provoke feelings of dissatisfac-
tion and restlessness among the people of Kleinmeer, embedded as they
were in the isolation of the desert? Did this new practice of watching
violence and nudity from other countries increase their feelings of being
marginalised? Or was it all simply too remote to matter beyond the
whiling away of so many hours each evening?

In Noubos, a nursery school called Rainbow detained us for a while
with its bright painted murals and the incorporation of half a bus body
built into the facility as a kitchen. Inside the single classroom we met a
talkative middle-aged woman and also Mandy, one of the young teachers
who seemed too shy to do much more than nod. The classroom was
well-equipped and the walls crammed with colourful posters. One of
them proclaimed: 'Forward with early childhood development – pilot
project'. And a hand-written list of names was displayed – Mary-Jane,
Porsha-Lee, Micaela and others – no doubt of the children who attended
each morning. In another place were assembled pictures of black, brown
and white people and the caption: *Different but together*. The whole of
Rainbow School was an unexpected monument to what had happened
since 1994. The middle-aged woman saw us looking at the assembled
pictures and said cheerfully: 'We need to be part of the whole picture,
even here in Noubos.' Mandy nodded. Her eyes were bright yet defen-
sive. She was a small young woman, small-boned, and her skin was pale
and yellowish. I guessed her to be of Khoisan descent.

At one point, as we continued on our way, my companion braked
suddenly. I could see the Bushman couple sitting together under a thorn
tree whose canopy afforded some mottled shade. They were dressed in
scanty animal skins, otherwise naked. The woman's breasts drooped in
flat Vs against her bony chest. The man's limbs were thin and small and
sinewed. The woman wore stringed adornments around her neck and
wrists. The man held a bow and arrow which he hoped to sell as a curio.

My companion got out to talk with them. They offered their wares which lay on a cloth laid out on the sand: artefacts of bone and wood and the shell of ostrich eggs and dry rattling pods. They had built a small grass shelter by the roadside. They looked up through wizened faces at my companion who momentarily squatted to talk with them.

'Same old story,' he said when he returned. 'They're almost certainly farm workers somewhere here. There are still a few white farms. To earn extra income they display themselves as tourist attractions.'

MY COMPANION, an Afrikaner named Hennie Swart, was a man in his late thirties, dressed in khaki trousers and a striped cotton shirt. I had met him first as he sat behind a table filled with posters and pamphlets advertising the work of an organisation called the Northern Cape Rock Art Trust. He told me immediately of his interest in Bushmen, those small people who had graced so much of southern Africa with their cave paintings and engravings chipped onto the surface of countless rocks. He told me even then of the problem he had with the nomenclature surrounding the indigenous peoples. The term Bushmen had been used derogatorily so often that it had become more acceptable to speak of the San, or Khoisan, that generic term used to describe the stone-age peoples of South Africa in both their main branches – Bushman and Hottentot. But even San, antiseptically academic as it sounded, had apparently some hint of insult in its history.

To get around the problem, Hennie told me, he had reverted to Bushman. It was unpretentious; and also it was the term most widely understood by the small yellow people themselves, particularly in its Afrikaans version – Boesman. This version had deeply embedded connotations of insult and belittlement, but I never heard even the faintest hint of such things when he used the term.

Not long after our first meeting, Hennie wrote to me about the Bushmen. He told me of his involvement with those most celebrated Bushman groupings who had served as trackers with the South African army in the war in northern Namibia and Angola. One grouping had originated from central Angola and was called the !Xun; the other, the Khwe, came from Caprivi. After the war ended with Namibian independence the !Xun and Khwe trackers and their families could hardly be left among the communities against which South African soldiers, with the help of their Bushmen trackers, had perpetrated considerable violence. They had therefore been brought to an army camp at Schmidtsdrift in the Northern Cape where they had lived under canvas for more than a decade. Indeed, they were still living there when my association with Hennie began, although by then they had been provided with a tract of land outside Kimberley, on a farm named Platfontein, for permanent resettlement. Hennie had at first taught at the school in the Schmidtsdrift camp. He had then been employed by these displaced !Xun and Khwe Bushmen as manager of their Communal Property Association through which they were to take possession of their redistributed land. And finally he took charge of the Northern Cape Rock Art Trust whose headquarters (a museum and tourism centre) was situated near an ancient rock art site on Platfontein.

Yet the chief concern expressed in Hennie's letter related to the passage of these Bushmen, traditionally such a gentle and spiritual people, from their Stone-Age past into the complexities of the modern world. What was happening in their heads? Would the arrangements on Platfontein – a form of permanent, almost suburban, settlement for nomads – lead to bloodshed between the !Xun and Khwe, or between the Bushmen and the people of Kimberley in general? And beyond these specifics, larger questions loomed. What would be the eventual impact of South Africa's land restitution and land redistribution policies? It seemed to boil down to questions of separation or assimilation. Should the latter be encouraged, even when the policies (designed to redress past wrongs) could have the practical effect of setting ethnically defined communities apart – itself a form of marginalisation? But how, considering the infinite adaptability of *Homo sapiens*, could the process of assimilation be permanently resisted? And should it be?

These questions were as valid in the Kalahari as they were in relation to the unique situation of the !Xun and Khwe. That is why I had arranged for Hennie to travel with me as we made our excursion to Rietfontein and then headed through the heat and dull red dunes towards Witdraai, a small settlement not far from the main gate into the Kalahari Gemsbok Park. Witdraai: this spread-out conglomeration of buildings – including a safari lodge for tourists visiting the Park – was the headquarters of the Khomani San.

Over lunch, which we ate under big ceiling fans at the lodge, Hennie told me that the Khomani San had lived in the Kalahari for thousands of years. Gradually the land had been enclosed for farming and nature conservation. Claims under the Restitution of Land Rights Act (1994) had been successful, and six or seven large farms around Witdraai had been purchased for the Khomani San; and some share in the takings of the Kalahari Gemsbok Park was also being worked out. In 1996, the Communal Property Association Act was passed, this legislation making provision for the communal ownership of land. So it was the Khomani San Communal Property Association (CPA) that owned the land and administered an accompanying trust fund.

Although the !Xun and Khwe, living in their tents 500 kilometres away, were not historically South African, land was nevertheless redistributed to them in compensation for their services and in recognition that they had nowhere else to go. The farm Platfontein had passed into the ownership of their CPA, the organisation that had not many months previously been managed by Hennie.

But Hennie's attention was, for the time being, concentrated on the Khomani San. He had heard that the Khomani San CPA council had been suspended and then dissolved. It was the second time this had happened. 'Corruption and mismanagement,' he said, his expression one of disappointment and concern. 'The CPA council isn't doing its job. There's a huge amount of poaching on the farms. No proper administration for the CPA has been put in place. Factions within the community are grappling for power. At the same time, CPA councillors are insisting on getting paid.' He shrugged his shoulders, a slightly dejected gesture, mopping at his perspiring face at the same time.

Hennie was, for me, the gentlest of men. He was heavy-jowled, slow-moving and considered in his actions, even in his physical movements, but with boyishly curling hair on his forehead, and kind and thoughtful eyes. He spoke English well, but with a definite, slightly guttural, Afrikaans accent. He had grown up, he told me, not far from Nelspruit, on a farm specialising in timber and bananas, the younger son of well-to-do Afrikaner Nationalist parents. I recalled the plantations of Mpumalanga where blue plastic bags protected the big hands of bananas from destructive birds; with the black stems of wattles in steep rows disappearing into mist.

Now I saw some amusement in Hennie's expression as he told me – to illustrate his parents' political pedigree – how his mother used to weep with relief when the results came over the radio during general elections and they heard that the National Party had won another seat. He chuckled at the memory, but he did so with fondness rather than with any malice.

There were zebra skins on the dark stone floor of the safari lodge. The sky had turned overcast, as if it might rain, and the heat lay burning against the skin, burning the more fiercely, I thought, because it was trapped and motionless beneath the clouds. We walked briefly in the grounds of the lodge. Outside the gate, at some distance, we could see the figures of near-naked Bushmen beckoning to the occasional vehicles that passed.

'I keep telling myself,' Hennie remarked, 'that even if the CPA fails, nevertheless the Khomani people have the land. They have parts of their old home returned to them. And yet,' he said after a moment, 'they are also imprisoned here. There's nowhere else to go. The major asset, the land, is locked into the community as a whole. It's not divisible. So tourism becomes the only resource. The curiosity of outsiders provides the underlying economic rationale – like that couple under the tree. But is it sustainable?'

THE SETTLEMENT of Witdraai had few attractions. It was built at a T-junction, the main tarred road giving direct access to Upington on the Orange River in the south and to Rietfontein (although the tar ended long before the border was reached) in the north-west. The turn-off was to the north-east, a stony dirt road that ended only at the entrance to the Gemsbok Park some sixty kilometres away. At the T-junction stood a general dealer's store, a tree, and some outbuildings. A few hundred yards further along were the big gates marking the entrance to the Molopo safari lodge. Interspersed between these land-marks, and sometimes built on the slopes of the surrounding dunes themselves, were humbler structures of corrugated iron or of those more pliable materials – fabric and grass matting, in particular – favoured by nomadic people even after they had been obliged more or less to settle. But most dwellings were out of sight of the roads. Sparse tufts of grass and thorn bushes grew on the terracotta dunes, and only a few shade trees graced the flatter places between.

In the slightly lessened heat of the late afternoon we ventured out into Witdraai to meet a woman named Betta Steyn who, among other things, ran a crafts project there. She came out to meet us in her bare feet, an ample woman inside a flowing kaftan-style garment. Her hair was enclosed in a doek and she wore pendant earrings that gave her appearance a vaguely vagabond or gypsy quality. Yet her handshake was firm and her smile wide and attractive.

We went into a building close to the general dealer's store. I had a glimpse of books (a small community library, Betta said); a refrigerator and stove; a computer-generated A4 poster that proclaimed *Kalahari San Youth – together we can make our dreams a reality*; and some smiling women on the floor, working on what looked like a large counterpane. All this as we passed into Betta's office which housed a dusty computer and a fiercely rattling air conditioner.

We sat talking for a while, Hennie and Betta making their exchanges with a familiarity that I recognised as a mark of their similar positions in the Afrikaner scheme of things. It was a position, this position of the rebellious Afrikaner, that had flourished in the years immediately before 1994. Afrikaans university campuses, often in spite of themselves, had bred a new generation of Afrikaner youth that had assisted in, perhaps even led, the assault on the old hegemonies. Here were two of this generation, caught in a warmth of recognition and conspiracy, talking of mutual acquaintances and what their generation was doing now, who had remained interesting, who had disappeared into the suburbs with mortgages and babies. Betta had a tattoo (or perhaps it was something less permanent) of a large ant crawling on her right foot.

'I came to the Kalahari in 1999,' she said to me. 'I came up with artist friends – I was married and living in the Natal midlands at that time – to baby-sit their children. And I never went back.' She gave me a careless gypsy smile. 'You ask why. Because there's something about the space here. There's lots of texture, yet it's so open. Your soul can travel forever. You know all the clichés. If the Kalahari sand gets on your feet, you're caught.' She opened her hands, palms up, and shrugged away the intimacy of the words.

Betta's ten-year-old son sidled into the room. He asked if he could buy a cool-drink at the store. She suggested a glass of water. He demurred. She succumbed. He skipped off with the money. She laughed. 'He knows exactly when to ask,' she said. 'He can see I'm busy with people and therefore won't argue too much. His timing is always perfect.'

I had heard that Betta, having left her husband in the Natal midlands, now lived permanently with her son in an old bus parked on a nearby dune. She told me: 'When I first came to the Kalahari I stayed at a place called Welkomhartbees. They were salt-of-the-earth people there, and I made friends all over. I lived in an old café, staying for a few months; and then things started to happen. That's when I bought the bus and came here. The crafts project started two years ago.'

Hennie asked how she had moved the bus. 'I got it towed. I think now I should have fixed and driven it. Wouldn't it be handy to have a mobile home? I can see my father's expression as I turn into the drive at home,' she said with one of her rich and ready smiles.

We spoke together about the Khomani San Communal Property Association committee, recently suspended. 'This is the second time, hey,' Betta said. 'It's just not working. Maybe my ideas are worth nothing, but you can't successfully impose a Western-style system onto the Bushmen. Several problems stand out. In the old Bushman system there was never one leader. Elders from family groups came together to decide policy. But for the CPA you have to have a leader. Then there's the CPA constitution. This is written by lawyers sitting in Cape Town and not really understood by local people. One of the clauses says that CPA committee members have to be literate. That one clause alone ensures that most of the real leaders in this community won't ever get onto the committee. So there's constant friction and feuding while the committee is simply discredited, even ignored, which means that the way is wide open for nepotism and all sorts of petty cheating.'

We walked round to see the craft shop. The sun had broken through the clouds, slanting into lingering dust, a dramatic end to a day still scorching, and with such a heaviness about the heat that even the birds, usually active in the late afternoon, could hardly be roused. The track was soft with a dust turned to fine powder by the constant passing of vehicles. We saw one of them parked in the shade of the building where the shop was housed. Other vehicles were little more than shells, wheels lying nearby; and chickens scratched at the earth while thin dogs lay panting in the heat.

Adjacent to the shop stood an old farmhouse, its walls clad with thousands of small stones not much larger than the eggs of farmyard hens. It gave the house a strange lumpy appearance – and I suddenly realised that this must have been the home of the white farming family before the land had passed to the ownership of the Khomani San. The crafts shop had therefore been established in one of the farmyard out-buildings.

Had the farming family laboriously attached the stones to the walls to save on plaster or because they thought it beautified the building? In any event, they had created a remarkable piece of Kalahari kitsch. Awnings had been attached above each window. The metal frames were still there, but the canvas hung in shreds. And the deep veranda was filled with people resting and small children crawling on a blanket.

Betta introduced us to two old San women in particular. The one had white peppercorn hair and opaque spectacles that concealed her eyes. When I took her proffered hand, she did not smile. She had withdrawn completely behind those milky lenses. She was suffering from high blood pressure, I heard. The other woman was excruciatingly thin, but with lively eyes. Whatever Betta said to them (she spoke with an easy familiarity in Afrikaans) the thin woman laughed delightedly and her eyes grew mischievous.

'These are our exhibits,' Betta said. 'In 1936, I think it was, they were taken to England, to some exhibition, and put on display there as genuine Stone-Age people.'

The thin woman clapped her hands in delight.

It was interesting to see Betta among the ragged band of Bushmen who seemed to have taken occupation of the old farmhouse. They engaged her as she moved about in her doek and bare feet. An inebriated young man with dreadlocks and a Department of Land Affairs cap stood before her for a while. Betta smiled and shook her head. Then a woman with a young body and wizened face accosted her. The woman wore a white petticoat and blouse and a bright red hat, the brim dipping low over her decidedly tipsy eyes. She clasped Betta's hands in a gesture of entreaty. Betta laughed in her expansive way, exchanging pleasantries, and then disengaging herself.

Later she said to me: 'The biggest enemy here is dependency. It started a long time ago. Those women going to England as exhibits; maybe that's when it started. When we had finished trying to exterminate them, we began to view them as Stone-Age curiosities, and now finally as remnants of a romantic lifestyle superior to our own. Don't the wide-eyed New Age people pour out here from all over the world, from Cape Town especially, to experience the Bushman way of life, the trance dance, the simple interdependence with nature. Back to the earth – that's what the Bushmen offer. Out the New Age disciples come with their medicinal wheels and their obsessive vegetarianism. They come for the spiritual experience. They sit in the darkness, hands clasped, while the Bushmen give them a trance dance that is no more than a drunken whirl to some scratchy gospel music powered by a car battery. And just out of sight of this spiritual experience, one night, there were four buck carcasses, probably poached, dripping blood into the sand. Bad, extremely bad news for the vegetarians.'

Betta laughed quite gaily at the picture she had painted. '*Ons tol met hulle.* That's what the Bushmen say. We are taking advantage of our fans – this is what they mean. They wink and nudge each other. Tol means a tribute or a price. In fact, the dependency has turned into an expectation. We have made these people special by idolising them. They understand the Laurens van der Post myth, and now they are using it to exploit us.'

THAT EVENING, in an airless prelude to a storm, we sat together in the Molopo lodge, Hennie and I, Betta and an Afrikaans woman visiting the crafts project. Thunder snarled across the red and stubbled dunes. Betta added to her dependency-to-expectation thesis by recounting a personal experience.

She had been driving at dusk in Andriesvale, a neighbouring settlement. A young man had leaped without warning in front of the vehicle. She had swerved and skidded and stopped. Perhaps mistaking her for a New Age tourist, the young man had said: 'Owe me two rand. I'm a

Khomani San.' Betta's reply had been immediate. 'So fucking what?' she had shouted. 'You owe *me* two rand. I'm a Boer.' Dumbfounded, the young man had stepped away.

Thunder crashed overhead. We ordered more drinks. Hennie told of tourist buses seeking out Bushmen in their 'fancy dress' and people taking photographs through the windows. There had been unpleasant incidents with half-naked Bushman girls.

'How long are these people going to stay on display?' he asked. 'It's like a form of prostitution, isn't it?' Later he said: 'That is why I say, giving people back their land is not the full solution. Also, there is something about funding that makes it difficult for people to take responsibility. And the combination of the land and the funding is also feeding that sense that they are special, that someone can always be found who is willing to pay. I am convinced that this is helping to stunt fulfilment. It's certainly slowing down the Bushman's assimilation into mainstream South Africa.'

Once at Platfontein, he recounted, a financial crisis had been discussed at a !Xun and Khwe Communal Property Association meeting. One member of the CPA committee had said: 'What's the problem? Call Mr Overseas.' This seemed to illustrate a dangerous level of financial ignorance and misunderstanding, and also a little about the level of Bushman expectations.

Betta said, but with a certain light-hearted humour, she sometimes thought that people who worked with the Bushmen, people from 'the outside', invariably had some sort of ancient curse put upon them. 'I'm talking about capable people. Professionals, academics. All too often they end up sitting in the sand with the Bushmen, smoking dagga to get their feeling, becoming entangled in their endless feuds, and then bearing the brunt of the anger and resentments that erupt when they feel they are not being fairly treated, or when another party or individual is perceived to be more favoured than themselves.'

As the evening wore on, they began to talk again as Afrikaners. Betta's son had no doubt read the symptoms of a late evening because he pushed two easy chairs together to make a bed. The tone was of easy yet deadly serious commitment to the country. There was also some pride in what they were doing. 'If you can make it in Africa you can make it anywhere,' someone said. 'I'm sorry to say this,' Betta commented, 'but it was the English-speaking liberals who ran away.' She looked at me with her gypsy smile, her earrings flashing. 'And yet, I hear that every second doctor practising in Canada these days has an Afrikaans name,' Hennie countered.

Lightning illumined in a series of flashes the garden beyond glass sliding doors. 'Mind you,' he went on, 'I think the first wave of running away is now over. There's something a bit sissy about going now. There's a growing positive feeling in our age group now. There's a sense that we can build the country, that things can work, that the effort will be worthwhile.'

Betta's bare feet rested on the dark stone floor of the Molopo lodge. She looked from face to face around our circle. Her son slept. Hennie's face had become quite animated, and I wondered what had impelled him, from a home where his conservative Afrikaner mother wept over positive election results, into the troubled heart of the problems associated with marginalised communities and land and reinterpreting the future. These young Afrikaners, all in their thirties, sitting in the airless lounge with its high thatched roof and glass doors onto the veranda with garden beyond, waiting for the rain.

At last, in the darkness, it came. But it was no deluge, simply a short sharp shower that splashed down through the reeds covering the veranda for a few moments, and then was gone. And afterwards, a drenching humidity was added to the heat.

IN THE morning, under a merciless sky, Hennie and I spoke to the Bushmen who daily gathered across the road from the entrance to the lodge. We went early to their place, and some of the men who would work there that day arrived after we did. A large thorn tree offered meagre shade. The men would strip off their jeans and T-shirts (and other western-style clothing) until they were naked save for a loincloth made of animal skin and sometimes a headdress of similar material. One elderly man wore on his head the skin of an animal complete with eyes and nostrils left as holes after the skull had been removed. They were all thin, many of the older ones hardly more than wizened skin and bone. Their bodies were small and sinewed, their skins yellow-brown, their faces seeming prematurely wrinkled. And they were all barefooted, standing or sitting on their haunches, working and waiting for the cars to pass. They worked with simple tools – side-cutters, awls, sandpaper and knives – taken from a small grass shelter in which they also stored their western clothes. A small fire had been kindled under the tree in which they heated implements to burn patterns onto ostrich egg shells and pieces of bone.

One young Bushman – he said his name was Tjan, aged 18 years – crushed soft red pebbles into a paste, mixing with water to the desired consistency and then painting small whimsical figures onto the surfaces of flakes of rock. His dexterity was beguiling. We asked if he had seen any rock art in caves or overhangs. He nodded. 'Once in the mountains at Kagga Kamma I have seen it,' he said in Afrikaans. Had once been enough to embed in his memory the style of the originals? Or perhaps he had seen such figures as he drew depicted in photographs in the tourism brochures. He applied his dull red paste to the grey rock fragments scattered about him.

The Kagga Kamma to which Tjan referred was a privately owned nature reserve high in the Cederberg mountains near the Western Cape town of Ceres. It was close to 1 000 kilometres by road from Witdraai. The owner had encouraged Khomani San families to settle in the reserve and earn their living by doing Bushman things under the curious gaze of tourists. Before land had become available in the Kalahari, Kagga Kamma must have been a realistic economic option for desperate families. Tjan's family had spent 14 months there, then they had come home. I asked why. Tjan said there was too little money in Kagga Kamma. Only R50 each for a trance dance, he said. 'There's not much money in the Kalahari either, but at least I know I'm at my place.'

Hennie alluded to the failure, once again, of the committee of the Khomani San Communal Property Association. '*Dinge gaan baie deurmekaar daar*,' the Bushmen said; things are very mixed up there. Hennie also asked them about the tensions between their various factions. They chuckled easily enough.

One man said: 'We hold onto our traditions because we care about them. Others say we use our traditions to beg for food. There are those Bushmen who scorn us for wearing this.' He tugged at the skin he wore like a pair of briefs. 'There has been a letter written to our leader, Dawid Kruiper. The letter says we are like animals with our skins.'

'That we smell like shit,' another voice said.

Hennie asked who had written the letter.

The reply came from several voices at once. 'They think they are very modern. The westernised Bushmen. Where do they live? In Upington. And in Witdraai here. Dawid Kruiper is the son of old Regopstaan Kruiper who has died. Dawid Kruiper is our true leader. Now they insult him. Yes, we wear the traditional things. Yes, we trade with tourists. They sit with their computers and talk like monkeys on their phones.' Bared teeth were brought jittering together in a stylised imitation of speech.

Hennie asked directly: 'So there are the westernised Bushmen and the traditionalist Bushmen. Here in the Kalahari. Will you soon begin to kill each other?'

The Bushmen laughed quite gaily, and then their attention was redirected to an approaching car. We saw young Germans clamber out. One of them asked me to take a photograph of them with their arms familiarly slung about the slight shoulders of the Bushmen gathered under the tree. Everyone smiled. In the mouth of one of the most emaciated Bushmen only one stained tooth remained.

Hennie and I went in search of Dawid Kruiper. We conjectured on the names. We wondered about the older names behind the Afrikaans ones. Or had Afrikaans, and the domination that had come with it, obliterated too much of the general background? Kruiper meant crawler or creeper, and at first it recalled for me the classic crouching pose of Bushmen in the hunt. It also, though, had connotations of servility and sycophancy. And then if one added the first name of Dawid's father, Regopstaan (upright-standing), the conflict of meaning turned into a crisis of fundamental identity. This reflection of the Bushman history glared out of the dull red dunes at Witdraai. The contradictions were also a reflection of the current cleavage tearing through the heart of the sad little community of Khomani San. Traditional and perhaps servile, on one side; westernised and progressive on the other.

At the general dealer's store, we found a dignified old man in a sports jacket who said he could take us to Dawid Kruiper. The leader had recently moved his household to a new position, returning to traditional ground 'behind the dunes'. Our guide said he knew the way. We drove along a track beneath an avenue of mature trees that led to another white farmhouse. Chickens and children, in a flurry of wings and protruding brown stomachs, were tumbling out of the front door when we arrived. We drove slowly through the yard, avoiding pieces of metal and rusting farm machinery and then onto a sandy track that began to twist steeply into the dunes. '*Gee vet*,' our guide said. He meant us to accelerate (literally, to give grease) to avoid sticking in the sand.

I asked the old man about his children. Most of them lived elsewhere, as far afield as Cape Town and of course Upington, and several of his sons had found their way into the police. His face became animated as he spoke about his family. But at the same time he painted a picture of steady depopulation, of Witdraai inevitably becoming a settlement of children and elderly. What would be the future of this remote ancestral ground, won back after so many decades of travail and wandering in a landless wilderness? The old man provided me with no reply, saying instead that his eldest son had recently been promoted to sergeant.

On a level stretch of dune, but bounded on one side by sharply rising higher ground, stood Dawid Kruiper's house, a small structure made of grass fixed to a wooden frame. Naked children wandered in and out. An open-air kitchen had been set up, and two young women were working inside this enclosure. A little distance away, a truck stood with the bonnet open. A few young men repaired a tyre in the sand, crouching in the shade of a twisted thorn tree. A small girl kept staggering away with the steel lever used for manipulating the tyre off the rim.

Dawid Kruiper wasn't at home, they said when our guide had introduced us. Hennie asked them about the Communal Property Association. Their replies were noncommittal. Hennie said he had heard that poaching was one of the problems, that R750 000 worth of game had been taken from the Khomani San farms. One of the young men disengaged himself from the repair work and stood before us, but without belligerence. He wore a black T-shirt and a wide-brimmed straw hat.

'We have no guns,' he said. 'We don't even have bows and arrows' – a comment that raised some laughter around the tyre.

'But are the buck disappearing?' Hennie asked.

The man in the black T-shirt gestured towards the dunes. 'You can see for yourself.'

Someone else said: 'It is the others.'

Hennie asked if they knew about the insulting letter. They nodded. The one in the black T-shirt added. 'It is inside the house.' He had a strong face and seemed more robustly built than most of the others. His eyes switched slowly from my face to Hennie's.

Someone said: 'The *indringers* (interlopers) at the top. There is no communication about the property meetings. They want to push us out. They think they are so modern.'

'Come,' the man in the black T-shirt said, and he led us into the grass abode.

It was surprisingly cool. Beds and mats covered most of the sandy floor. A few hens had settled in a corner, no doubt to lay. On one wall was attached a colour picture (a broadsheet pullout from a newspaper) of the South African rugby team. The man produced the letter from a transparent plastic bag containing an assortment of papers and documents.

The letter had been painstakingly and amateurishly typed on a blank sheet of paper, now much folded. It said that it was impossible to sit near to Kruiper and his traditionalists. They smelled of '*kak en piss*'. They smoked dagga. They were generally disgusting. The letter was neither signed nor dated.

Hennie handed it back, so it could be once more folded and put away. He asked when Kruiper would be back. Everyone shrugged their shoulders.

We shook hands with everyone and left. We returned our guide to the general dealer's store, and drove back to the Bushmen outside the gate of the Molopo lodge. They greeted us and pointed. There through the heat and dust (a wind had once again sprung up) came Dawid Kruiper.

He weaved slightly as he came towards us. We introduced ourselves. He stood unsteadily before us with bloodshot eyes. He took the cigarette that Hennie offered. He said that the taking of photographs would have to be negotiated through his lawyer. This also applied to note-taking. He said he had been a film star in many films: *The Gods Must be Crazy*, *Red Scorpion* and others. He said he expected large sums of money.

We sat down in the sand under the thorn tree. Hennie spoke to him about the Communal Property Association. His replies rapidly degenerated to irrelevancy. He kept referring to himself as a doctor and sometimes as a lawyer. In his mind, too, there appeared to be little difference between the now suspended committee of the Khomani San CPA and an organisation called the South African San Institute, not to mention WIMSA (the Working Group of Indigenous Minorities in Southern Africa) and the National Geographic Society of America.

All at once, his wife appeared and Hennie and I rose to greet her. She seemed a pleasant woman with an engaging smile – and she immediately asked for money.

We returned to our conversation with the leader of the Khomani San. He was suddenly lucid in the way inebriated people sometimes are. The letter troubled him. Why had they come to kill him? He leaned forward and began to draw a diagram in the sand. He had reached a crossroad, he said, drawing it. Here at the cross his head would be severed from his body. But how then was he to reach the destination over here? Or were there other paths? If so, where were they? Or was violence inevitable? He looked at me with his discoloured eyes, then lit another of Hennie's cigarettes.

And I thought, as I sat in the sand under the thorn tree with a few four-wheel-drive vehicles speeding past without stopping, of what Betta Steyn had said about the ancient curse that all too often came to outsiders, even professionals, when they had dealings with the Bushmen. They ended up sitting in the sand and smoking dagga with them to get their feeling, she had said, and then becoming caught up in their endless feuds and resentments. I remembered her brilliant gypsy smiles and those pendant earrings that occasionally flashed, and I hoped that the tattooed ant would stay on her right foot forever.

6
Finding the past

A PLEASANT Canadian at the Upington office of the South African San Institute told Hennie and me that the mission of the Institute was to mobilise resources for the benefit of the San people in southern Africa. In particular, he said, the recovery of the San past was of vital importance. To illustrate what he meant, he made a telling analogy.

'Their past is like an earthenware vase that has been thrown on the floor and smashed. Some families may have a few individual pieces, but nobody knows what the whole vase looked like. It is essential that somebody assists with the piecing together of the original vase. It is a basic human right to have a known ethnic identity rooted in the past.'

I asked if this was not in some ways a return to the preoccupation with ethnicity that had characterised apartheid and separate development.

The Canadian, whose name was Nigel, disagreed. He said, yes, apartheid had been based on the premise that there was a direct correlation between language and race and territory, and that it was up to the state simply to administer what God had originally ordained. That was certainly the basis of the homeland policy of separate development: following the natural ethnic and linguistic divisions with their enforced separation.

'This occurred largely with black Africans in the eastern parts of the country,' Nigel went on. 'But when we jump to the western side, we see that something much more pernicious has occurred. In the western parts lived brown people with many different ethnicities and pasts. But under apartheid they were all thrust into the 'Coloured' category. Out of necessity they all learned to speak Afrikaans, although of course this hid a more complex reality. The crudities of apartheid had smothered the history of San and Khoikhoi and Nama alike ...'

Even, I thought while he spoke, the descendants of those slaves imported from the East in the 17th and 18th and early decades of the 19th centuries were lumped into this 'Coloured' category, not to mention all the varying gradations resulting from liaisons between these groups and their white masters. They were all past-less Coloureds, as devoid of history as they were of any essential status.

Nigel was telling us that the Khoisan gene pool was 'the oldest on the planet'. In fact, he said, black African and white European were more alike than either were like the Khoisan. I glanced at Hennie, who sat attentive and absorbed. It seemed all at once a strange place for the son of a wealthy Mpumalanga farmer to be, sitting here with Nigel (whom Hennie knew from his own work with Bushmen) and listening to this darker side of a policy his mother had always been so anxious to see perpetuated.

'Yet the irony for the San,' Nigel said, 'is that even though they're aboriginal, they feel awkward in post-1994 South Africa. They're not black enough. They don't feel African. After tens of thousands of years! There is linguistic evidence to suggest that the southern and east African hunter-gatherers separated 80 000 years ago. But they don't feel African because their past has been blotted out by apartheid. They're simply "coloured". That is why it is essential that their past be rediscovered.'

Land restitution was an important part of this process. It proved and publicly proclaimed that the San had roots. The intention of the San Institute was to help them to come to this realisation, and in this way to get in touch with their own past, finally thus equipped to stand on their own feet. The resuscitation of the old languages was crucial to this whole process as well, Nigel told us.

He was himself a linguist, working through the Institute to assist what he called 'San activists' to standardise an alphabet and develop the capacity to work with the governments of South Africa, Botswana and Namibia – the three countries where most of the surviving 90 000 Bushmen lived. I had read somewhere that of the 14 known San languages in southern Africa, at least four were extinct, and all the others were under severe threat. Nigel told us that the language used by the Khomani San had very nearly been extinguished, but that a few elderly people who could still speak it had been unearthed. Apparently, the two old women I had met in Witdraai, those who had been placed on display in England in the 1930s, could still speak it. In addition, there were two women living here in Upington. In fact, they were both related to members of staff at the local Institute office, those smiling young Coloured women (now identified as San) who had greeted us as we came through that morning to have our chat with Nigel.

Talk turned to the community at Witdraai in the South African corner of the Kalahari. Nigel told us that some families from Upington townships, as well as from the desert towns of Rietfontein and Welkomhartbees, had joined the community living on the 38 000 hectares of farmland owned since 1999 by the Khomani San Communal Property Association. I remembered the rift we had begun to witness between the traditionalists and the westernised people from Upington and elsewhere, 'talking like monkeys on their phones'. Hennie remarked that the elected committee of the Communal Property Association had once again been suspended.

Nigel nodded. He said with surprising vigour that a collection of 'insane people had come out of the woodwork: kings, chiefs, queens and sundry leaders' all in search of a slice of the land restitution and funding pie. 'Opportunists and slime bags,' he called them, 'seizing on the collective hope of a national identity for individual gain.'

UPINGTON SEEMED not much more than a blur of heat and the glittering river, of palm trees and scant shade, of dusty townships and a dome of inhospitable sky that depressed the horizons, thus increasing the impact of the shimmering space and brutal blue fire above. As Hennie and I went about our business there, we put together a brief chronology of the Bushmen of the Kalahari.

These ancient people, the San, living in southern Africa for at least ten thousand years, hunting and gathering, wandering in small self-sufficient groups. It was by the conquest of others, both black and then white, that the Bushmen trekked north and west, gradually adapting to the increasingly arid conditions that they encountered there. Then, from about the middle of the 19th century, hunters and traders from South Africa and Angola began to disturb the relationship between the Khomani San and the wide spaces of the Kalahari desert. San children were sometimes captured as slaves. Later, permanent settlement of Boer farmers further restricted the old Bushman lifestyle – and finally destroyed it. Fences were erected, water sources rendered inaccessible. More damaging still was the European perception that the San were less than human, more animal than *Homo sapiens*, remarkable most of all for their apparent lack of morality and any recognisable social organisation or predictability. It had not always been so. In the hunting days, when ivory and ostrich feathers had been the prize, the Bushmen were praised for their tracking and stalking ability. But when over-hunting brought these lucrative trades to an end, the Bushmen were themselves often ruthlessly hunted. They were subdued as farm labourers or simply eliminated. San women and children found themselves working in the kitchens of Boer families. The destruction of their former way of life was completed by the drought and Great Depression of the 1930s. Even those few groups that had more or less survived as nomads, still roaming the great spaces now comprising the Kgalagadi Transfrontier Park, were deprived of their land when the original game reserve (the Kalahari Gemsbok National Park) was created. Although in the 1960s a small piece of the new park was fenced off for the Bushmen, there were complaints about poaching and they were finally evicted from their ancestral land. They too became wandering farm labourers. Their leader was Regopstaan Kruiper. At last some of them settled as tourist curiosities at Kagga Kamma. But when the chance came for land restitution, the Bushmen left the inhospitable mountains of Kagga Kamma and returned to the Kalahari. In 1996, Regopstaan Kruiper died in a squatter's shack less than five kilometres from the gate of the Park. He was as old as the century. The loss that he and his people had suffered, and the yearning for the red sand of his boyhood, both were immeasurable.

By then, the laws of the land were changing. The old Kalahari Bushmen (the Khomani San) laid claim to all land north of Upington, including the park. The Department of Land Affairs contested the extent of this claim. The South African San Institute (for which Nigel worked) began a cultural and linguistic mapping of the area to prove their lengthy habitation. The matter went to court. The Khomani San won their 38 000 hectares just south of the park. Witdraai became their capital. A trust account was established, to be administered by an elected council of the Khomani San Communal Property Association.

'The rest we know,' Hennie said. 'The fight for councillors to be paid. The lack of proper administration. The absence of improvements or any development on the newly acquired land. The huge thefts of game. Was there an audit of the game? In any case, the CPA council is now suspended. For a second time. The Department of Land Affairs will act as caretakers and organise new council elections. Then the same disaster will occur all over again. We can be pretty certain of that.'

We sat at a formica table in a gathering of such tables, drinking aerated water from plastic bottles. Hennie's attitude seemed to be one of a constantly developing doubt, yet built as a superstructure above a primary level of concern. The beads of perspiration stood out on his upper lip. His brown eyes were gentle and interested: these were the characteristics of his concern. And again I found myself wondering what sequence of events and convictions had brought him from the lush banana groves of Mpumalanga, or for that matter the plush Pretoria suburbs where he had lived as a young teacher, to these desert places and these forlorn San people on the other side of the country.

I expressed this thought to Hennie, adding that I would soon need to ask him to tell me his full and unexpurgated story. Hennie laughed.

WHEN IT grew less scorching in the afternoon, we fetched two smiling young women from the office of the South African San Institute and drove with them to their homes. Our interest in them was as Nigel had intimated. Both were the daughters of San mothers and black African fathers (one from Malawi, the other from Namibia). Both were educated and urbanised in the sense that they lived and worked in Upington and carried no outward trace of their Bushman links, although both were members of the Khomani San Communal Property Association.

The elder of our passengers, a thick-limbed woman named Anna, directed us to her mother's house in a suburb of small houses and dusty streets not too far from the centre of town. She told me that she had no wish to live in Witdraai, or anywhere in the Kalahari, although her mother would need no persuasion to return, she said. In responding to a question from Hennie, it appeared that Anna was working in some way for Dawid Kruiper (the traditional leader with whom we had tried to converse as we sat under that roadside tree in Witdraai). But when Hennie alluded to the suspension of the CPA executive committee she became evasive and vague.

We sat on the veranda with Anna and her mother and Anna's elder sister who was visiting from Saudi Arabia where she was contracted as a nurse. 'From one desert to another,' she said with a faint smile. But she seemed to be an unhappy woman, her face set in an almost haunting expression of discontent. The mother was attentive and bright, but saying little as the conversation unfolded. When Hennie mentioned her linguistic skills she laughed shyly. She sat flat on the veranda, her fat legs stretched before her on a blanket. In this company, as though it might afford some sort of protection from questions she had no wish to answer, Anna became more forthcoming. She had been a member of the previous CPA executive committee, she said, and she guessed that the present problems were financial ones. The government should step in and elect another executive committee, and then install a mentor to assist them. Services were needed to upgrade living conditions on the sand farms (her term for the 38 000 hectares of desert farmland that had been restored to the Khomani San), especially in terms of health and welfare services and education. But development in these spheres should be financed by the state in the normal way, not by the CPA.

The small houses of the suburb pressed in against us as we sat. A few small dogs were barking at the fence. Hennie's pleasant questions directed the conversation. Yes, she, Anna, had been born in the Kalahari Park; as had her mother. There were no doubts concerning their authenticity as Khomani San. But for many others it was not so.

'All these wannabee Bushmen,' Hennie said, and everyone laughed.

Our other passenger, the younger and prettier of the two, and sincere almost to the point of naivete, lived 15 kilometres out of town in Sesbrug, a small township standing cramped inside a perimeter fence and close to the northern bank of the river. Her name was Ruth. As we drove, she told us she had grown up as a 'coloured' girl, essentially unaware of her San ancestry. It was only later, through the restitution of the Kalahari farms and her association with the San Institute, that her consciousness had grown.

Her mother was sitting under a karee tree in the front garden, no doubt to take advantage of the slightly cooler evening air that had begun to stir. She was small and thin and animated, with hand movements like the fluttering of birds. She laughed frequently, seemingly from out of the centre of a life of great contentment, and she could raise her voice to a high-pitched falsetto to provide emphasis for what she was saying. She said, smiling happily at us, that long ago when she was young the Boere had told her that if they ever heard her using that Boesman language they would kill her. So of course they hadn't used it, learning to speak Afrikaans instead. Now, she was the only person in Sesbrug who could speak it. She spoke a few words characterised by clicks and small explosions in her mouth, and then laughed gaily. Yes, she said, she remembered the old days among the dunes of the Kalahari when her father had hunted. Then they had worked on the farm. She had worked in the kitchen. She darned socks. She sewed. Her reward was bread and tea. The Boer woman shouted at her every day. The Boer woman said she did not know why the Lord had created the stupid Boesmans, and perhaps He hadn't created them, these '*skepsels*' who were half human and half animal. How gaily the old woman under the karee tree laughed as she related these hardships.

Ruth, her daughter, seemed slightly pained by the woman's mirth and high spirits. She told us earnestly that it was only now that her mother was elderly that she found the courage to talk of all the oppressive darkness of the past. She, Ruth, also needed courage to acknowledge her Bushman heritage. But she was not ashamed. She wanted to be proud. Her soft face seemed tensed into steadfastness, and her almond-shaped eyes looked shyly at us. She was a small, round young woman, and her skin was smooth and dark, no doubt a gift from her father. Her very posture – the shoulders pushed back slightly and the head erect – reminded me of the work being done by Nigel and the San Institute. Here was the reclamation of another piece of the earthenware vase that had been so degradingly smashed to the floor.

A five-year-old child appeared somewhat warily at the door of the little house. Ruth went to him with a laugh and brought him out. 'This is my son,' she said. He hid behind her skirt. When he was reprimanded for not greeting us properly, he approached with some hesitation. We shook hands, a gesture which turned into an embrace. The child stood looking shyly at the ground. Ruth laughed in her pretty way. The old woman clapped her hands. A gathering of small birds with white eyes fidgeted momentarily in the branches of the karee tree, and the woman raised her face towards them.

Later, we ate a few grapes together in the last of the afternoon sun. A taxi rattled past on the pitted roadway beyond the gate; and a slight taste of dust permeated the sweetness of the fruit. Hennie spat his pips one by one in arching trajectories into a patch of succulents adorning the garden. It seemed such a relaxed and amiable gesture, bringing a sense of ease to us all.

The talk continued. Ruth and Hennie talked of people I did not know. San claimants who could not speak the old languages, and whose names were not on the lists that had been compiled. Names like Springbok and Vaalbooi, and of course many others, that had been traced back and were considered to be core names of the Khomani San. Others simply did not fit, and were consequently not on the list. In this way we came face to face with the difficulties of establishing San authenticity. In a country with hundreds of years of intermarriage and miscegenation, it seemed an impossible task. One stood staring into an impenetrable genealogical tangle. Suddenly the whole land restitution business seemed senseless. I thought of the intoxicated leader drawing lines in the sand under the Witdraai tree. I thought of Ruth with her lovely dark skin and almond eyes, those classic gifts from Black Africa. A San identity was like a passport into the future for her. Yet the opportunists, the slime bags as Nigel had called them, thought nothing of this. And who could tell how many omissions and false inclusions characterised the list of the members of the Khomani San Communal Property Association? It struck me, as I watched Hennie spitting his grape pips in those perfect arcs, that for a country so historically obsessed with racial purity it had nevertheless been filled with assimilation and the blending of cultures and the blood that supported them. Perhaps one of the effects of the attempts to recompense the marginalised would be to arrest the process of assimilation. But at what cost would be this temporary delay in an inevitable process?

And yet. There were these doubts everywhere, like shadows, as evening came at last to the crowded little township of Sesbrug. The restoration of the vase could not be stopped. The validity of Ruth could not be denied. And when we rose to say our goodbyes, the old woman who remembered so clearly her own hunter-gatherer past astonished me. She did not rise. She clasped my hand, as she did Hennie's. And stooped towards her I saw clearly the tears on her creased old face. Was it the too-blithe recollection of old times and old humiliations that had brought her heartache? Or were the tears simply a manifestation of her joy, or perhaps an inkling of her daughter's joy, that the long eclipse was over?

BEFORE WE began our 350-kilometre drive east to Schmidtsdrift and Platfontein and more San complexities, Hennie took me to see some Afrikaner artists he knew who were living in Upington. It turned out that these were the people whose children Betta Steyn with her doeks and gypsy earrings had first gone to the Kalahari to baby-sit. The man was away, but his wife Catharina made tea which we drank at an old table in the profusely overgrown garden. The grass was uncut, and through dense foliage I could see the harsh aridity and boulders of a vacant piece of ground beyond the perimeter of this well-watered oasis. Yellow weaver birds with black faces and red eyes chattered noisily at nests attached to the long pliant branches of a willow tree.

Catharina was dark-haired, and she told us she was one week away from her 40th birthday. She wore spectacles behind which her eyes showed very calm and strong. It was the strength born of a tempestuous relationship, it seemed, for I soon gathered that her husband's absence might have had something to do with his problems with alcohol. He was nevertheless a talented painter, a realist who often depicted the unsightly relics and through them the failure of white settlement in platteland South Africa. But it was not about art that Catharina and Hennie spoke. It was at first about mutual acquaintances. The conversation, conducted in animated Afrikaans, reminded me of Hennie's exchanges with Betta Steyn. There was the same conspiratorial tone, the same camaraderie between Afrikaners outside the mainstream, people who sought new meaning among the relics of the profound difficulties that constituted the Afrikaner past. Finally, Catharina asked Hennie about his work with the Bushmen.

112

This question began a conversation on the difficulties surrounding the restitution of land. Here were the Griquas claiming everything they possibly could, Hennie said; and the San activists claiming, or promising to claim, every yard of territory that had a rock painting or engraving on it. So much so that some farmers were no longer willing to admit to any rock art on their properties, thus making the task of preservation (an aim of the Northern Cape Rock Art Trust for which Hennie now worked) much more difficult. Soon there would be no land left not under dispute. They laughed. Catharina said in her calm way: 'I don't want to live anywhere where I'm not welcome. Maybe, in the end, this will have to be on a boat anchored off the coast.'

Then Catharina said: 'Oh, talking of Bushman art, I must show you something quite remarkable.'

She disappeared for a moment, returning from the house with an exercise book filled with drawings by a Bushman soldier illustrating his experiences with the South African military in Angola. He had been 21 years old when the war ended. Now he was living under canvas at Schmidtsdrift. It was not clear to me how Catharina had been in contact with the soldier, but it was she who had encouraged him to record his experiences by making the drawings. The result was a collection of meticulously made drawings of helicopters, armoured troop carriers, jet aircraft and other weapons, bleeding figures lying on the ground, homesteads ablaze, faces in agony and horror. Catharina said knowledgeable friends had told her that the detail of the military hardware depicted in the drawings was unerringly accurate. The visual memory of an illiterate, we said. Hennie looked at the drawings in silence, turning the pages again and again. Perhaps the story of the Schmidtsdrift ex-soldier drawing his experiences of war with a ruler and ball-point pen had come unexpectedly to penetrate his central preoccupation, and had in a way lowered his guard.

The story that had culminated at Schmidtsdrift, as far as I knew it, returned to me as well.

The !Xun and Khwe Bushman communities, respectively from Angola and Caprivi, had become embroiled in the Angolan war of independence against Portugal, serving on the Portuguese side. So had the old ways of life been mortally damaged. When Angolan independence

113

had been achieved in 1974, these Bushmen communities had fled south, all the way over the border into northern South West Africa. They were soon recruited as trackers into the South African Defence Force that was then engaged in fighting supporters of SWAPO (the South West African People's Organisation). The !Xun and Khwe trackers and their families had been housed in an army camp called Omega. They lived there for 16 years. When South West Africa gained independence as Namibia in 1990, the homeless !Xun and Khwe flew south, literally, in military aircraft carrying them to the tents at Schmidtsdrift.

Hennie sat with the exercise book lying on the old garden table between the three of us. 'A little while ago,' he recounted, 'I found some photographs that had been taken at Omega. I showed them to a group of !Xun and Khwe at the Rock Art Centre on Platfontein. At first there was some excitement. Young men and women recognising themselves as kids; or a relative who had since died; and so on. And then – it was shocking – one by one they began to weep. I had never known what it must be like to be homeless. Then I knew. Omega meant so much to them, that dismal army camp, and the wrenching away from it was so awful. They showed me one young girl in the photographs. Her baby had died just hours before the aircraft left. She was too terrified to speak. She flew all the way to South Africa, and came all the way down to the tents at Schmidtsdrift with the dead baby clutched in her arms. To catch sight of such dislocation is almost unspeakable.'

We sat silent. The weavers chattered in the willow tree. A slight breeze turned the pages of the exercise book, showing glimpses of the machines of war. Catharina looked at him with one of her calm smiles, a light of understanding deepening her eyes. It was as if, I thought, she supported him in the sudden desolation of those moments.

'I WAS BORN in Nelspruit in 1965. I grew up on my father's farm near Sabi. I went to the primary school in Hazyview by bus. My grandfather was well-travelled. We were wealthy, although of course I didn't realise this at first. We were very strongly into the Dutch Reformed Church, and it was a powerful influence in my upbringing. The church and the volk were everything.'

This was Hennie talking as we drove through the green of the riverside agriculture to Groblershoop, turning east there towards Griqua-town and Campbell and then Schmidtsdrift and beyond. He spoke easily enough, yet with a slightly mocking tone at times, as if some of the things he knew he must say embarrassed him in the actual saying.

'So there I was, the model Afrikaner boy. Going to church, going to school, listening to my grandfather's stories, honouring my parents, idolising my elder brother, living in my small protected world like any other normal child. Of course, I was soon aware of the people around me on the farm. There were four hundred Zulu labourers doing the bananas and timber and some oranges; and we also had a Malawian house boy in a white tunic. I have a very vivid memory of listening to the drumming that would come sometimes from the compounds for hours and hours in the night. And I always seem to remember this as being accompanied by a bright moon shining. The romance of Africa, hey!

'Of course, I played with the Zulu boys from the compounds, but I was conscious of my superiority. For example, I used to race down the hills in my box cart, with the Zulu boys running beside me, and then they would push me back up again. Inexorably, though, my world began to expand.

'When I was in standard five, I started listening to *Patrolie 333 Charlie*, a programme on Springbok Radio about our war in Angola. This intrigued me. I wondered where Angola Patrol 333 actually was. But it was only after I started high school in Nelspruit that the military real-ity began to live with me. You are a boy; therefore you will be a soldier. For two years this will happen. This was inevitable, inescapable, unques-tionable. Your enemies will be black people. You are going to kill and perhaps be killed. Such things weighed heavily. My future was being shaped for me. And also I was becoming more and more aware of the distances between white and black. Any sort of synthesis was out of the question.

'Let me tell you about one memory. It's funny now, I suppose. But I used to go shopping in Nelspruit with my father sometimes and see black people from Lesotho driving big cars. This always annoyed my father, and he would always say: *waar die donner kry hulle die geld vir so 'n motor?* (Where the hell do they get the money for such a car?) The implication was not so much that they might have stolen it, but that they (the black people) were encroaching on our space. They had no right to be as wealthy as we were. It was unseemly. It was also the first step to an unthinkable equality.

'When I was in standard seven one of my women teachers took an interest in me. She called me sometimes after school and tried to encourage my reading and writing. I found out she was an alcoholic. She said she was very concerned about the future of the country.

'But my overriding consciousness in those years was of the war. In Nelspruit, I saw films like *Kaptein Kaprivi* and *Kariba Meer*, which showed brave white soldiers in conflict with terrorists. The links between South Africa and the war going on in Rhodesia were obvious, and constantly pointed out. White people were fighting for their survival. It was western civilisation against communism. I remember someone we knew getting killed in an army accident. It was immediately *die vokking terroriste* (the fucking terrorists) that were to blame. We used to get letters from Angola, from my elder brother, with lines and words blacked out by the censors. Then he'd come back and talk about "contact" and all the horrible things he'd witnessed. The whole war thing was very close around me as I grew up. It dominated my thinking.

'Once, when my brother was home, a black boy named Dick – I suppose he was more of a personal servant for me on the farm – began to admire the rifle and other bits of my brother's army equipment. He said he also wanted to be a soldier. I remember the awkwardness. I remember trying to explain the situation to him, that being black he could not join the army, that in fact he should be part of the enemy, and how irritable I had got that day. I remember kicking things in my anger.

'By now it was 1983 and I was in matric. We began to have discussions with our teachers. One day a boy at the back of the class asked directly: "What is this ANC? I hear things. I want to know." I realised that he spoke out of the secret places that were aching in all of us. But those three letters had been openly said. They were in the air. The teacher – I remember he had a big moustache – went pale. He told the boy to sit down immediately. The discussions stopped. The boy who had asked the question was removed from the class. He was severely beaten, not once but several times.

'So there was this anger and curiosity simmering in me all the time, and coupled with it was this looming necessity to kill and perhaps to be killed. The alcoholic teacher was teaching us Afrikaans literature. She lent me books by Etienne Leroux and a few others that seemed to me to challenge a great deal of what we were taught. So I would go from my lonely alcoholic with her books and unhappiness to the history class to study the barbarism and treachery of black people being pitted against the reasonable God-fearing white men at Blood River. So in these ways I began very seriously to doubt.

'After matric, I went straight to a training college in Pretoria. I had decided I would become a teacher, a course of action that would defer my military obligations for another three years. My parents saw to it that I had my own flat in Sunnyside, and also my own car. I was definitely a privileged white student. The sense of freedom was highly exciting. For some time, I forgot all about the war and the deepening contradictions of the country I was living in. I was young. I made lots of friends. We used to go to Rockey Street in Johannesburg and mingle in the non-racial coffee shops and night clubs there. It seemed a very worldly thing to do. We went to the Market Theatre and sometimes looked at dissident Afrikaans plays, and we definitely listened to the dissident Afrikaans music that began to come out in the middle eighties. You know, people like Johannes Kerkorrel and his friends. There was a big world out there, especially for a *plaasjapie* (country bumpkin) like me, and I plunged into it.

'But one couldn't escape the other reality. At the college, one of our subjects was *geeste weerbaarheid*. What's that in English? I suppose something like spiritual defence or spiritual resistance. The lecturer was passionately anti-communist, anti-socialist, and as passionately Christian nationalist. His job was to build our inner strength so we would be able to cope with the total onslaught. I felt the mockery coming into my throat sometimes. I was learning all this crap and writing it down, but secretly realising that it was okay to think of it as crap. We used to go to the Union Buildings for picnics in the gardens sometimes. To amuse ourselves, we'd make up stories of all the terrible things going on in the corridors and offices of this seat of power of the Nationalist government. My disdain felt like a combination of merriment and bitter anger. I found myself directing it at the church, at the Afrikaner establishment, at the military. The army was a favourite joke on those picnics. We would go, if they forced us, but we would do so without any conviction. And then,' Hennie added with a laugh, 'we'd deliberately piss on the roses when we were drunk.'

I had asked Hennie to drive, to enable me to take a few notes. So he rarely looked at me while he spoke, and I saw him only in profile. The kindly, heavy-jowled face, the hair curling boyishly onto his forehead, the often cutting honesty of his words – and beyond this aspect of him the big hot country stretched away in an endless repetition of thorn scrub, ant hills and flat horizons.

He told me that after his teacher training had been completed, he moved immediately to the university to study educational psychology. It was during this time that the whole system of conscription had seemed slowly to collapse, or at least to lose its absolute power. At the university, he became friendly with political activists working for democracy, but he had not seriously become involved. He had also married during this time. He finally graduated in 1989 and secured a post as school psychologist in a big suburban high school in Pretoria. He was 25 years old.

'Then of course in February of 1990 Mandela was released. The feeling at the school I had just joined came as a shock to me. My years at varsity had in a way prepared me for what was to come. All my professors had been young Afrikaners, many of them quite radical; and the classes were racially mixed, of course. But now, at the school, the feeling of dismay was universal. Elections were on the way. One-man-one-vote was on the way. That would be the end. Nobody saw it as a step forward, as they might well have done in Afrikaner academic circles.

'Once a month or so, all the male teachers at the school got together to have a braai in someone's garden, and to get drunk. It was a kind of release for them. They talked interminably of rugby, of how they hated their jobs, of being locked into suburbia and sexual frustration. They had an end-is-nigh attitude to everything. In five years, the whole situation in education would change, they said. Half the big suburban high school where they all taught would be black. How could they teach black kids? There would be no discipline. It was a dark, dark cloud coming towards us. And hadn't I heard that the ANC was buying up properties all over Pretoria North using white fronts? Later there would be black occupancy. Then property prices would drop. I must say I didn't enjoy their negativity much.

'By contrast, the boys were so optimistic. I went on a tour with them to Waterval Boven. It really opened my eyes to the changes that were taking place. The teachers showed them numerous films on nature conservation. That was the first change. In my day, in the seventies and early eighties, we would have been shown exclusively military stuff. The boys' attitudes were invigorating for me. One small group had begun importing takkies from Lesotho and selling them to friends. We're going to make money, they said; fuck the rest. One of the features of these school tours was the meditation times. When I was a schoolboy, you had to take your Bible and contemplate the trials and tribulations of the chosen people. The group I had charge of said they didn't want to read the Bible or pray. They wanted to talk about the ANC. So we had a smoke together and talked about the future. They seemed so young and enthusiastic. It was wonderful.

'Going to Schmidtsdrift was really very easy,' Hennie said. 'Although I was doing well – I even had my own office and my life was very pleasant – something lacked. Then my wife, herself a teacher, heard about the need for teachers at this place called Schmidtsdrift. We had no idea that there were Bushmen there. My wife suggested we make the telephone call. I forgot all about it. She made the suggestion again. I telephoned. Yes, of course I had heard of the Bushman tracker Battalion 31. The need was desperate, the voice said. I spoke to my headmaster. He said: you're completely crazy. Then he said: go and look, otherwise you'll never be satisfied.

'We drove down in my brand-new bakkie. We couldn't find the camp. It was hot. We were looking for a place near a river in the Northern Cape. That's about as much as we knew. At last, after directions upon directions, we saw the tents stretching out in the bush. Here were thousands of Bushmen. We stood in the blazing sun in front of a crowd of ragged children. Someone played a tune on a piano accordion. I recognised the hymn, *Wie is Hy wat op die water loop?* (Who is He that walks on the water?). Then those little yellow-brown children began to sing it in their Bushman language. It was a moment of almost shocking emotion

119

for me. Something cracked in my head. I signed immediately. We found a house in Douglas.'

We drove in silence for some time. There seemed little, for a few moments at any rate, that could usefully be added. Hennie glanced at me with a slightly rueful grin.

'These Bushmen,' he said, 'had very nearly been destroyed by African colonial politics. Me, I had all my life been fucked around by South African politics. Now there seemed to be a coming together of all the different pieces of my life. I had never before experienced such a sense of peace and certainty as then.'

WE TOOK a detour, on our way to Schmidtsdrift, to the town of Douglas where it huddled not far from the confluence of the Vaal and Orange rivers. Seen from a slightly elevated distance, the intensive agriculture along the banks looked golden, as if everything at once had become ripe for harvesting. The town itself displayed a distinct sense of wellbeing, the buildings low but not derelict, the residential streets graced by mature trees. The green and white house rented by Hennie and his wife was still there, but now turned into a bed-and-breakfast establishment. Even the old garage now had lace curtains at windows installed as part of its transformation into a quaint and diminutive *Africa Cottage*.

Hennie had another story yet to tell. He spoke of the fear that had gripped the town in 1994. When the Bushmen had first arrived, a petition had gone out from the farmers here that they should be settled elsewhere. It could not have been easy to contemplate the thought of several thousand expert trackers and hunters on your doorstep, hunters moreover who needed no rifles for the hunt. Even more difficult was the uncertainty generated by the pending general election.

'We got involved with the white community preparing for "the end",' Hennie recalled. 'They were very good to us, and by that time I was a deacon in the church in Douglas. But we lived this double life. We taught at Schmidtsdrift by day, and by night we were drawn into what amounted to nothing short of plans for the defence of Douglas. The conviction was that when polling began, Douglas would be attacked by hordes of ANC supporters who would kill all whites and plunder white properties. We planned the defence with maps. Bakkies were turned into military vehicles with weapons hidden among agricultural litter. All access roads would be defended. On Saturday nights we had our braais. The men would go over the check lists for the bakkies, the women would do the same for all the emergency supplies, everything from tinned food to hand cream and insect repellent. Then we would all have a few drinks, eat the braai, and go home.'

The sense of unreality for Hennie and his wife increased when they became volunteers for the Independent Electoral Commission, helping to put up banners and organise the various polling stations.

'About a week before the elections, a resigned calm settled over Douglas. It was almost a pathetic thing. *Ons kannie poep teen donnerweer*, people said; we cannot fart against thunder. The Boere came to church in huge numbers, making their peace. And I was with them, checking the vehicles and the emergency supplies. These people genuinely thought they were going to have their heads blown off. Then, the final straw was De Klerk and Mandela conversing on the television. De Klerk, their last resource, had grievously betrayed them. They knew they were going to die; they knew equally that they would die fighting.'

On the morning of the first election day, Hennie said, the bakkies guarded the access roads to Douglas as planned, while he and his wife, as part of a team comprising black and Coloured people and also an Indian woman, manned the polling station at Schmidtsdrift. No hordes appeared; and no one died. The right-wing Freedom Front distributed some pamphlets. A few combi-loads of black youth came from Kimberley to toyi-toyi for a while. The Bushmen voted in a desultory way. In Douglas it was even quieter. In the darkness of the first evening of the elections the militarised bakkies stole away, and the possibility of peace dawned in the troubled hearts of many whites.

We took a final glance at the garage that had once housed Hennie's brand-new bakkie and was now transformed into the picturesque *Africa Cottage*. We savoured the irony. Then we turned our thoughts more fully in the direction of the tented camp at Schmidtsdrift.

7

Sacred sites

THE SCHMIDTSDRIFT town of canvas presented a cheerless sight from the dirt road running along one side of the fenced area of bush that contained it. Hundreds of khaki tents stretched away between the thorn bushes and yellowing grass of the veld. This had been home to 4 500 Khwe and !Xun for more than a decade. Now they were waiting to be taken to the brick-built houses at Platfontein. I thought of the young man who had drawn the helicopters and tanks in the exercise book fluttering on Katrina's garden table. I thought of the teenage girl clutching her dead baby through all the hours of transit from Omega to here. They were in this sun-blasted camp before me; somewhere close by they were living out their lives in the twilight between old and new, between known and unknown.

It seemed a cruel twist that after the wrench away from their homes in Angola and Caprivi to Omega, and then the wrench away from Omega, now these communities must endure this new upheaval, this time as they moved to Platfontein. Most of them had lived all their lives in this state or expectation of transit, the physical reality perfectly reflecting a much deeper spiritual process.

Why could they not be left where they were at Schmidtsdrift, living along the river on land once owned by the military? The answer drew one onto another land-restitution level. For the military to take occupation of the land in the first place, it had to be purchased from white farmers. Living on the land before the farmers arrived had been Tswana-speaking people from the Batlapeng clan. They stayed on as farm labourers in a system of serfdom. But when the farms were sold they could not remain: the army wanted to use the land as a practice firing range for artillery and strike aircraft. So about four thousand Batlapeng were forcibly removed to a piece of the old Bophuthatswana homeland near Kuruman, 200 kilometres to the north. Any hopes that the Khwe and !Xun Bushmen might settle permanently at Schmidtsdrift were dashed when the Batlapeng land claim was lodged. The Tswana-speakers would therefore return to their ancestral land and the Bushmen would move 80 kilometres further east to Platfontein. The houses were currently being built.

'Land restitution is unarguably fair and humane,' Hennie said. 'But there is another side. In a way, I suppose, it recreates a definite physical segregation – especially for small groups like the Batlapeng and the Khomani San. Probably for the !Xun and Khwe as well. And there is also the element of greed,' he went on. 'I remember once, Coca Cola giving a donation to our Schmidtsdrift school of thousands of litres of free coke. Children and their parents were actually coming to blows for more than their fair share. I've sometimes wondered whether this isn't a fairly good analogy for what happens when there is free land up for grabs. People want to get as much as they can for themselves out of the windfall.'

We drove in via a wide road and stopped for a moment at the heart of the camp. Here were permanent structures of brick and corrugated iron. A little distance away an elevated water tank broke the skyline, and beneath it in every direction stood the tents, many of them stained and sagging, and into which well-trodden roadways dispersed.

'We came from Douglas in a school bus,' Hennie said. 'Most of the teachers lived there. In those early days, a cloud of uncertainty was hanging over Schmidtsdrift all the time. Everything was so temporary, and especially because the elections were coming up, and who knew what would happen after that. Perhaps the Bushmen would be sent back to Angola. There was no job security for white staff. Some thought that there would really be no life at all after the elections. But of course the elections came and went and life went on.'

It did not take long before Hennie was promoted to head of department, and then he became the deputy headmaster. Under his care was a combined primary and secondary school with over a thousand pupils being taught in large marquees. He had acted swiftly to make improvements. He changed the syllabus, throwing out the old Afrikaans material and matching the new to fit more closely with the children's life experiences. He also worked on the attitudes of the teachers.

'There was, to begin with, not much rapport between teachers and learners,' he said. 'So I brought the teachers into much closer contact with the community by taking them every Friday into the residential tent towns where their pupils lived. It certainly helped to modify their attitudes.'

Finally, Hennie himself had moved into the camp at Schmidtsdrift. He pointed out the house where he and his young family had lived. It seemed hardly larger than two rooms. There was no garden, just the sand and gravel of the open space upon which it stood, as if at the edge of a parade ground.

'In many ways I made my peace with the army here,' he said. 'They were very helpful, very organised. And the people were all right: like all the rest of us they were just trying to do their jobs.'

We drove slowly along the roadways that passed between the tents. The sides of some tents were rolled up, and we saw people lolling in the shade. Others sat under thorn trees. Everything was dusty. Sometimes people waved – particularly when we got out of the car and they were more easily able to recognise Hennie. He spoke to them in an easy and familiar manner. Two old women staggered past, almost paralysed in their drunkenness. Some youths stopped to talk. They had just written matric at Hennie's old school. One said he was going to Johannesburg with his girlfriend.

Hennie said: 'What about Platfontein?'

The youth shrugged his shoulders. 'I can always come back.'

At another place, we stopped to look at a few women making crafts. One of them took us to see her garden, a patch of hand-tilled earth filled with half-grown plants behind her tent. The heat struck upwards from the terracotta earth. 'Goodbye, *liefies*,' Hennie called as we drove off. He showed me the school: corrugated-iron classrooms with open ventilation spaces all round the walls just under the roof. 'My office used to be in that military vehicle over there,' he said. 'As hot as hell in summer; quite nice in winter. And see that rostrum? The army built it for me and that's where I stood to hold morning assemblies and also to address the school on special occasions.'

We drove on through the high heat of the day. He said: 'Incrementally, but very organically, I became involved in Communal Property

Association business. It was a logical extension of my position at the school. It didn't take too long, and I was their de facto chief executive officer. Then the CPA sold some diamond royalties attached to Platfontein. They were then able to pay me, so I made the break. But it was difficult for me: wrenching myself out of education and into the huge responsibility of the CPA.'

We traversed a piece of open ground between two gatherings of tents. Hennie referred to this as the no-man's-land – between the !Xun on that side and the Khwe on this. I remarked on the seeming emptiness of the camp. Hennie explained that many of the men, and some of the families, had abandoned the tents and were living in shelters that they had made along the banks of the river.

'They're sitting down there making bows and arrows,' he said. 'So you can see why I'm nervous about the move into those neat rows of houses at Platfontein. They're like suburbs: one for the !Xun and one for the Khwe. Will they be too close together? Will they fight? The good news, though, is that the young people are much happier to mix than their parents. They've been to school together for the past decade. It'll be the new generation that will begin to heal the old antagonisms. Of course, it's always the new generation that takes the process of assimilation another step forward.'

We passed slowly along the rutted roads through the interminable drabness of the tents. Children ran beside the vehicle sometimes, calling to Hennie and laughing, but the heat suppressed their persistence. Hennie's eyes were alert, interested in everything. In this way I saw him in his own milieu. I saw where he, the wealthy Afrikaner boy from Mpumalanga, had been able to make an impact. But most of all I caught the symbiosis between the man and the situation that had transformed his life. The piano accordion – I remembered the unconscious poignancy with which he had recounted that moment – and the singing children had caused something to crack inside his head. It was at that moment that this dreary and degrading camp had become a hallowed place.

THE ROCK art site at Platfontein was easily accessible via a tarred road from Kimberley. Indeed, there was parking there, and also the modern building (museum, auditorium, restaurant and crafts shop) where

Hennie now worked as director of the Northern Cape Rock Art Trust. The building was painted a pinkish terracotta colour with a pale grey roof. It had been symmetrically built around a central skylight, and there were mosaics made by !Xun and Khwe artists set into the floor. The architects, Hennie told me, had at first suggested something rather different. But the Communal Property Association had issued specific instructions: 'traditional' or 'cultural' structures, or even imitations of these, were not wanted, but rather a proper modern building made with conventional materials like bricks and plaster, doors and windows, and an iron roof.

So this is what had been provided. In the modern terracotta building, tourists were shown a few films in the auditorium. On the morning that I attended, San music played – a male voice accompanied by plucked strings – as tourists from a luxury bus drifted in. It had been suggested, by the architects and others, to have a stage in the auditorium where the Bushmen could do traditional dances, and perform the fire-making ritual, for tourists. But this was not seen by the Bushmen themselves as an opportunity. The idea had come from outsiders, and again any artificial return to things traditional was rejected by the !Xun and Khwe. Then the auditorium darkened and the images began.

First, we were shown an expanse of savanna and a depiction of volcanic action – close-ups of molten lava and plentiful sparks – all happening 2 600-million years ago to create the current landscape of Wildebeest Kuil. This really was Eden, the commentary said, one of the venues for the start of the human adventure. The San diaspora had been brought about by Bantu-speaking peoples (and European settlers when they arrived) forcibly dispersing them from the eastern seaboard of southern Africa and driving them north. Another set of images showed how the religion of the ancestors had been replaced by 'the new Christian God'. This had happened fairly effortlessly, according to the time spent upon it. Later, they had fought for the Portuguese as that colonial power had struggled to retain Angola, and finally on the side of the South Africans against Sam Nujoma and SWAPO. I recognised, as the result of the latter allegiance, the expanse of tents at Schmidtsdrift, the bare ground, the dust, the torn canvas. Children queued with mugs, waiting for sustenance. I remembered Hennie telling me how children

and adults alike had fought for their fair share, or more, of the free Coca
Cola that had once been offered. Then the combined housing subsidies
of the !Xun and Khwe had bought Platfontein, and now everyone
would be much happier.

At some point in this basic chronology, we were shown a trance dance
– 'famous for its spirituality'. There was such a heaviness for me in seeing the people dance. They were connecting with their cosmology, the
commentary said, with their spirit world. (There was likewise vomiting
involved, and a teeming array of phosphenes – although the film did
not touch on these aspects.) The dance also carried a healing function
for Bushmen. The San believed in two gods: the healing god and the
other one who came to the fore at death. But my heaviness was not pro-
voked by these details. Rather, it was by another memory. This time
delivered by the woman I had met in the Kalahari, Betta Steyn: the
trance dance in the Kalahari, performed for a rapt New Age audience,
that was little more than a drunken whirl to some scratchy gospel music
powered by a car battery.

Throughout the showing of the film, one of the tourists kept taking
flash photographs of the screen. There seemed in this action to be a true
fog of misunderstanding. Would the light on the screen not be obliterated by the brighter light from the flash so that in the end the tourist
would be left simply with snapshots of a blank screen? All at once, for
me, the tourist's action – particularly the persistence of the flashes in
the darkened auditorium – became illustrative of the more general
attitudes displayed towards Bushmen in their largely unhappy contact
with a more sophisticated world than their own.

The early response to these extraordinary people was to exterminate
them as vermin. They were too close in behaviour and impulse to more
'civilised' observers, and yet too distant in dress (or undress) and
hygiene and habit for any comfort. And, besides, they were expert stock
thieves. So to exterminate them and obliterate their way of life seemed
a logical response. Yet so did the next much more romanticised response: to hold them up as examples of an essential human mutuality
and happiness, and to begin to worship them as particularly saintly
examples of the noble savage. This new perception came into prominence after the brutalities and disillusionments of World War II when

people, particularly Europeans, longed for an escape from the Cold War struggles and the suspicions and lack of trust and insane piles of armaments that came with that time. San communities were seen as exemplifying everything that the modern world was not. No wonder they were (and are) worshipped. The cameras flashed away, obliterating the realities, particularly those relating to the inevitable changes that would come as Bushmen rubbed shoulders with the wider world. The constantly flashing cameras obliterated all trace of the processes of assimilation and transition. The awful sight of unwashed and largely naked people wandering around in the bush was replaced by the ennobling vision of primitives at peace with themselves and their neighbours.

The film did provide a deeper insight. An historian named John Wright said that these people (the San) were not relics from the past but essential elements of the present. This perception brought me closer to the current reality: that glimpse of ordinary human beings struggling to come to terms with new demands and in so doing testing to the limit their powers of adaptability. I was certain that this was what Hennie had seen when he first went to Schmidtsdrift; and what the tourist with the flashing camera missed completely.

When the film ended, we filed out of the auditorium. The tourists were provided with small tape players and earphones. They then passed through glass doors at the rear of the building and into the searing sunlight of the sacred site. I lingered, going instead into an exhibition room that provided me with some of the background.

Wildebeest Kuil presented the visitor with traces of history stretching from the ancient past into the present. On the sacred site itself, a low and rocky hill directly behind the tourist centre, later Stone-Age hunter gatherers, ancestral to the Khoisan, lived and made rock engravings about a thousand to two thousand years ago. The engravings, and their setting in the landscape, hinted at a spirituality that could also be sensed in many other sites across the subcontinent. Pre-dating the engravings were hand axes and heavy stone flakes found at the edges of the nearby pans. In later times, these Stone-Age people had been caught up in a struggle for land as the colonial frontier advanced inland. Many had fled further north towards the desert regions of the Kalahari and beyond. Those who remained were absorbed into colonial society. In the exhibition space, as well, hung the representation of a wildebeest engraving (the animal standing alert with its horns at a perfect angle) that had been dated at 4 000 years old.

Outside in the brightness of the day, once one's eyes had made the adjustment, the landscape was of red earth, grass waving in a breeze, dark stones and boulders littering the flat places and collecting in more concentrated configurations in the direction of the low hill some five hundred metres ahead. This was where the rock engravings could be seen.

Closer at hand stood thorn bushes with large white thorns in pairs, and other bushes adorned with pale green pods. The prescribed tourist route to and from the engraving site was circuitous, and I did not follow it. The tourists walked from station to station, according to their taped instructions. I walked more directly towards the hill. Above me a clapper lark soared into the air, working its wings, then fell in a steep descent accompanied by a protracted whistle. I passed one station – station 10 – from which the skyline of Kimberley could be seen. The view was reproduced in a landscape photograph protected under perspex. The caption read: *To the east is Kimberley, a city of about 200 000, and the capital of the Northern Cape province. It was born in the 1870s, in the dust, dreams and disappointments of the greatest diamond rush the world has ever seen.* But I pressed on towards the low hill, seeing tourists spread out over the summit, heads bowed as they searched for engravings, and sometimes taking photographs before moving on.

The hill, when I gained it, seemed saturated with engravings, representations of animals and a few humans, chipped onto the faces of individual rocks. The rocks lay dark among the grass and among themselves, and it sometimes took a moment for the eye to adjust so that the engravings could emerge. Here were buck of every kind, and elephants and rhino and ostriches. I became aware – and the realisation came slowly, incrementally – of being surrounded by hundreds of depictions made by human hands identical to my own. One engraving showed figures dancing: a trance dance perhaps. I wondered what it must have been like, then, with the sound of stone on stone, with the sight of game grazing on the surrounding plains, the huge blue sky touched in places with thin wisps of cloud, and the sound of children's voices similar to the voices that Hennie had heard when he listened to the singing of a Christian hymn the first time he had gone to Schmidtsdrift.

A sign at the hill-top station instructed me. *As the hill rises above the surrounding plains, so the spirit world under the earth may have been seen to 'break through'. At such a place as this some engravings show animals of the spirit world as if they are emerging from within the rock, while others 'connect' with the spirit realm above.* Here was this ancient concept of human occupation of the earth, of living on the surface, but of being irrevocably connected to those other two spheres: the underworld and that wondrous sphere above our heads. The breeze blew across the hill top, waving the grass, cooling the engravings as they baked in thousands of years of sunlight and gradually decomposed.

Hennie told me once that he had taken a group of !Xun and Khwe young people from Platfontein into Kimberley to do some errands. They were in a shop with television sets everywhere, and they saw an aeroplane flying into the side of a tall building. The date was 11 September. The young Bushmen enthused over the images. 'Wow!' they said. 'Aren't the Americans clever to make such things happen for the cameras.'

I could not clearly understand why that story, with all its veracity and its glimpse of the impact of limited knowledge on our deepest human responses, should seem so apposite as I stood on that beautiful and persuasive hill called Wildebeest Kuil.

IN THE restaurant area of the Wildebeest Kuil visitors' centre, beyond the little sea of tables, an array of San curios and crafts was displayed, and framed artworks covered the far wall. The tourists strolled in, returning their audio equipment to impassive young men working behind a counter, then moved in among the crafts, buying a few things, or settling at the tables for a little refreshment. A low chatter of conversation filled the restaurant. When they had gone, filing with their colourful clothes and dangling cameras onto their luxury bus, I spoke to the two young men behind the counter.

In fact, at the suggestion of Hennie who was working in his little office at the front of the building, they joined me at a restaurant table. I bought tea and cool-drinks, and we sat looking through closed glass doors over the flat veld, now shimmering in heat, to the skyline of

Kimberley. The young men told me that Platfontein, where they would soon live, had been incorporated into the same local authority that administered the city.

Both young men were !Xun, and both had been born at Omega, the military base in northern Namibia. Jaoquem had been in his early teens when he arrived at Schmidtsdrift; Titu had been a child of nine. They had spent the better part of their lives in the tents. They had gone to school in tents, no doubt both taught by Hennie or his wife, and both had matriculated there.

Jaoquem's father (Hennie had told me) was probably Portuguese. The young man before me now was light-skinned, bright-eyed, self-assured. Titu was darker, quite thickset, but shyer and seeming more nonplussed than his companion. They smiled politely at me, then looked away through the glass doors.

I asked if they ever thought of going back to Angola, to their roots.

'To look, yes. And to Namibia, to Omega. But not to live there again.'

One of them had an uncle in Grootfontein in northern Namibia, who sometimes came to visit. He drove down all the way in his car. I had a momentary vision of the men in the dunes at Witdraai, at David Kruiper's house, repairing a tyre in the sand, crouching in the shade of a twisted thorn tree, while at some distance from where they worked stood an old truck with the bonnet gaping open like a mouth. To get from Grootfontein to Schmidtsdrift or Platfontein would be a journey of around two thousand kilometres. And yet such cross-border journeys were being made.

We talked about life in the Schmidtsdrift tents.

'The people feel confined. They are surrounded by a fence. They can't go out onto the free land. Most of them live at the river now. They make bows and arrows for self-protection. No, not for shooting other people's animals. That's not right,' they said with pleasant smiles.

I asked about the relationship between the !Xun and Khwe.

'Those of us who went to school together no longer really want to fight. But the older people – those who didn't go to school – they still keep away. Yes, at Platfontein we will be quite close together. Yes, there will be conflict sometimes. There will also be conflict with the people of Galeshewe, we think.' (Galeshewe was a large township attached to

Kimberley, housing for the most part Tswana-speaking black Africans.)
'It's going to be hard,' one of them said, 'but we've got nowhere else to
go.'

Jaoquem said he wanted to be an aeroplane pilot; and Titu, his gaze
averted, said that his dream was to train as a doctor. His dark eyes
flickered across my face. The light-skinned Jaoquem said that many
Bushmen joined the police force. 'This is good,' he said. 'It means that
they are becoming South Africans. But we don't want to be completely
integrated. We want our own identity.'

I chatted to them about the various processes of assimilation: marriage, all the imperatives of economics, and all those of sport and entertainment. They looked at me in silence. The terms Jaoquem had used –
'integration' and 'own identity' – seemed to jar slightly against the rest
of his English usage, as if the terms themselves had been assimilated
from the slogans of others. 'What about music?' I asked. 'What do you
enjoy?'

'I like love songs,' Jaoquem responded. He thought some of them
were American. But he could remember no names. Then slowly he
remembered Steve Hofmeyr and a few other Afrikaner entertainers.

I tried to talk to them about their communal property association, but
they sat before me in their casual western clothes – jeans and T-shirts –
looking perplexed and saying they did not understand. Once or twice
they said things to each other in their own language.

Then Jaoquem surprised me by saying: 'I voted in the elections in
1999. But the government has done nothing for me, or for any of the
Bushmen.'

'Except given you land,' I said.

Titu said, and it emerged as a blurted statement: 'I don't ever want
to vote.'

Suddenly, as if it had come to him in a small explosion of understanding, Jaoquem said that the CPA was more important to them than
the central government of South Africa.

There was a sense of schizophrenia in the way they jumped from one
thing to the other. The security of tribe and place seemed to be in conflict with the adventure of the new, the cell phones and aeroplanes of the
modern world. Both boys seemed animated by the prolonged thrill of

vacillation. The inevitable dislocation of their people had been exacerbated by wars and confused allegiances. They – or certainly their fathers –
had done their duty by the army. It was a livelihood: Battalion 31;
Omega military base. And then they found that this allegiance was
quickly obsolete because they had unwittingly aligned themselves to
the notorious apartheid state. Now they sat by the river making bows
and arrows that they would carry with them into the bungalows built
in the suburban style on Platfontein. While some outsiders anguished
over the preservation of their traditional way of life, the next generation
(born in Omega and schooled under canvas) dreamed of cell phones and
satellite dishes, and of flying above the murk and confusion of their own
particular clouds.

I BOOKED INTO a hotel on the outskirts of Kimberley called the
Kalahari Lodge. It was topped with mature thatch and looked quite
graceful in its garden setting studded with indigenous acacia trees. But
there were conferences going on in Kimberley and the only room available was tiny, with an even tinier bathroom. It seemed so at odds with
the space suggested by the desert in its name.

The Kalahari, a desert that stretched away in the imagination forever.
I sat on the edge of my bed, making a few notes, and remembering
another film that Hennie had put on for me after my conversation with
Jaoquem and Titu had ended. I sat alone in the auditorium, while
Hennie worked in his small office at the front of the building, and saw
a Land Rover overlanding in the Kalahari in its search for Bushmen living their natural life in the wild. A half-naked man loped in front,
assisting in the search. The film had been made in the 1940s and 1950s
by a Danish ethnographic film-maker named Jens Bjerre. In 1997 Bjerre
returned to southern Africa, found the group of Khomani San living at
Kagga Kamma in the Cederberg mountains, and showed them the film
that I now watched in the auditorium of the Wildebeest Kuil visitors'
centre. Hennie had also showed me a newspaper cutting that recorded
Bjerre's 1997 visit. *He spent* (in the 1940s) *seven months living with and
filming ... hunters and gatherers in action, storytellers around a campfire,
trance dances, rituals and myths*, the newspaper article said. This is what I
watched on the screen. Here was *a filmic tapestry of a time the Bushmen*

want to reclaim. And they had reclaimed it – at Witdraai and other places. But the purity of the experience had gone. The reclamation of land could not deliver the past to a dislocated people. The message drummed in my head as I sat in the auditorium, and again as I sat on the edge of the bed in my tiny hotel room.

The film ended with images, added as an addendum, that showed the degradation of being marginalised. Bushmen living in iron shacks with rubbish and broken cars littered all around. This was in Botswana, where the government would not allow them to hunt. All game was a state asset reserved for tourism as an economic activity: expensive hunting parties from overseas; tourists with binoculars and cameras. What struck me was the contrast between the primitive Bushmen in the body of the film – those cheerful dirty faces of people who never washed, the commentary told me – and the filth of the shacks and the squalor and incomprehensible grief of people diminished into flotsam dying of alcohol and floating as trash on the rolling desert plains.

Kalahari Lodge. The dining area had been set out pleasantly enough on two levels beneath a high ceiling of vaulted thatch. A mutilation of Joaquin Rodrigo's *Concierto d'Aranjuez* floated from loudspeakers somewhere up there near the grass. Strict tempo muzak to accompany diners tackling immense racks of lamb with their fingers, and drinking from glasses with small umbrellas attached. Why should Rodrigo's music, stirring and impassioned and tragic as it was, cut through me even in this bloodless version? Was it the recurring memory of the moment at Schmidtsdrift, also musically induced, when something had cracked in Hennie's head? Or perhaps the devastation of the final images in the Bjerre film? Or more likely, despite the cheap twanging of the *Aranjuez* theme, the sense of forfeiture articulated through the original, that haunting sense of a flamboyance from a period in Spanish history that had gone forever long before the music was first composed. The echoes of the Bourbon reign now mingled in my head with the echoes of the Bushman innocence.

On one wall of the dining area had been painted a mural of a watering hole surrounded by animals. The game of the Kalahari park, no doubt: whetting the appetite for Africa's plentiful excitements.

IN THE morning, I returned with Hennie to the Schmidtsdrift tents. He had agreed to take me to see the chairman of the !Xun and Khwe Communal Property Association, a man named Mario Mahango. We drove in once more on the wide road and came to the scattering of permanent structures at the heart of the camp. There was the small house where Hennie had lived. But we turned down in another direction, heading for the mobile home that served as Mario Mahango's office. Perhaps because it was a Saturday, several groups of people were standing about the central square. I caught glimpses of creased yellow skin, of small bright eyes darting across our presence, and I saw darker complexions and rounder features, evidence of the intermingling with black Africans in Angola or Caprivi or northern Namibia. On the side of a battered caravan I read the words *!Xun and Khwe Jeug* (youth), and somewhere else some graffiti was scrawled: *Hou die liefde vas* (hold firmly to love). A sudden breeze raised dust on the sandy tracks.

Mario came out to greet us, standing on the steps of the mobile home. He was a large man, powerful-looking, and his handshake was firm; but there was a gentleness in his eyes, and in a polite way he invited us inside. Of course, he knew Hennie as a friend, and for a while they chatted together, asking after their respective families, and then talking about their respective responsibilities: Mario's in the CPA, Hennie's with the Northern Cape Rock Art Trust.

We sat on easy chairs in the central part of the mobile home. The floor creaked whenever we moved. On the wall hung a biblical text and an outline map of Africa, with a bold circular arrow beginning on the southern coastline, sweeping up halfway towards the equator and then returning to end in South Africa again. The map bore a prominent caption: *Die sirkel is voltooi* (the circle is complete).

Mario noticed me looking at the map and said. 'Do you understand? The San peoples were pushed north by black African and European expansion. They stayed far north for a long time. Now we've come home. *Deur genade alleen*,' he added, which I took to mean, by God's grace alone. 'This is reassuring for displaced people.'

He told me he had been born in Angola, and that he had never considered that he belonged anywhere else. Then he got to Namibia – to Omega military base – and saw that San people were in Namibia and

Botswana also. In 1979 he travelled to Cape Town and found that South Africa also had them in the Kalahari. 'We had been chased further and further north; we were separated by colonial boundaries; but our original land was deep in South Africa. So that is why many San people feel unhappy that they – the original South Africans – are constantly being referred to as displaced people. And this is also why people are wrong when they say that we don't belong in South Africa and should go back to Angola and Caprivi.'

We spoke together in Afrikaans. He agreed that the whole of the world's history was a history of one thing overlaying another. People were constantly putting their marks on people who had gone before, fighting with them and taking their land. The possession of land provided power. In South Africa, a disastrous attempt had been made at segregation on the basis of people's ethnicity. Land was provided to justify this segregation. The result was a hugely unequal development process and the generation of poverty. Perhaps the division of land had been unfair. Perhaps separate development had been unfair because it was forced on people by the apartheid state. But, I asked, wouldn't the process of self-determination based on land restitution, equally rooted in ethnic identification, yield similar results?

He appraised me in silence for a few seconds. Then he said: 'The black people made us their slaves just as the white people did. We had soft natures; we weren't militarised. We were easily driven northwards.

'The new government has thrown out the old white government. When they were struggling for power, they said to the Bushmen, join us and regain your freedom. Yes, to some extent they have helped us. But it sometimes seems to us that the four most important things they have done are these. They have saved the whales. They have saved the penguins. They have tried to bring peace to Burundi, sitting and talking at all those meetings at Sun City. And they have helped the Mozambicans in the floods. But what about us? We long for the black government to acknowledge us as the original inhabitants. Or would that do something to threaten their moral high ground?'

It surprised me that there was such an undertone of sarcasm, and also of conviction, in what he said. 'I feel sore in my heart,' he added. '*Ons was uitgeroei.*'

Uitgeroei meant uprooted, exterminated, eradicated. Now his tone expressed some bitterness, but he was not angry. He smiled pleasantly at me. 'White people have to do something that accords with the idea of international human rights,' he said, 'especially now that they have lost political power.'

I smiled in return. We sat for a moment in silence. He sat with his hands planted on the tops of his thighs as if the more squarely to face the darkness of his own perceptions. I directed his attention to the biblical verse on the wall. *Jesaja 40:31.*

He nodded. 'I am NGK (Dutch Reformed Church), a *predikant*,' he said. I have told you I went to Cape Town in 1979. That is when I was ordained as a dominee. Yes, of course, this is the colonial influence. In Angola the influence was Roman Catholic. In Namibia it was protestant. There was a fellowship group at Omega. That is where it started. Now many of us here are NGK.'

I had two thoughts. One was a memory of the dilapidated church at Rietfontein, the plaques that showed the passage of the church from Rhenish missionary times to that fateful date in April 1994, the queues of Coloured voters, how many of whom were of Khoisan origin I did not know. The other thought was of the young woman clutching her dead baby to her breast all the way from the Omega military base in Namibia to the torn and dusty tents stretching away outside the mobile home in which we sat. Had she found courage or at least solace in the Afrikaners' protestant God? Or was it to the animals occupying the space both above and below her simple human torment that she turned?

We spoke – Mario, Hennie and I – of religious belief and how certain elements in traditional San belief had found an echo in Christianity. There was the emphasis on blood, of the worship of something greater than themselves, of the spirit of community.

Mario said: 'There was no reason among traditional San to insist that people should love their neighbours as themselves. That happened automatically. It was an imperative for survival.' He had brought his mother to the church, he added, and she had been satisfied. In other words, she had given her stamp of approval.

But there were other rituals that seemed not to prefigure Christian beliefs at all. Like the killing of the rain beast and the marking of the land with its blood, to encourage rain to fall. And the mapping of the land, the profound rootedness in the land of these nomads who drew their heritage and intellectual power from the earth underneath their feet, that medium from which I had seen the engraved animals emerging at Wildebeest Kuil. But for Mario, it seemed to me, he longed for a continuity from the old to the new. He longed as much for his protestant God as he longed for his pre-Christian traditions. It was as if he looked out at me from the difficult and arid places of transition, and from within the clinging coils of a reluctant assimilation, but saw only the circular sweep of his long journey home as it was depicted on the wall of his office.

And there on the wall so close to the depiction of the circular journey was the biblical text. *But they that wait upon the Lord shall renew their strength; they shall mount up with wings as eagles; they shall run, and not be weary; and they shall walk and not faint.* Perhaps, when the ancient linkages of a people to the earth had been sundered, like the final snapping of the connective cord, when all the old certainties had been broken and were disintegrating into irrelevance, these would be words of genuine comfort.

And what did all this mean to Hennie? I could see that the conversation had interested him. His heavy-jowled face was thoughtful yet animated, his gentle eyes deepened with inner feeling. But it was only as we drove away from the tents that he made his response.

He said, almost in alarm: 'There I was, sitting in this ancient culture and expected to be a Moses for these people. It was terrible. The never-ending responsibility. People talking to me, looking to me, rather than to their own leaders. Moses? Ha! I didn't know what staff to use to part the Red Sea. I didn't even know where the Red Sea was. Everything was so new. It still is. And who can we SMS for advice?'

I realised he was talking from a position that was placed roughly a decade after those first moments in Schmidtsdrift when he had heard the San children singing. There was always a sadness and disillusion that came with human experience, a dulling through knowledge and complication of the first hot sense of glory. It could not be otherwise. We drove in silence after that.

PART THREE

Umtata, Kei Mouth, King William's Town

1994 has left black people worse off in a number of ways.
There's much more loneliness, fewer jobs, much more uncertainty.
My children say to me: you guys were lucky. You had a common enemy,
a common goal. What do we have? All we seem to do now is compete,
fighting for the top jobs.

8
Old homeland

AT FIRST, as the light increased, I saw the earth stretching away as a lumpy expanse of cloud. Uniformly grey this expanse seemed, and low against the monotonous flatness of the land. In the east, as the sun rose, the cloud blazed white like snow. Later, dark protrusions appeared. They were the summits of hills and outcrops piercing the white. They looked like archipelagos in a dazzling sea, lying scattered to the horizon. I tried in my mind to draw a straight line from Johannesburg airport to Umtata, and in this way to establish more accurately where I was. Perhaps the eastern Free State already; perhaps somewhere approaching Bethlehem; and perhaps these protrusions below me were sticking straight up through the clouds from Golden Gate.

The cloud cover soon disappeared and the mountains of Lesotho appeared. A few thin wisps lingered momentarily, then they too were gone. The mountains lay below, uncovered and uncompromising, ridge after jagged ridge of them, looking like broken black teeth. Now we were flying over precipitous places, seen perfectly in the clear air, the gouged hills between which silver streams and waterways seemed to wriggle like fossilised serpents. The geomorphology of a small country was exposed in its totality for me, the unutterable rationality of time and erosion intensified now by young sunlight glancing across the heights. There were no trees and no signs of human habitation for some time as we flew, only this gaunt and lucid picture. Later the mountains did flatten and the snowlike clouds returned, but this time in broken patches only, with empty country showing below as grey-green hills mottled with dark shadows cast by the clouds.

The descent began.

The vision I had witnessed of an entire country, each rock and river explained and in its place, lingered in my mind. The clarity of the vision was the vision's allure. An understanding on that gigantic scale, the grasp of the logic of gravity and running water across an entire kingdom: how could one transfer that to the tangle of pain and loss and arrogance and power into which I now flew? The mountains of Lesotho were behind me; the Eastern Cape, with its reputation as the most corrupt and inefficient province since its delineation in 1994, lay before. Here was the old homeland of Transkei, further east the nightmare that had been the Ciskei. Thereabouts, too, was the Border region, that shifting demarcation between black and white through the 18th and 19th centuries that had caused nine wars and such a plentiful supply of death and devastation. All this was now incorporated into the Eastern Cape.

It was a faintly bizarre concept to grasp, this one of a border deep inside a unitary state. They even used the concept in the names of sports teams. The Border Bears, for example, those brown-clad cricketers reminding one perpetually of the collision of two expanding forces, the victories and defeats, the emergence of defiance and power, and new countries passing like swift shadows traversing green hills, and then the afflictions and moods of the unitary present. Could I find a point of view that would clearly show the logic and continuity of all this?

The green hills lay distinct and separate beneath the aircraft now, and sometimes I saw small collections of huts on higher ground, with tiny roadways and rivers curving through the valleys. For a time, plantations spread out over large tracts, but always defined by straight lines, on one side of the line the deep green of the trees, on the other the pale monotony of grass alone. The settlements grew larger; corrugated iron flashed in the sun; small vehicles travelled on tracks running from one settlement to the other. Now we were low enough to see the contour ploughing, and also the ragged wounds of soil erosion. People looked up at us from the fields. Then we flew over some water, the aircraft banking as it turned. We rushed above tree tops in a blurring green landscape; and in a moment the wheels bumped down and the roar and drag of the brakes filled the cabin.

'Welcome to Kaiser Matanzima Airport,' Willie said as he greeted me inside the small terminal building. 'That's what it used to be. I don't know what we're supposed to call it now.'

WILLIE WAS as thin as on my previous dealings with him, and his beard, trimmed at the throat and bushy on his jaw and cheeks, was as I remembered it – although perhaps more uniformly grey than the salt-and-pepper colouring of five years previously. Probably in his middle sixties now, he was still wearing those khaki shirts and shorts from which his scrawny sun-browned limbs angularly protruded. He had lived for the majority of his life in Umtata, and had, before retiring early, worked for a mining recruitment agency there. He spoke fluent Xhosa, to which Xhosa people invariably responded with pleasure, and his eyes were quick and observant in a slightly impertinent way.

My previous dealings with him had involved travelling to some rural schools in the old Transkei. So we had found ourselves grinding along some impossible roads to Port St Johns and Lusikisiki and Flagstaff; and on another day to Qunu (where Nelson Mandela had grown up) and Elliotdale and Hobeni. An enduring vision was of him standing, one morning, with one boot up on the front bumper of his four-wheel-drive and talking to a group of people who had assembled outside a collection of huts painted a light turquoise but now needing a second coat. They laughed easily with him, conversing (it seemed to me) in a way that found pleasure for them in his command of their language. His knowledge of the language was inevitably accompanied by a knowledge of their customs and etiquette, which meant that he met them on equal terms, being neither condescending nor obsequious before them. So there he stood, his boot on the bumper, a long-peaked khaki cap pulled down over his eyes, his even teeth suddenly appearing in his beard as he smiled.

When he was alone with me, however, he tended towards a knowledge of 'them' which veered close to cliché sometimes. Yet there was an admirable honesty in him also, as when he told me how he had been hijacked one day.

'Just outside Umtata. Actually on this airport road. A policeman with white gloves put up his hand. Naturally, I stopped and rolled down my window. And here was a nine millimetre pistol aimed at my eyeball. He gets in the back and says: Go. Where to, I asked. Drive, he said in a very unpleasant way. I drove. We went on the Queenstown road to Cofimvaba. Drive on, he said. I tried to make conversation but he didn't speak. I concentrated on the driving. Near Queenstown, he said: turn left. It was a small dirt road. Suddenly I was terrified. He was going to kill me. Will I hear the shot? When will they find my body? I can't really remember how, but suddenly we were driving south to Cathcart. We passed through the middle of Cathcart. About four kilometres from Stutterheim he told me to stop. The moment had arrived. But he got out and began to walk down a path. My 270-kilometre joyride was over. I went to the police station in Stutterheim, and I stood there it seemed forever fighting back the weakness and trembling. Luckily we have friends in Stutterheim. When I got to their house, I don't mind telling you, I broke down and wept,' he added, his impertinent eyes sharpened by the emotion still resident in the memory, yet covered by a slightly disdainful smile.

I asked if the hijacker had ever been caught, and Willie merely laughed in reply.

He told me of his experiences as a child in Umtata, herding cattle and milking cows and standing barefooted in the cow dung when it was still warm; and waiting for what his parents told him was the bogey man. His family had lived on Alexander Road (now Nelson Mandela Drive) and he would watch from the gate, seeing the lamps swaying and coming up the road. When they were close, he would rush inside, hearing the clatter of the buckets, and afterwards the silence returning to what had been little more than a quiet country town in those days.

Now Nelson Mandela Drive was filled with traffic and noisy taxis, especially at the intersection with Madeira Street. Empty grandstands belonging to the sports field – open green seating describing horizontal lines across a blue-grey sky – occupied the southern side of the street, and the old Bhunga Building the other. On open space below the stands, rows of taxis stood, and rows of hawkers on ground blackened with the oil left by running repairs, and a long concrete wall with graffiti proclaiming the virtues of water conservation. The air seemed grey with fumes; and a banner draped on a footbridge across the road advertised an event that commemorated the tenth anniversary of the assassination of Chris Hani, leader of the ANC's military wing, Umkhonto we Sizwe. That was when the country had staggered closest to collapse. White extremists had killed Chris Hani outside his home. Photographs showed the blood on his driveway. I had glimpsed the aftermath: the marching, the fists and shouting, the suburban windows freshly smashed, the stampeding legs, the tear smoke swirling through. That was near Alexandra township enclosed in Johannesburg's northern suburbs. I pulled myself back from my own small experiences of the price of the freedom dance to the results of that dance. Yet it seemed to me that the price should never be forgotten: it helped the more intensely to contextualise the results.

In the days after Willie had told me of his hijacking, he related other stories as well. I had heard that helicopters were being used to subdue what the media still insisted on calling 'faction fighting' by tribesmen high in the hills around Lusikisiki. People had been killed. These events seemed to trouble Willie. He told of a friend who had run a trading store on the road to Port St John's, and how his property had been attacked by men with AK47s while his wife hid in the bedroom. He told of the uprisings of 1960 that had been caused by the conflict between chiefs over the development of the Bantustan idea. The uprisings had centred in the wild places to the north of Lusikisiki. The South African army had intervened, killing at least a dozen as they tried to disperse those opposed to Bantustans, an action that drove many into an alliance with urban groupings in Durban also opposed to the ethnic division of the country.

It appeared that Willie too had been opposed. He railed against the stupidity of the old border post between Transkei and South Africa that had been built at Umzimkulu. 'It was all for show,' he said. 'The rigidness and arrogance of the South African immigration officials when you could walk unchallenged across the so-called border at any other place!'

We stopped at a settlement close to the coast. On the last of the hills before the sea, a row of holiday cottages had been built, some with satellite television dishes to offer diversions when the view of the broad expanse of Indian Ocean began to pall. But closer at hand was Willie with his boot on the front bumper of the vehicle talking to villagers about the roof of a school that had collapsed. He explained to me later that he had told them that he needed a unified decision from the village. He did not want some oxen pulling one way and some oxen pulling another way, while the plough remained stationary in the middle and

145

no ploughing got done. 'They're a wonderful people,' he remarked, as we bounced inland once again.

To one side, the rolling treeless country revealed only huts gathered into innumerable villages, the occasional wound of soil erosion, and behind all this the darkened sky as rain built up and then came down in swarthy shards, and mists obscured the distance.

'But the old customs are being slowly eroded,' Willie continued. 'They're still there, but fading – especially among the youth.'

I asked him what he thought impelled the youth these days.

'High expectations,' he said. 'They're waiting for the promised houses, jobs, prosperity. Like all of us, they're looking for security. Yet the people who led them to freedom have disappointed them. They see themselves as worse off than before 1994. So they're seeking a direction. I sense a deep confusion.'

In Willie's analysis, however, they would continue to vote for the ANC for several reasons. First, there was no alternative to that party. Second, there was intimidation during the elections. Third, rural people were easily led. 'They're easily intimidated when they're out of their own environment. On the mines. In the trade unions. I have no truck with the unions,' he said with some severity. 'They have often used these people as cannon fodder.' His views were a jumbled mixture of paternalism, genuine respect, and socio-political conservatism.

On my first visit to Willie, he had driven me through the downtown streets of Umtata in search of a civil servant named Mr Govender. Willie had told me that many of the old Transkei government buildings were half empty, most of the functions having been moved to the new Eastern Cape capital of Bisho. People were squatting in some of the buildings, he told me, and in others civil servants sat at empty desks or before switched-off computers, waiting for pay day.

I saw some of these things as I went from floor to floor in one particular building, looking for Mr Govender. I was conscious also of the security pads into which numbers needed to be punched to get deeper into the building. The doors invariably slammed behind me and the security guard who accompanied me; and discarded papers were banked up along the walls of empty offices. The sense was certainly of take-over, and also of disorganisation. Now, on my second visit five years later,

146

things seemed more settled. Computers were on. The front desk was in operation. And among a litter of papers on an empty table, I came across a modest pile of pamphlets entitled From Liberation to Transformation that seemed recently to have been issued by an organisation called the Moral Regeneration Movement. A butterfly was depicted on the cover. On an impulse I took one away with me.

I RETURNED one morning during my second visit to Umtata to the old Bhunga Building in Nelson Mandela Drive. In fact, the main entrance was around the corner in Owen Street, a thoroughfare with mature conifers gracing a narrow central island. Built in 1927 in a neo-classical colonial style, the pale double-storeyed Bhunga, complete with dome and colonnaded entrance, had changed its use between my first and second visits. From being the erstwhile home to various legislative bodies, including that of the pseudo-independent homeland of Transkei between 1963 and 1994, the building now housed the Nelson Mandela Museum. Two large boards at the entrance announced that this was so. The museum had been opened on 11 February 2000, said a plaque, exactly a decade after the world's most famous political prisoner walked out of jail to become South Africa's first democratically elected president.

The Mandela exhibit comprised a chronology of his life in the context of his times. This remarkable story was told through simple text, blow-up photographs, and supplemented on occasion with artefacts and film or video footage running on appropriately positioned television screens. The exhibit was divided into four sections: A Country Childhood: 1918 – 1941, The Struggle is my Life: 1941 – 1964, The Dark Years 1964 – 1990, Long Walk to Freedom: 1990 – 1994.

So it began with hills and villages and huts in Mvezo, Mandela's birthplace, and also in Qunu where he grew up and went to school. During my first visit, Willie had taken me to Qunu, hardly forty kilometres south-west of Umtata, and there he had driven up a hill to the junior secondary school that Mandela had attended. It had recently been painted brown and white, and according to a board at the entrance electrified by way of a grant from the Norwegian government. A few of the window panes were broken along the back wall, and through one set of windows

I glimpsed rows of test tubes. But I remembered most clearly how the long grass in the playground had waved noiselessly in the breeze. In the museum, remembering these things, I read of Mandela's school days and particularly of how his 'imagination was fired by the glory of these African warriors (Sandile and Maqoma) against Western domination'. Those two names in particular turned my mind towards the British arrogance and treachery of the frontier wars. But the chronology unfolding in the museum claimed my immediate attention.

Here was a youthful Mandela in boxing gloves and shorts, his fists raised to fight. And the context of this section of his life was clearly enough described. The defiance campaign; the women's campaign against the pass laws; Kliptown 1955 and the Freedom Charter; the Treason Trial dragging on for nearly five years; resistance to the imposition of the Bantustan system via the Pondoland uprisings; the massacre at Sharpeville; the establishment in 1961 of the Republic of South Africa; the armed struggle beginning through Umkhonto we Sizwe. And then Mandela's own arrest, his trial, the clashing shut of the metal gates.

But freedom had come again, and with it the release of the aspirations of an entire nation. A two-metre photo assemblage depicted a voting queue in April 1994. In a series of S-bends, the queue doubled back on itself as thousands of people waited to make their crosses. The euphoria was part of South Africa's legacy now.

Another assemblage, even larger, showed the long and symmetrical Union Buildings in Pretoria on 10 May, the day Mandela was inaugurated as president of a democratic South Africa. Tens of thousands of people filled the gardens in which Hennie Swart and his university friends used to have their sacrilegious picnics. Here was the dance personified, scorched into the history of a nation. And to one side of the assemblage, a television screen brought everything to life. The dancing and singing and the aircraft overhead, and the world leaders arriving, and the swarming crowds waving the flags, shaking the trees, carrying the posters, dancing in the streets with V-signs and raised fists waving in the air. The delirium of a new beginning, the impact of it on such a scale.

Mandela's words, delivered during his inauguration speech, stood outside of the visual images. They stood as it were to one side, printed as a simple text, a credo, a road map for all those years that would follow the dance. Almost inevitably I thought of that young man I had met high in the hills between Mozambique and South Africa. Mpumelelo, the poet of the crash. He had spoken so ingenuously about tragedy and love and enemies. And as I looked at Mandela's words, I suddenly realised that a key to understanding Mpumelelo's contradictions was rooted in the high ideals articulated before me now. All that ennobling thought; all that striving and responsibility. This is what would endure long after the rigours of the dance had been forgotten.

We have not taken the final step of our journey, Mandela had said, *but the first step on a longer and more difficult road. For to be free is not merely to cast off one's chains, but to live in a way that respects and enhances the freedom of others. The true test to our devotion to freedom is just beginning.*

I sat on the low wall surrounding the Bhunga Building, watching the taxis pass and occasionally stop to disgorge a part of their loads. At my feet a broken manhole cover revealed a collection of bones and the cobs of eaten mealies. I began to page through my booklet on moral regeneration while I waited for Willie to telephone. I noticed then the subtitle of the document: *living the Values in our constitution.*

WE DROVE out, Willie and I, to a school in the countryside just outside Umtata to talk to the principal, a man named Mr Kunene. Willie had recently helped with a survey of schools in the eastern districts of the old Transkei, travelling around in a helicopter; and I had asked him if he could take me to a school where I might chat to the principal.

Mr Kunene's school seemed typical of many in the old homeland: two low buildings housing classrooms and facing each other across a space of trampled veld that acted as the school courtyard. It was criss-crossed with red pathways through the grass as they led from one building to the other. A small group of teachers was sitting on plastic chairs in the sun, and children were emerging with their books and passing in leisurely fashion out of the schoolyard gate. Willie spoke to the teachers, who smiled and chatted easily with him because his knowledge of their language and its built-in etiquettes was seen as flattering.

Mr Kunene, it turned out, was down at the bottom of the hill coaching rugby. So we bounced down in Willie's truck and for a moment watched a crowd of boys tearing around some uneven ground defined by two sets of rugby posts made of wattle poles. Mr Kunene said: 'The main thing to start with is that we have to teach them how to tackle and be tackled. Otherwise they hurt themselves.'

He was a man in his thirties, friendly, confident, enthusiastic about rugby and about his school. 'Yes, things are going along,' he said. He shouted some instructions to the crowd of boys and then turned his attention more fully to us.

Willie observed that he had surveyed the physical infrastructure of Mr Kunene's school the previous year, and that he noticed that the broken windows had been replaced and rainwater tanks installed. 'But what about the toilets?' he asked.

Mr Kunene laughed and shook his head. He looked at me. 'We have 720 learners but no toilets. And there's only one pit latrine for 23 educators. We are now short-listed for toilets. There was cholera in this district last year. But we've still got no toilets.' He laughed again, enjoying the irony of the situation: a school in a cholera area being short-listed for toilets, as if for some great honour.

'There is instability in the education department,' he explained. 'There are too many political bosses – you know, the MECs, one after the other – with different policies. There are too many changes. I don't know why they can't find an MEC who will stay. Now there's a new Superintendent General as well.'

Yet his good humour remained. He seemed enthusiastic about education in general, and he praised the keenness of his teachers. Some of them had given up their holidays to prepare the school choirs for a big competition. The parents, too, were loyal to the school, making sure that school furniture borrowed for weddings and other community occasions was returned. And the results of the school were steadily improving. The entire district was improving: increased grade 12 pass rates, but not yet at 50%.

Willie seemed anxious that I take much more careful note of the problems. 'When we did the survey,' he said, 'we found that not a single school had not been burgled. On the other hand, quite a few schools were electrified, but there were no photocopiers, computers, televisions and video machines in any of these schools – Mr Kunene's included – so what was the point of the electrification?'

Mr Kunene chuckled, turning our attention to his own career. He said that after his training at Butterworth Teacher Training College (and a degree through Unisa) he started teaching at Elliotdale in 1992. Then he spent two years in the office of the South African Democratic Teachers' Union in Umtata. But when he had been offered a post as acting principal (which soon turned to a full principalship) he had been obliged to choose between the union and promotion into the management structures of education. 'You can't have your bread buttered on both sides,' he said in his amiable way.

I asked him to share with me his perceptions about pre-1994 and post-1994 conditions in the old homeland schools.

'Maybe I am too young to ask,' he said. 'But my view is that in some aspects things are very much better, and that other things are not as good. Take the new education methods: they are learner-friendly and outcomes-based. This is very good. Although the ANC orientation to history – especially the history of the struggle – has meant that some other subjects have been neglected. And there seems to be less in-service training now than before. For years there has been nothing. Those subject-based training sessions were very valuable, especially for isolated rural teachers. All right, here we are close to Umtata. But many of our children have never been. We are deep rural, even here. The teachers have no television and certainly no internet. We are seriously isolated.'

Then he laughed pleasantly and said: 'But we can't keep lamenting. Freedom doesn't mean that you have to eat a chicken with every meal. So let me sum up. I think the district managers are really trying hard. The overall policies are much better than before. But the administrative commitment from Bisho – it's not there.'

Willie snorted. 'Ask Mr Kunene to tell you about the conference on work ethics. Not a single senior education manager turned up. What does that tell you?'

Mr Kunene laughed. A few sheep came grazing past us, pulling grass off the clumps growing among a little grove of flowering aloes. The boys were yelling as they chased the doubly unpredictable bounce of rugby ball on uneven field.

'Yes, there are major administrative problems,' he said. 'Take the teachers' payslips. These always come long after the actual pay. The job of generating the payslips has been outsourced, and the system is in chaos. These days, you have to bribe someone to get your payslip in time; and unauthorised deductions – often organised by unscrupulous insurance salesmen – are common.'

Other issues were also raised. Sport was increasingly being recognised as an important developmental tool. Rugby had been identified as particularly important. But there was also talk of increased activity in cricket, tennis and swimming. Mr Kunene spread out his hands with a rueful grin. 'But how – without facilities?'

'For God's sake,' Willie said. 'They sit in Bisho, governing by remote control. Sport, like the provision of toilets, is all centralised in Bisho.'

Mr Kunene laughed again in his pleasant way. Another problem was the financial predicament of thousands of rural schools. 'Each child pays R50 a year,' he explained. But it wasn't easy to extract this amount from parents, many of them living in poverty, and many of whom, via the child grant system, were exempted from paying. Out of school funds, however, everything needed to be provided, even blackboard chalk. 'We haven't had any new allocation of school furniture for 15 years. In our entire district there are 140 schools, and only five are budgeted for furniture this year. But if you complain, you're seen as problematic, a troublemaker.'

I wondered, as I looked into his affable young face, how much more frustration lay beneath his obvious commitment and cheerfulness. I did not ask. Meanwhile, the rugby practice had ended. The boys greeted Mr Kunene as they began to trail home. I saw a bleeding knee among the strong brown legs marching slowly past. Mr Kunene said: 'I've been looking for a rugby kit – you know, jerseys and shorts and socks for the whole team – but the cost is around R5 000. Of course, completely beyond the means of our school fund.'

Willie shook his head in commiseration.

Mr Kunene said pleasantly, and yet with the clear intention of establishing a balance in all he had said to me: 'It's going to take some time to come right. Senior management is top-heavy, bloated. The whole department is in need of intensive care. But no wonder. There have been six MECs in the past nine years. But I don't think that striking will be a solution – not at this stage.'

On the way home, Willie told me that the practice of outsourcing had brought chaos to many areas in the education and health departments of the Eastern Cape, as it had to social welfare and pension payouts. 'The results have been terrible,' he said shortly.

The education theme lingered with me throughout the day. When we got back to town, Willie invited me into his house for a cool-drink. We passed through his dining room to get to his bar, an especially manly place complete with a pin-up or two, where he stood behind the counter with one of his boots resting on a shelf, much as he used the front bumper of his vehicle when travelling out of town. At his dining room table I had seen a black youth poring over a scattered collection of books as we passed through.

'Nothing special,' Willie said in an offhand way when I asked. 'I knew his father well – we worked together – but now his father's dead. He's a bright boy. One of his sisters is paying for him to do something in mechanical engineering. But he can't live at home: his mother's an alcoholic. So we're chipping in with accommodation for a few years.'

And then that evening I had supper with a cousin of mine named Elizabeth. She ran a unit attached to Fort Hare University that provided in-service training for teachers leading to a bachelor's degree in education. She and three colleagues, a Ghanaian man and two pleasant Xhosa woman, were in Umtata for a few days to evaluate those teachers in and around Umtata participating in the programme.

Elizabeth told me that the programme had been designed to take into account prior learning and service. Two years were recognised in this way. Then there was one additional year of more formal work, including a project conducted in the schools where they taught. One participating teacher they had evaluated had taken as her project the building of an additional classroom. She had invited every learner in the school to ask their parents to donate at least one cement block. Volunteers had done the building. In this way, the programme had the effect of animating whole school communities, while at the same time preparing teachers for the challenges of outcomes-based education and improving the general level of teacher qualifications.

The conversation turned to more general things. One of the Xhosa women, Paula Batya, had lived abroad for a long period and her daughter had returned home with a distinct English accent. 'I get so cross when she mispronounces her Xhosa,' she said, 'just like a European.' We all laughed. And her son had come to her one day saying that he wanted to undergo Kweta, the Xhosa manhood initiation ceremony that involved circumcision. She had allowed him. 'But I made damn sure he was properly protected against infection,' she said with considerable vigour.

Later, I asked how many teachers were involved in Elizabeth's programme. The answer was that the first graduation ceremony would confer degrees on more than two hundred teachers, and that obviously the programme was ongoing. This seemed a significant contribution, even in a province containing 6 400 schools and well over seventy thousand educators with varying qualifications.

LATER THAT night, in my room, I read the pamphlet on moral regeneration. In fact, the pamphlet was an account of the launch of the Moral Regeneration Movement, an event that took place at the Waterkloof Air Force Base in April 2002 and was attended by President Thabo Mbeki, several cabinet ministers and provincial premiers, as well as religious and other community leaders from all over the country.

The purpose was to restore 'the moral fibre of our nation' and to 'transform the anti-social acts which threaten our country'. These acts and tendencies were set out in detail in the brochure. *Murder! Robbery! Rape! Violence! Drugs! Embezzlement! Racism! Muggings! Hijackings! Abuse of women and children! The gap between the haves and have-nots! Perverted religion! Backbiting! Greed! Corruption in state and civil society!* And then in bold type, the crucial question is asked: *Why is it happening to us?*

Several answers are given. Mbeki remarks that 'as we were our own liberators in resistance against apartheid so today we should act as our own liberators in dealing with its legacy'. This argument was repeated later in the pamphlet, when reference was made to 'the legacy of colonialism and apartheid, which twisted our thinking and our attitudes, educated us badly, and left us with vast practical problems'.

There is also a recognition of less politically obvious causes. *Do pos-*

sessions and power move the focus from a vision of a new world to the quest for personal power and greed in that world? How can we regain the moral high ground – when money becomes the god many people worship, when our economic systems make most people poor, and when spiritual values are frequently neglected?

What were the solutions to the moral decline? The pamphlet described what happened at the launch event when delegates broke into smaller discussion groups and came up with specific focus areas such as: the family, education, youth, media, religion, leadership and government as agents of change. A photograph in the pamphlet showed important components of national leadership with their heads bowed in prayer; and there were several references in the text to the RDP (Reconstruction and Development Programme) of the soul. But what lingered most in my mind was that cry, almost anguished in its presentation on the page, where it was both italicised and emboldened. *Why is it happening to us?*

EVERY MORNING as I drove from my bed-and-breakfast accommodation into the centre of town I passed a signpost that pointed the way to the Umtata Child Abuse Resource Centre. I asked Willie about it, and he asked his wife who was active in various fund-raising endeavours. The result was that I was able to arrange an appointment to see the director, a woman by the name of Nokuku Sipuka, on the afternoon of my last day in Umtata. Willie was working out of town, so I spent the morning wandering about the central business area, buying a few necessities, seeing what sights I could see and generally mixing with the busy thriving of the streets. Some graffiti somewhere: *Human rights for all* and the tantalisingly unfinished *The death sentence is* ... Some of the traffic lights were out of order. Patient-looking Xhosa women attended to ranges of clothing laid out for sale on black plastic sheets spread over areas of sidewalk. Around the town hall and the open space on several sides of it, with the formal gardens, the statues, the shaded avenues, there was a sense of colonial times being overtaken with new life. Like the Bhunga Building itself, a block or two away, sedate with the colonial sense of limited decision-making powers for the natives, now bursting with the vigour and courage of the greatest native of them all. It was like a submersion of the old, with only a few high points still visible above the torrent of the new.

The Umtata town hall, built in 1907, was solidly colonial, but requiring paint, seeming indeed in great need of scaffolding to protect it. On the walls of the interior passages the hand-to-shoulder band of grime looked almost like a deliberate dado. The main hall smelled of wet wood and stale cigarette smoke. Velvet curtains had been tied back in sensual folds to reveal the stage; and on the auditorium floor several hundred plastic garden chairs had been pushed together in a sea of gaudy turquoise blue. Again there was that sense of the old being steadily swamped.

Beyond the formal gardens to the north of the town hall's main entrance lay a pedestrianised square giving access to the municipal offices that were housed in a building called Munitata. A crowd had gathered on the sunlit square to listen to a man speaking through loudspeakers. Indeed, many of the people were seated in rows, and frequent applause rattled lightly over the proceedings. I drew closer.

The square was surrounded by trees and shrubs. I saw a few pigeons alighting on the dome of the town hall, just visible through this surrounding foliage. I searched for the meaning of the gathering. Was it political? Did it have something to do with the anniversary of Chris Hani's death? But more likely it had a religious intent – to judge by the pseudo-American accent of the man with the microphone. Then I began to decipher the posters. Some were in Xhosa. But I found some in English. *Jaywalking kills: cross alert*, said one. *Traffic safety: your responsibility*, said another. Then I noticed the logo of the Department of Transport as well as the logo of the national Arrive Alive campaign. 'Amen and hallelujah, O Jesus,' the man intoned through the microphone. Then some women, all wearing Arrive Alive T-shirts stretched over their ample chests and waving Arrive Alive flags, rose to sing. The rhythms of the song were seductive. People began to dance. Passers-by joined in. People came dancing out of the automatic glass doors of Munitata. I changed my position, moving round the outside edges of the attendant crowd. And in so doing finally I saw it, the explanatory poster. *Our Voice. The Church Forum. We are praying. No more senseless blood spilled through negligence on our roads.*

'Hallelujah, Hallelujah,' the man said. A speech followed. I noticed rows of seated women dressed in their red, white and black church uniforms, some of them shielding their faces from the sun with Arrive Alive flags. Then a band (perhaps it was from the police or Correctional Services) with big brass instruments struck up a surprisingly timorous tune, individual musicians struggling to find a rapport with the rest to deliver a unified sound. While the band performed, young women moved among the crowd, distributing pamphlets. I expected something on road safety. What I was given was a trio of government publications. One was 'a people's guide' to the next budget. The central message on the front page seemed to be that growth and development spending was up while personal taxes were down. Another pamphlet was entitled *The tide has turned: build a people's contract for a better South Africa*. And in the third, I read about a special month in the year having been dedicated to the rights of children, with a strong response coming from 'religious leaders united under the banner of the Moral Regeneration Summit'. I looked across the faces of the hundreds of people gathered on the square to deliberate the slaughter on their roads. They seemed a contented people. Some shielded their eyes with the little flags. Others read the literature that had been handed out. Others listened as the band huffed and puffed their way through a final tune. There was a sudden sombre note for me in this manifestation of the powerful new wave. The dome of the town hall seemed to be subsiding beneath it. The sun shone. The people were enjoying the proceedings. They were always ready to listen to speeches, always ready to dance. The fruits of majority rule were coming their way. The literature held the details. Nevertheless, the sombre note remained.

Across the street – it was Owen Street but without the adornment of conifers – stood what I found out later was the Universal Church of the Kingdom of God. Across its plain facade had been slung a large banner. *Don't miss the distribution of the Holy Oil from Israel*. There followed a biblical text, Mark 6:13. *And they cast out many devils, and anointed with oil many that were sick, and healed them.*

It was not the overlaying of the colonial old by the democratic new that had struck the sombre note for me. Rather it was the emerging character of the new. Was I seeing the conversion of a nation of idealists

157

and freedom fighters into something else entirely? Those words from my butterfly-adorned moral rearmament booklet stood stark before me – *do possessions and power move the focus from a vision of a new world to the quest for personal power and greed in that world?* – and the sombre note, as from a tuba, boomed deeper.

SHE WAS a large woman, and she walked slowly, as if she might be in some pain. Her face was slightly strained, indicative of pain, yet this might have been from the nature of her job as much as from any malfunction of her legs or hips. This was Nokuku Sipuka, and we met at the offices of the Umtata Child Abuse Resource Centre, a neat building in one corner of the equally neat grounds of the General Hospital. We sat facing each other across a boardroom table. She said her office was too hot for afternoon use. She told me, by way of introduction, that she was a registered nurse and that the Resource Centre was privately funded. She dealt with me warily at first, weighing me up. But once I had passed her tests – if that in fact was what I had done – she spoke to me with an almost ardent candour.

She said that they, the field workers in her organisation, were experiencing a large number of child rape cases, and that there appeared to be several main causes.

'The first,' Nokuku explained, 'very definitely relates to the virgin myth. It's a widespread belief that intercourse with a virgin, or a very young child, will cure and prevent HIV infection in the male. As the epidemic shows more and more frightening results, so the victims get younger and younger.'

Then there was the matter of simple incest, she said, folding her big brown hands before her on the boardroom table. Or perhaps it wasn't so simple.

'You need to understand a thing called grooming. We believe it's traditional, but it's always been very secret. As the child grows up she is sexually groomed in various ways for later sexual activity which usually begins at age twelve or thirteen. One of our approaches is to give educational talks at schools. I can often see by the changing expressions on the girls' faces who has been or is being groomed. The sudden shock of recognition as she realises we're talking about her own experience.

Sometimes the children simply break down. Often disclosure is traumatic and emotionally draining. But at least, afterwards, we can take the appropriate action.

'Don't think that this happens only in traditional households,' Nokuku went on. 'Well-educated families are sometimes involved. Even professional men are not immune, although they normally get a lawyer to defend them.'

She looked at me in silence. I asked if the incidents of grooming were on the increase. She shrugged her shoulders. 'We are definitely saying they seem to be on the increase. But we are also asking: was this thing there before? Almost certainly it was, but probably people didn't report. There were no services, like ours, to provide this outlet. Also, we're looking at the subservience of women. But those days when the subservience was complete are over. We live with a constitution that protects women and children, and people are becoming more aware that such behaviour – like grooming and abuse generally – is a criminal offence.'

Nokuku identified some of the aggravating factors. Drugs and alcohol. Unemployment, which meant that the man was always at home, and that often the mother would be out working. Situations where men were in positions of power without accountability: like teachers and ministers of religion. And most common factor of all: that the abusive man would have a history of himself being abused as a child.

'Yes,' she said. 'We're in a crisis.'

I steered her back to the idea of power without accountability. She looked heavily at me, an expression suggestive of some pain in her eyes. 'It's true,' she said. 'There definitely seems to be a connection between corruption – theft and fraud – and sexual abuse. Do both become possible for people breaking into freedom for the first time? Perhaps that is true. Now there's democracy, people say, I'm free. I can do anything. Democracy has become a playground for gratification and self-indulgence. Perhaps it will take a long time for responsibility to catch up with the idea of the blossoming of rights.'

I asked her if she had any statistics. She rose and went into her office, walking slowly. She returned with a sheet of paper. The figures it contained were for the year 2001/2 and related to the eastern region of the old homeland.

A reported total of 2 580 children had been sexually abused; 2 266 had been criminally neglected; 856 had suffered physical abuse; 380 had been abandoned; and there had been 59 cases of child prostitution.

'These are the official reported cases,' Nokuku said from across the table. 'Underneath, though, the real activity in these categories must be huge.'

9
Girl at the river

LEAVING UMTATA in the early morning, I came across an unexpected image of sheer optimism. For a short distance, a track ran at a converging angle with the main road on which I travelled, and along this track a young boy, perhaps twelve years old, rode a grey horse with richly ornamented bridle. The sun had just risen, and the new day's light came slanting across green hills and illuminating both horse and rider from the front. It was as if they rode directly into the light, seeking its source. The boy was standing in the stirrups, his sleek chest bare, his unbuttoned shirt streaming out behind him, as did the horse's tail as it cantered boldly forward. Here was such energy, such buoyancy and joy, such a purposeful optimism, that the image lingered with me for some considerable time.

The road was crowded as I drove down, following the south-westerly sweep of the continent's bottom edge, towards the Border region, that endlessly contested and bloodied country defined by the Great Fish and Great Kei rivers. For the entire period between 1779 and 1878, black and white had tussled with increasing bitterness, hatred and paranoia. The rivers were hardly 150 kilometres apart at the coast, yet in that limited space were laid the foundations for the racial brutalities and inequities of 20th-century South Africa as a whole.

The road's verges teemed with school children, and with elegantly erect women carrying baskets and bundles on their way to the markets that enlivened every village that the road passed through. In the larger of these, traffic slowed my progress: a strange assortment of the shiny cars of the *nouveau riche* – the civil servants at various governmental levels, the politicians, probably a few businessmen – mingling with the buses and taxis and trucks of the more staple transportation businesses still booming in the old Transkei. The hills were full of houses. At one

161

point, the road curved over the top of a high ridge and the vista of the country became enormous. As far as I could see, houses inhabited the rolling green hills until in the distance they were simply like dots. Far away on the horizon, the hills formed into a greyish ridge of mountains below which in the valleys the morning mist and cloud still lingered. The sun brought depth and richness to the scene. The green and tree-less hills, the constantly repeated settlements of circular huts topped with thatch and surrounded by ragged fields of sorghum and maize; and always in attendance, cattle and goats, long-tailed dogs and often naked children, rounded and brown, playing in the swept spaces between the generally immaculate abodes.

Impossible not to return in one's mind to the history of the occupation of such a place. It had been inhabited to begin with by Stone-Age Khoisan people. I remembered Mario Mahango, leader of the !Xun and Khwe, and the outline map of Africa on the wall of his mobile office at Schmidtsdrift. The arrow on the map had begun in the southern extremities of the continent (where I now drove), then had swept in an arc halfway towards the equator before returning to end in South Africa again. That was, roughly speaking, what had happened to the Stone-Age Khoisan inhabit-ing the South African coastal regions. They had been pushed towards the arid north by the powerful Xhosa people. The Xhosa forefathers were part of the great Bantu migrations begun about two thousand years ago in the armpit of the continent. And it was as the Xhosa drifted slowly west-wards, assimilating new land to accommodate the needs of new-generation Xhosa chiefs, that they had met the European settler expansion from the Cape coming in the opposite direction.

The accretion of new land that had finally pushed the Cape's eastern border more than five hundred kilometres from Cape Town was hardly on the agenda of official Dutch colonial policy. It occurred more through the lifestyle of the South African frontiersmen of the 18th cen-tury, those semi-nomadic pastoralists, the Dutch-speaking trekboers, who grazed their cattle in ever-widening and ever-eastward-looking directions.

The advance settlements of Xhosa and trekboer met in the 1770s on a strip of land known as the Zuurveld. It was on the western or colony side of the Great Fish River. As more and more people from both sides moved in, so tensions rose. Cattle theft and accusations of cattle theft, raid and counter-raid, became the order of the day. In 1779 a trekboer cattle raid left a Xhosa herdsman dead. Tensions boiled over. Widespread fighting swept the Zuurveld. This was the first Frontier War; it ended inconclusively only in 1781.

The early-morning cloud had cleared and the Transkei hills shone brilliantly green. Rectangular bungalows were interspersed among the huts, and all over the changing landscapes the glinting of corrugated-iron roofs caught the eye like flashed messages in code. I wondered if the message said that some prosperity had indeed found its way into the Transkei hills. A similar message came to me from the quality of the road: recently upgraded and well-signposted, three lanes in places, wide verges, wide concrete drainage gutters.

Just beyond the larger town of Idutywa, I saw a neatly made cricket oval, white stones marking the boundary around the central square. The whole field had been laid out on slightly sloping ground, the wicket going with the gradient so that fast bowling from the top end must have been a fearsome affair. Close at hand was a rugby field with regulation goal posts soaring into the blue air, and atop one of the posts a large black bird, probably a crow, preening in the early sun. Impossible not to think of the smiling Mr Kunene then, and the important place that sport, and indeed other extra-curricular activities like the school choirs, occupied in his view of education.

Indeed, I was travelling down to Kei Mouth, a small resort that nestled in the coastal bush where the Great Kei River, the eastern boundary of the Border area, flowed into the sea. A training conference for school-teachers involved in planning the preliminary rounds of a huge national multi-sports event was being held there.

But my attention as I drove had returned to the western boundary of the Border area, the Great Fish River, and to the troubled Zuurveld beyond. I had asked Mr Kunene whether the Frontier Wars were taught in Eastern Cape schools. Of course, he replied. And they always had been. Hadn't I visited the Mandela Museum in the old Bhunga building? There I would see how, as a child, Mandela's imagination had been fired by the glory of African warriors like Sandili and Moqoma.

In the early 1790s drought had come to the Zuurveld, placing an added strain on limited resources. Black and white, already suspicious and fractious, began fighting over reduced grazing and other resources, and before long the Zuurveld was aflame once again. Contested areas of land changed hands several times in fighting that continued through two clearly defined Frontier Wars and well into the first years of the 19th century.

During this period, of course, a new power had entered the South African picture. The British first appeared at the Cape in 1795 and then returned to stay in 1806. The chaos on the Eastern Frontier became an immediate focus of attention, and the British soon concluded that the two warring groups should be separated. This meant that the Xhosa advance should be halted. Indeed, Xhosa settlement should be pushed out of the Zuurveld altogether and back over the Great Fish River. In fact, they should be pushed even further back to allow for thousands of new settlers who would establish agricultural enterprises on the eastern banks (the Xhosa side) of the Great Fish River. The eastern regions of the colony would thus be adequately protected by this formidable double barrier of settlement and river. The military campaign required to achieve this plan (the fourth Frontier War) began in October 1811 and lasted six months. British troops assisted by settler commandos and Khoisan irregulars destroyed crops and villages and confiscated thousands of head of cattle as they forced the Xhosa from the Zuurveld and over the Great Fish River. The then Cape governor, Sir John Cradock, remarked (in his report on this brutal war to London) that there had 'not been shed more kaffir blood than would seem to be necessary to impress on the minds of these savages a proper degree of terror and respect'. Within seven years of the end of the war, the military garrison of Grahamstown was established in the middle of the Zuurveld.

But more manoeuvring and downright treachery, as well as another Frontier War, were necessary before the eastern banks of the Great Fish River were cleared for the planned settlement that would go to make up the desired dual barrier between the Xhosa and the eastern regions of the Cape. After deliberately dividing the Xhosa against themselves, the British took the side of a Chief Ngqika who was occupying the area planned for settlement. They defeated his rivals in the fifth Frontier War, and then demanded as compensation for military assistance the very land upon which the hapless Ngqika had settled. In this way, the Xhosa were forced not only to retreat – but also to sign a treaty ceding all the land to the east of the Great Fish River (up to the Keiskamma River) to the Cape Colony. Thus was the land to the east of the Great Fish finally opened up for the 4 000 English settlers who landed in Algoa Bay in 1820.

It was out of the obvious resentments of this perfidious dispossession that the sixth Frontier War emerged. There were other factors as well. For a start, the English settlers were subject to frequent Xhosa guerrilla attacks from the east. It soon occurred to the newcomers that cattle constituted the major reason for these attacks. They therefore started to farm with sheep, to which the Xhosa attached little value. The two sides also began to trade together. Weekly fairs were held, where settlers and Xhosa rubbed shoulders, and increasing quantities of produce and money changed hands. Relationships at the frontier jostled along in this way until the middle 1830s. Matters were then brought to a head, exacerbated by the effects of another drought and increasing disease on the Xhosa side – as well as pressure from present-day KwaZulu-Natal and Lesotho.

This came in the shape of refugees fleeing into Xhosa territory from the Zulu-inspired Mfecane, the great dispersion of people that gripped the whole of southern Africa during the first third of the 19th century. Suddenly a thread of desperation had entered into Xhosa actions. They were in dire need of land to ease the relentless pressure. They therefore attacked the colony, Xhosa warriors charging across the Keiskamma River in defence of their autonomy, even of their survival. The date was 1835. Within a year, however, they had once again been severely beaten.

At a town called Butterworth, the streets choked with taxis and shopping, I turned off the main road and headed south towards the sea. Almost immediately I had a sudden sight of poverty: people living in shacks, people who seemed to deal in old tyres and bales of cotton waste, the earth around their abodes blackened with what looked like oil, the faces of the women and children bearing the imprint of hardship. These were the heirs of the growing Xhosa desperation of 170 years ago. So were the women I saw later, when I had regained the countryside, stacking firewood in neat piles by the roadside. The villages seemed poorer:

mud collapsing from the walls of the huts; broken cars rusting in the grass; some dogs eating at a dead cow lying bloated in a corner of a field. I saw an old Xhosa man with white stubble on his face, leaning on a fence and holding in his gnarled old hand a collection of sticks and a folded umbrella. We greeted each other as I passed. And then, from a suddenly breezing high point, there was a glimpse of the straight blue line of the distant sea.

After the sixth war had ended, the Cape governor Sir Benjamin D'Urban annexed the whole territory between the Keiskamma and Great Kei rivers, naming it Queen Adelaide Province. A mission station that had been established a decade before was renamed King William's Town and declared the capital. But this ill-considered action was reversed by the British colonial secretary, not least because of its arrogance. D'Urban himself was censured for the long series of aggressions and systematic injustices perpetrated against the Xhosa, while the destruction of Xhosa huts and crops (executed under the command of Sir Harry Smith) and the killing and mutilation of Xhosa chief Hintsa received the same official treatment. But this action by the British government tended merely to harden settler racism, particularly when the fledgling King William's Town was destroyed by the Xhosa immediately the territory had been handed back to them.

So the desperation and the hatred remained, as did the intercourse via trade and missionaries. The traditional Xhosa way of life was being corrupted and their resolve weakened. Indeed, the general Xhosa predicament increased through more drought as the 1840s dragged on; and on the white side attitudes were exacerbated by simple land hunger, particularly with which to exploit the burgeoning wool industry, already the Cape's most valuable export. So both sides, reading belligerence into each move made by the other, drifted towards the seventh Frontier War. It began in March 1846. The settlers welcomed the opportunity to put the Xhosa in their proper place. Even the missionaries were enthusiastic, seeing the war as retribution for Xhosa obduracy against the Christian message. But the war began with a significant Xhosa victory and, as if to revenge the mutilations wreaked on Hintsa ten years before, the body of a British officer killed in early fighting was similarly dealt with and displayed.

But the outcome of this most expensive and brutal of the Frontier Wars thus far, dragging on for nearly two years, was militarily inconclusive even though the Xhosa had exhausted most of their resources. The supremely arrogant Sir Harry Smith had reappeared in South Africa, this time as governor of the Cape, and he had no hesitation in re-annexing the territory that D'Urban had called Queen Adelaide Province, but this time with the full approval of the British parliament. In a special ceremony in King William's Town, Sir Harry assembled the Xhosa chiefs, proclaimed the new territory as British Kaffraria, and then obliged the chiefs, as a mark of subservience to the sovereignty of Britain and to the superiority of Sir Harry himself, to kiss his boot as it rested in the stirrup.

In this way, the border between white colonial control and the independent Xhosas was shifted all the way east to the banks of the Great Kei. Since the 1770s, when contact had first been made on a significant scale, the Xhosa had lost ground at an average annual rate of around three agonising kilometres. The damage to the Xhosa psyche was even more profound. It had alienated them and (in the words of historian Noel Mostert) 'turned them fatally towards a growing conviction that if they themselves were incapable of driving the English back into the sea then conceivably the shades might come to their assistance'.

This comment points obviously forward another ten years to the notorious cattle-killing episode of 1857. Thousands of Xhosa were convinced by a prophecy that instructed them to kill their cattle and await the arrival of salvation from their own spirit world on a specified apocalyptic day. The results were catastrophic.

The sea lay close between the mounded green hills as I made my descent on a rough dirt road towards it. I had turned right at Kentani, venue for one of the final great battles between black and white in 1878 when, according to my guide book, 5 000 Xhosa attacked a British fort established here – only to fall beneath heavy gunfire and a cavalry charge. Now in Kentani, as I looked for my road, I passed a shop called Power Save Cash and Carry with American rap music belching from the entrance. Then I was on the rough dirt road. From each hill top the sea reappeared closer than before, and finally I was overlooking the Great Kei River where it entered the ocean spread out in a deep blue haze before me.

But I was still thinking of the slow yet inexorable defeat of the Xhosa people. At the turn of the 19th century, the Cape's eastern boundary was fixed at the Great Fish; by 1819 it had advanced to the Keiskamma; and in 1847 to the Great Kei. But that was not the end. By 1858 it had swept across half the rolling green hills of Transkei, and by 1878 (at the completion of the ninth and final Frontier War), virtually the whole of Transkei also lay under the Union Jack. In 1894, with the annexure of Pondoland, the eastern border of Cape Colony met the southern boundary of British-controlled Natal, thus bringing to finality the political and economic destruction of the once independent Xhosa-speaking people.

I drove down the steep hill to the bank of the river. A pontoon, plying in a wide arc across the river mouth, came to fetch me. I stood on the pontoon. Looking seaward I saw waves breaking against the low sand bank, sending up a spurting barrage of spray from choppy waters. I thought I saw a horse and rider charging through the surf. The sun glittered sharply on the calmer water of the river, so I could not be sure. Yet the glimpse reminded me of that boy standing in the stirrups of the grey and ornamented horse outside Umtata, going boldly forward into the light of an eternally renewed sun. Subjugated, I thought, destroyed in the pages of history, but unmistakably there.

THE IDEA of the Xhosa people being unmistakably there, rather than merely a part of a tragic colonial history, became a recurring theme at the training conference for schoolteachers that I had been invited to attend. The conference had taken over a complete hotel resort, and in every corner of the sprawling establishment – in the lounges, the pubs, the swimming pool clubhouse – breakaway sessions were in progress when I arrived. The delegates were all teachers in their twenties and thirties from rural schools in the old homelands of Transkei and Ciskei. The plenaries were held in a large hall on the landward side of the hotel and were invariably opened with vigorous singing: nearly two hundred young teachers harmonising in controlled and reverberating song. To sit in the hall at those times was to sit in the engine-room of a great and spontaneous vitality.

The conference organisers went out of their way to ensure that my visit was comfortable and worthwhile. To begin with, they put me in a room with a view of the sea. Indeed, I looked down directly onto the beach and onto the stretches of black rock that took the brunt of the waves when the tide was high, and that when it ebbed left scores of pools filled with shells and smoothed stones and occasional small sea creatures clearly visible through the crystal water. The further view was of ships, predominantly container vessels, plying the coast between Durban and East London; or, if they were further from the shore, heading around the bottom of Africa and then turning north in their various passages towards the wider world.

A youngish man named Zuki Makazi explained to me the importance of the sports events they were training the teachers to organise. 'We don't prescribe to them how to run the games. We want only to empower them to do it themselves. This is now the third year they're doing it. They start at school level. They mark the sports fields out in the bush. They compete at a district and a regional level. The games become a big community thing, cementing all segments of community around their own schools. So in this way, the games are much more than sport, much more than extra-curricular activity. They're giving whole communities a new sense of purpose. And there's also the HIV/AIDS messaging that gives the games an added weight. Then they compete at provincial level, and finally at the huge national games held in Durban every year. We call them the loveLife Games: that's the name (loveLife) of the AIDS awareness organisation that does the messaging and financing. But in fact the games are organised by the teachers themselves, under the auspices of USSASA, the United School Sports Association of South Africa.'

Someone at lunch said: 'Teachers in the Eastern Cape, especially from the rural areas, are very enthusiastic, sucking up information and the opportunity for camaraderie like a sponge.' That is certainly what I saw. The jovial camaraderie of people working together at something they considered to be worthwhile. And I remembered Mr Kunene teaching boys how to make rugby tackles without hurting themselves at his school in the bush outside Umtata. That pleasant face nearly always smiling and positive, even when regretting the loss of the fellowship of the old subject-based in-service teacher-training sessions. How he would have loved the fellowship here next to the pounding Indian Ocean at Kei Mouth.

After lunch I watched the start of a breakaway session. The facilitator drew her group into a series of light-hearted games, jokes, even physical exercises. The teachers' laughter rang out through the gentility of one of the hotel lounges. They played a game resembling musical chairs. They filled their lungs and their arteries with a good supply of oxygen, and then the facilitator, a young black woman with bright and expressive features, turned to a fresh sheet of paper on her flip chart and wrote: *effective meetings*.

Someone told me of a remarkable interchange at the opening plenary session. The tenth anniversary of the death of Chris Hani had been acknowledged and discussed. Someone had remarked that he had given his life for the freedoms being enjoyed today, and it was right that we should keep him in our memories. We should in this way revere the past. But was there, in our revering of the past, not also a yearning for it? And did this imply a lack for many people in the present and the future? An absence of solidity, perhaps. A sense of purposelessness, the post-struggle void, the post-struggle longing for direction and purpose.

I sought out Zuki Makasi and asked him about these things. 'I call it the post-1994 blues,' he said with a laugh. 'We never prepared for "after-the-struggle". Neither did the government. So there's a kind of emptiness, a kind of dull pain. Among the teacher population in the Eastern Cape, there is serious disillusionment. We're in a democracy now, but so what? So we're saying to them: there is life after the political struggle. It's right here. The games. And it's working. The games have brought in a completely new challenge, a new opportunity to once again become part of something larger than ourselves.'

A striking young woman from Soweto introduced herself as the training conference director, although she was quick to add that the training facilitators took it in turns to do that particular job. Her name was Lebo Komane, and she had a degree in communications science. She told me with an engaging smile that she had been born in Soweto, that her mother's family lived in the countryside, in the old Bophuthatswana homeland. She had visited – but never lived there.'

'I was still at school in 1994,' she said, when I had broached my subject. 'But it's true, I think, that after 1994 we black people lost the rhythm. We lost the unity of the struggle. We emerged almost without an identity. I think one of the problems was with the assumption that when apartheid went, a two-way cultural assimilation would be possible in a big way. But it just didn't happen This was my experience anyway. I was at a model-C white school in Johannesburg, and I was being assimilated into white English culture. There was no reciprocity. I was always the aspiring one. I was the one who had to learn the new rules. White people's attitudes seemed to be based on the assumption that the two cultures – the black and the white – weren't equal. And in a way it was true. English was dominating everything as we tried to become global citizens. So that is why we lost rhythm, I think, why some of us have been so severely at sea. We don't really know who we are.'

I asked if people were therefore trying to rediscover their roots, their collective pasts, much as the San people were being assisted in doing.

She looked at me in silence for a moment. She had large open almond-shaped eyes. She seemed, for all her confidence, suddenly vulnerable. 'I would say young people right now are less in touch with the realities of their past than they were before.'

'Would these teachers here all know – I mean have really absorbed – the realities of the century of Frontier Wars, for example?'

She smiled. 'You'll have to ask them. For myself, what is needed now is an affirmation of what people, these teachers especially, have known all along: that their rhythms and they themselves are intrinsically valuable.'

'And your hope is that they will find this affirmation in these loveLife Games?'

'Yes!' Lebo said with a laugh. Then she added: 'To an extent at any rate. These teachers can make an impact on their learners, their schools, their communities. They can find a spiritual and intellectual fulfilment. They can learn that the materialist urge on its own is never enough.'

In the half-light of evening I walked on the beach. The lights of a freighter hugged the horizon. I saw the imprints of a horse's hooves in the crisper sand closer to the quiet dying of the waves. In my mind I carried an assemblage of pieces that might at some point fit into a picture of the people with whom I mingled in the Eastern Cape. The first piece concerned the long travail of the Frontier Wars, the defeats, the resentments, the aching humiliations. The second piece concerned the certainties and comradeship of the 20th-century struggle. The third piece was fragmented. Here was the loss of rhythm, the post-1994 blues. Here was my butterfly-adorned booklet elaborating on the need for moral rearmament in a society in need of comprehensive spiritual repairs. And here was the pained face of Nokuka Sipuka of the Umtata Child Abuse Resource Centre talking about one aspect of this spiritual crisis. I wanted the erstwhile political struggle to act as the key to fix the pieces into a coherent picture. But it would not. There was something underneath the struggle – something deeper, something more terrible perhaps – that I would need to seek before my picture emerged. I turned in some anxiety from my own thoughts.

I heard the teachers singing on the hotel terrace. They seemed complete. The tempo of their song was *obbligato* vigour, *obbligato* power, *obbligato* optimism; but in the gloomy sand before me as I walked along the beach I could no longer see the imprints of the horse's hooves.

WHILE IN Kei Mouth I met a man named Alan Jefferies whose great-grandfather, Edward, had come to South Africa in 1820. That meant he would have been allocated ground to the east of the Great Fish River. There he had formed part of the settler barrier the British wished to establish against the Xhosa who, after military defeat and diplomatic treachery, were licking their wounds on the eastern side of the Keis-kamma River. But the original Jefferies found he was more suited to trade than to farming, and spent an adventurous life doing just that on both sides of the frontier. He died in 1855, in King William's Town, eight years after Sir Harry Smith had created British Kaffraria and two years before the prophecies of the young girl Nongqawuse had led to the fateful Xhosa cattle-killing.

The old man's son, Alan Jefferies's grandfather, was also an adventurer, and he too found himself as part of a settler barrier, this time on the Cape Colony side of the Great Kei. In 1864 he applied to the authorities for land and was granted a farm less than twenty kilometres inland from the river mouth. Other farms were added to the Jefferies estate over the years, until the family owned nearly three thousand acres on the western bank of the river. In 1877 the final Frontier War began, and the Jefferies family evacuated to several British forts for safety. They finally returned to their farms to find they had been devastated. All that remained intact, having escaped both burning and plunder, was an old chair that had remained in the family's possession ever since.

I knew these things because Alan Jefferies had written and privately printed a book entitled *The Absolute Border* which contained much family information, as well as an attempt at an overview of Kei Mouth history. An entire chapter of his book was devoted to Nongqawuse, the Xhosa prophetess of the cattle-killing, because 'the chain of events focussed no more than three kilometres from Kei River mouth as the crow flies'.

To provide a context for this most horrifying of events, I remembered again the long sequence of Frontier Wars that characterised the relationship between black and white through most of the 19th century. The seventh of these wars had ended in 1847 with Sir Harry Smith annexing British Kaffraria, thus pushing the eastern frontier all the way east to the Great Kei, and forcing the Xhosa chiefs of that region to kiss his boot while he sat imperiously on his horse. Such behaviour could hardly be conducive to peace, and the humiliated Xhosa chiefs and their people, now being forced to live under British authority, were open to any persuasion that might correct the blatant imbalance of fortunes to which they were being subjected.

This persuasion came in the form of a strange young man, Mlanjeni, who convinced many that he had a special contract with the spirit world that could help the Xhosa finally to defeat the hated British. He ordered limited cattle-killing and prescribed a special purple root that would render the bullets of the enemy harmless. The Xhosa rallied behind Mlanjeni, their new prophet. All over the eastern parts of the Cape Colony, Xhosa servants were absconding to be in the presence of Mlanjeni, missionaries lost their converts, and people streamed towards this new beacon of hope even from those tribes living to the east of the Great Kei. Such were the preparations that the Xhosa made for the eighth Frontier War, which began in 1850 and dragged on for three years, the longest of all the wars. In typical fashion, it began with some early successes for the Xhosa, but it ended with extravagant helpings of

British brutality and the final surrender of all the chiefs in British Kaffraria.

Then it all began again a few years later just over the Great Kei where I had crossed it on the pontoon. 'Not more than three kilometres from the Kei River mouth as the crow flies', Alan Jefferies had written in his book. In this remote corner of a troubled country, near a river called the Gxara, the teenaged Nongqawuse had heard voices. She herself had been orphaned, perhaps during the final brutal stages of the war that had just ended. She had been taken in by an uncle, Mhlakaza. He was a man who had spent time in Grahamstown and had been significantly influenced by the ideas of Christianity – but finally angered by his supposed inferiority in the eyes of colonial society. In any case, he and his niece were living close to the Gxara, and it was to her embittered uncle that Nongqawuse delivered the fateful message that the voices had relayed to her.

The message was that there was soon to be a great resurrection. To ensure its occurrence, however, all cattle should be killed, and there must be no cultivation of food. Then a new people would arise, and all the ancestors would arise, and these miraculous events would make it possible for the Xhosas to sweep all whites and unbelievers into the sea.

In the hands of Mhlakaza, who had influence in high Xhosa places, this message became like a potent drug to many thousands of households. Salvation was at hand. So the cattle began to die. One of the chiefs asked for a special extension so he would have time to kill all of his 6 000 cattle before the resurrection came. Although many Xhosas did not believe, everyone was dragged into the fever of the prophecy and the possibilities of a better future for a bruised and battered people.

In his book, Alan Jefferies wrote of 'hypnosis, mass-persuasion and rhetoric (being) recognised as a very real way of dominating and making subjects obey commands'. All over the world, he wrote, 'charismatic sect leaders have convinced their followers to obey their teachings without question, often culminating in many deaths ... I believe Mhlakaza was such a person, who firstly manipulated his niece and through her, the Xhosa King and his subjects along a road of no return'.

Perhaps all this is true, but one seeks a deeper and more organic explanation than hypnosis and mass persuasion. What makes such techniques workable? Perhaps only a depth of hopelessness that unlocks all the defences of the heart and brings a vulnerability that is akin to madness. Does it matter if we live or die? The bloodshed and humiliation that had been going on for nearly two generations had taken its toll. And underneath all that, there must have been a profound spiritual disturbance; this clashing of traditional and Christian cosmologies; this jumbling of images and ideas.

In this climate, Nongqawuse's message was (or in the embittered hands of Mhlakaza became) apocalyptic. The notion of sacrifice was magnified ten thousand times. Kill the cattle, scatter the corn, abandon the logic of agricultural routine. Then the resurrection will come. The resurrection would be of all the ancestors. It would be of a new people come with trustworthy assistance to a languishing nation. And after the resurrection and the destruction of the Xhosa enemies, a new millennial happiness would waft across the people like a welcome breeze. It would be a time that resembled exactly their idealised memory of the old times, before the frontier, before the white people and the British guns, those times of joy and peace and contentment.

So the killing of the cattle continued, and the reckless feasting continued, and the hope continued, and lookout posts were set up all along the coastal hills to await the arrival of the Xhosa salvation. On the cover of that most authoritative book on the cattle-killing, JB Peires's *The Dead Will Arise*, is a reproduction of an oil painting, obviously contemporaneously rendered and now housed in the Africana Museum in Johannesburg. It depicts a small group of people on the top of a steep hill overlooking what looks like a moonlit sea. It is entitled *Kaffirs Watching for the Return of their Dead Warriors*.

It is impossible not to be gripped by such a blatant manifestation of desperation and steadfast hope. Impossible, also, not to be haunted now by the sense of aftermath.

I HAD OFFERED to drive to his house, so as not unduly to disturb him, but Alan Jefferies came instead to the hotel. He suggested that we drive together in his truck. I had told him on the telephone that I was interested in Nongqawuse and Mhlakaza, and so he drove me straight to where the pontoon plied across the mouth of the Great Kei River. I could clearly see, on the far side of the peaceful water, the road on which I had arrived. It went curving up the first Transkei hillside like a narrow scar of brown against the green.

'Once you're on top,' Alan Jefferies said, pointing, 'look out for tracks leading off to the right. You need to get onto the second set. This track will take you straight down into the Gxara gorge. That's where the prophetess saw her visions.'

He was a large man, filling up the space behind the wheel of his truck. He wore shorts and open sandals, and his thighs were deeply tanned. His face was equally large, with a bristling moustache, and his features were marked with an habitual reserve that brought a heaviness, a sort of pondered gravity, to his whole demeanour.

I asked him if the prophetess still lived in the memory of ordinary Xhosa people.

'Oh, definitely,' he said, but offered nothing more.

'In what way?'

'As a sense of national shame,' he replied.

I asked what had happened to Nongqawuse and her uncle after the appointed day – in fact, there had been several – of the arrival of the ancestors had come and gone like any other. He said he had dealt with this question in his book. Yet even as I asked it, I felt a sudden rumbling of fear. The disappointment! The terrible collapse of dignity. I had never in any sense experienced a felt reaction to the facts before. Now the reaction suddenly shifted as this rumbling within me. All that waiting for nothing. The disappointment, I thought again. The disillusion must have been unendurable. The Xhosa were finally and unutterably deserted. It seemed too much, suddenly, even to contemplate as a thing of history as one stood there so close to where the painting on the cover of Peires's book had probably been made and where the starvation had begun.

I said as much.

Alan Jefferies made no reply. He started the engine and turned his truck on the slipway. His big brown arms manipulated the wheel. We drove back into the village. He took me to a few places of interest, a few vantage points.

'A sense of national shame,' he said once more, suddenly. 'What happened to Mhlakaza? Some people say he died of starvation. There's also a story that he drowned in the sea, and that his body was washed up on some rocks close to Kei Mouth. As for Nongqawuse, I've seen her grave. She was handed over to the British. She spent some time in the Paupers' Lodge in Cape Town. She also several times in her life had to flee from Xhosa people who blamed her and wanted to kill her.'

As we drove back to the hotel he told me he knew a blood relative of Nongqawuse who used to verify whatever he was saying by swearing on her name. 'Oh, they're conscious of what happened, all right.'

Before we parted, and I had been unable to penetrate the reserve that lay close around him like a cocoon, he said: 'I'm neither historian nor writer. But I wanted to write the history of my roots here, and the project just expanded into a contextualised version of my family's story.'

In my room, with the ocean crashing on the rocks below my window, I looked at Alan Jefferies's book once more. 'Surely,' he wrote, 'in this so-called enlightened age, we should learn from the past and those lessons must be used to build a better future for everyone. How dare we be smug and critical of the consequences of Mhlakaza and Nong-qawuse's actions nearly one hundred and fifty years ago when, right now, AIDS is taking a toll on human life that will make those (cattle-killing) casualties ... pale into insignificance.'

I could hear the sudden outbursts of noise and laughter that punctuated the work of the conference downstairs – organising a series of sports meetings that combined HIV/AIDS messaging with games and other extra-curricular activities.

I stayed with Alan Jefferies's book for a while longer. In his conclusion, he allowed himself some philosophical leeway. His attention focused on two Xhosa words: *Ubuntu* and *Umona*. The first was well known in post-1994 South Africa as meaning working together for the common good. Jefferies, who was fluent in Xhosa, took the meaning further. 'Humanity towards other human beings in the most unselfish manner, with no attached conditions. A person with *ubuntu* does not demand or expect thanks for any generous deed done to others ... they must assume that the receiver silently recognises their humanity and will pass the message on to others.'

Umona had an opposite meaning. 'This simple word carries a host of negative connotations for people afflicted with it. I say "it" because one is afflicted with *umona*, like with a disease, and people recognise your ailment, even if you are unaware that you have it.' Jefferies struggled with an exact definition. Jealousy and its resultant resentments was too simple a concept. *Umona* goes further. It 'goes back and forth in people's minds, simmering for long periods, sometimes with no noticeable consequences, but at other times exploding as the pressure increases to breaking point, resulting in uncontrolled rage and physical violence.' He gave a few examples of *umona* in action. The first focused on what he perceived to be a tendency in black society to drag high achievers down to the generally accepted level or destiny for all black people. The second example was to be found in the taxi industry, he wrote. 'The spiral of violence and death seems to take little account of the plight of innocent people (passengers and bystanders) because *umona* forces have become too powerful to allow consideration for them.'

These examples did not satisfy me. I searched for something more. I laid aside the book and stood staring out at the sea from which the dead warriors had never emerged. Was there a collective scarring in that experience, and indeed the whole experience of the Frontier Wars, that had encouraged a precedence to *umona* over *ubuntu*? Was there a kind of darkened eye of cynicism that had been opened in the collective psyche, like a flowing out of bitter black blood that even the triumphs of the struggle had not staunched?

Where was that bare-chested young horseman now?

A BRAAI AND dancing took place on the terrace of the hotel that evening. The training course was more or less complete and it was time to relax. Many of the women had dressed exquisitely for the occasion, and many wore tight clothes, jeans and sequined boob-tubes, even those with fuller figures. The men's eyes were laughing and dark. Everyone queued for meat and salads and sat to eat at long tables set out of doors. Then the dancing began. It took place in a special room leading off one of the bars. Soon the entire floor was filled with dancers, and the music thumped persuasively out onto the terrace and into the darkness beyond the railing.

At one point the dancers moved in unison, and the dancing began to resemble waves. Individuals danced within their own preoccupations, their faces intent, yet moving in perfect unison with the main movement: all facing the same way, all crouched, all extended with hands fluttering above their heads, all stepping to the right, all to the left, all backwards, all forwards, effortlessly together in a remarkable display.

I commented admiringly upon it to the young woman, Lebo Komane, who sat with me for a moment. She nodded. But she had come for another purpose. She looked thoughtfully at me with her almond eyes and said: 'We were talking about what has happened since the struggle, and I knew I wanted to add something.'

Her cell phone rang and I waited.

'I'm never off duty,' she said to me with a slight laugh. 'Anyway, here it is. The sad thing about the transition was that very many of us – increasing numbers of us – suddenly started earning large amounts. Comparatively speaking, of course. We felt like sports stars, pop stars, VIPs and we started going overboard. There was no period of preparation for this new life. So things became chaotic. Materialist gratification became an individual imperative.'

I was on the point of asking her if she spoke from personal experience, but her cell phone rang again, and she hurried away. I returned my attention to the dancing, the bodies, all facing the same way, flowing like a single wave.

The teachers danced in the morning as well. They had assembled in the hall on the landward side of the hotel for a final session. And before it began they danced in a conga line moving slowly down the central aisle and across the front of the hall. Their voices filled the space with exuberant singing. What made the dance unusual for me was that each dancer carried a piece of green from the garden: a palm frond, a young branch from a shrub, or sometimes smaller objects like a single twig or a single flower. They moved so gracefully, forward and sometimes back a step or two, now with the greenery extended upward as if in a salute, now with it held against their heads, the leaves tumbling against the foreheads of these teachers singing together for the last time. The voices of the men stirred in the stomach; the voices of the women pierced the higher air; and their gathered faces seemed to express above all a rich and undiluted life.

I asked someone close by about the meaning of the greenery. Did it signify a particular Xhosa ritual, perhaps one of farewell? My informant laughed. He wore a black loveLife T-shirt over a muscular chest. He turned his head to speak into my ear above the noise of the singing. 'Nothing like that,' he said. 'It's Palm Sunday, that's all.'

AFTER THE completion of the final conference session I climbed into my car and drove to the pontoon. I crossed the wide water of the Great Kei mouth once more, seeing the waves seething and spraying above the largely submerged sand bank at the river's exit to the wider sea beyond. Then I ascended the first hill in low gear and on the top looked for the tracks leading off to the right. The tall grass waved in a stroking breeze that smelled of the sea. The tracks were faint but unmistakable. I turned onto the first I came to, even though Alan Jefferies had said I should take the second. I felt a tightness of expectancy as I drove, almost a reluctance to intrude upon this heartland of the Xhosa pain. The grass was swishing on the underside of the car. Down to my left I could see what I guessed to be the Gxara gorge, cliffs almost obscured by thick bush, a village on the grassland above, and in the shadows below merely a glimpse, once, of a reach of dark water. I drove slowly on.

The sea stretched out before me now. I drove on a spur of land jutting towards it until I could drive no further. The land fell steeply away at my feet. I wondered if I was standing at one of the lookout posts. Day after day, waiting for the ancestors to emerge. Waiting for the Russian ships. Those far-off people who had inflicted a military defeat on the British during the Crimean War quickly became the allies of the Xhosa, in particular because they had killed a former governor of the Cape, Sir George Cathcart, at the Battle of Inkerman in November 1854. The speed with which this news spread through the eastern Cape Colony and in particular the speed with which it was transmuted into the fabric of the Xhosa hope revealed the extent of the Xhosa spiritual crisis. Explanations that the Russians where white, and that in fact Britain and her allies were winning the war in Crimea, were not believed. The Russians were black, and they soon became inextricably woven into the hope of the resurrection and the thrill of the ultimate triumph.

But the ships did not appear. The day of deliverance passed. New dates were set. They too passed. Throughout the frontier country, Xhosa turned against Xhosa, those who believed in Nongqawuse's prophecies against those who did not, believers blaming unbelievers for the failure of the prophecy, unbelievers desperate to protect their cattle and crops from starving believers. I turned from the unyielding blue of the sea, from the breeze blowing so pleasantly into my face, and went in search of the second track.

Easy enough to find, and to descend by it into a steep valley a little distance upstream from the Gxara gorge. The track deteriorated, so I walked the last few hundred metres. The cliffs of the gorge were above me now, and the air was humid with rank vegetation on every side. I got no glimpse of the water that many said had been disturbed with shadows and visions and omens of a resurgence of self-belief. But I felt the silence of the place and the tangle of the trees and shrubs and grass, and also I noticed small birds chirping obliviously close to my head as I tried to imagine the starvation moving across the hills. Even in the village above the cliffs. Everywhere, in fact, on both sides of the Great Kei. Some of the words describing those brutal times returned.

'They boiled up old bones,' wrote Peires, 'that had been bleaching in the sun for years and ate the broth as soup ... they ate food that they would not normally have contemplated, such as horses, pigs and shellfish. They stole and ate the well-fed dogs of the white settlers in King William's Town. They even tried to eat grass. In a very few cases, believers maddened with hunger attempted to kill and eat little children. The majority of believers, though starving themselves, were horrified by this last excess and hunted down and killed any who were suspected of cannibalism ... Parents snatched the bread their children had begged, usually taking the food from those liable to die and giving it to the older and stronger children who might still conceivably survive. On other occasions whole families sat down to die as one, and for years afterwards pathetic little clusters of skeletons might be found under the shadow of a single tree, the parents and their children dead together ... Those who survived were so emaciated that they "resembled apes rather than human beings", while the children looked more like monkeys or bats. Many had lost their voices, and could make only indistinct sounds in their throats like the chirping of birds. Mentally and emotionally, they seemed "stupid from want and indifferent as to their fate", moving more by instinct than by conscious will. And as this ghastly procession of skeletons converged on the capital of British Kaffraria in the desperate hope of some assistance, it seemed to one observer that the prophesies had indeed come true, that the dead had risen from their graves at last, and were walking towards King William's Town.'

The birds were noising about my head as I stood in the thicket in the Gxara gorge. I wanted to raise my arms to protect myself from them. They were the voices of ghosts crying out inside the Xhosa psyche. The number of cattle slaughtered had been about 400 000. Human deaths from starvation were estimated at above 35 000, with nearly 150 000 people displaced. The Xhosa population of British Kaffraria alone dropped from over 100 000 to less than 40 000, as tens of thousands migrated into the Cape Colony to look for work. What a godsend for white farmers who had been starved of labour ever since the abolition of slavery nearly fifty years before. And here in this gorge, with the birds chirping like the voices of death, was where this ultimate destruction had begun.

I felt unnerved, standing alone in the thicket. I returned to the car. I stood looking out towards the opening in the hills that carried the Gxara to the sea. I could not steer my thoughts away from the ghosts within the Xhosa psyche. The consternation, the anger, the hatred, the humiliation, the pale new hope, the obsession, the disillusion, the starvation and death. This was the road trodden by these ghosts. What then of the later triumph?

I heard a soft footfall. I turned. A young girl was walking up the path from the river. It seemed astonishing to me that she should appear like this, a young Xhosa girl of no more than sixteen years, using the paths that Nongqawuse would have used. Here was an unconscious defiance, an unconscious affirmation of the continuity of life.

As the girl passed, I greeted her. She stopped and turned to me. She carried a bundle of belongings and a child on her back. In English, she asked me for a lift. I asked where she was going. She said she must get to the pontoon. I said I was going in the opposite direction, to Butterworth, then I changed my mind and agreed to drive her the few kilometres back to the pontoon. I turned the car and she clambered in, holding her baby on her lap, as we began the steep ascent back to the road.

I asked if she was still at school.

'Grade nine,' she said. Her clear eyes shifted across my face. The child on her lap stared fixedly up at me, as if in a stupor of surprise.

I asked after the child.

'Yes, mine,' she said. 'He is a boy. He is five months.'

I asked her what was the name of the river down there in the gorge behind us.

'Gxara,' she said.

Had she crossed it?

She nodded.

I said I had come to the river because I was interested in a young woman from history. 'About your age,' I said. 'Someone who had seen visions at the Gxara.'

My passenger's eyes brightened immediately. 'Nongqawuse,' she said.

I asked where she had heard of Nongqawuse.

She said: 'At school.'

I asked her what she had heard. She shrugged her shoulders, suddenly noncommittal. I asked if she had heard good things or bad things. Again she shrugged her shoulders, and we drove in silence.

Only as the river and the pontoon came into view below us, at the bottom of the final hillside, did she speak again. She turned to me with a new brightness and said: 'My name is Nompelo.'

I noticed then that she was excruciatingly thin and that she had small ulcers in the corners of her mouth. She said she was going on the bus to East London to her mother. She clambered out with her baby and her bundle. I wondered suddenly if she was going to die of AIDS. She raised one thin arm to wave as I turned the car and drove back once more into those historic and tormented hills.

10
Dividing the spoils

PEOPLE LIVING in King William's Town sometimes tell visitors that their town is unusual in that it has been the capital of three different territories in three distinct periods. To begin with, of course, it became the capital of Queen Adelaide Province. This was in 1835. But the short-lived province disappeared hardly six months later when the whole territory was returned to the Xhosa chiefs. About a dozen years later, though, British Kaffraria came into being and there was King William's Town, still hardly more than a mission station, ready to do duty as the capital once again. By 1866, however, British Kaffraria was incorporated into the Cape Colony, and the town was left to amble along for over a century before its next prominence. It is true that there was an opportunity for King William's Town to be incorporated into the independent homeland of Ciskei in the late 1970s, possibly as capital, but a referendum among white residents decided that this should not be the case. Bisho was built instead, albeit on the north-western outskirts of the town. So only in 1994 did King William's Town reclaim some status, this time in combination with Bisho, as capital of South Africa's newly drawn Eastern Cape Province.

Bisho is a collection of modern buildings that stands, even today, as a blatant visual monument to the folly of separate development and also, more subtly perhaps, to an unsightly autocratic power. When Ciskei took independence in 1981, it did so without popular consent; and the early cost estimates of R100-million for this so-called capital seemed obscene for a homeland without an economy (95% of employed Ciskeians worked in South Africa) and where 20% of children died before they reached five years. The buildings of Bisho's central business district, the majority of them government offices, crowd together a trifle foolishly on an otherwise largely empty skyline. The commercial aspects of the town have long ago failed, and the arcades and walkways are filled with litter and the pervasive stench of urine. The decorations on some of the buildings are grandiose, like the leopard gargoyles sitting along a ridge near the top of one office block. There seems to be nothing to justify the place. It has no internal dynamism nor any reason for being there. It is simply itself, unexplained and pretentious, the embodiment of an autocratic mindset. Certainly this was the case in the days of Lennox Sebe, first president of the independent nation of Ciskei, and even more so in the days of the military dictator Brigadier Oupa Gqozo, the ill-conceived nation's last. So there they were, King William's Town and Bisho – the one an English colonial town (although most of the English people have stolen away) filled with old colonial buildings; the other an inappropriate and unjustifiable post-modern conglomeration smelling in too many places like a public toilet – forming the capital of the Eastern Cape, arguably the most poorly managed province in South Africa.

But the two towns, clinging to each other in this unlikely partnership, did not exist in isolation. They found themselves incorporated into a new (at last geographically logical) local authority region called Buffalo City which included: the port city of East London; the sprawling township of Mdantsane to the left of the main road to King William's Town; Ginsberg and Zwelitsha just south of King William's Town; and Dimbaza, a bizarre apartheid creation on the road to Alice.

Dimbaza came into being in the late 1960s as a place where people redundant to the apartheid scheme of things began to be dumped. As South Africa's notorious forced removals gathered momentum, so Dimbaza filled up, with a high percentage of children. And a high percentage of the children died there in the tents and wooden huts on the treeless slopes of the Ciskei uplands. The graves of the children are still there, forming a sombre centrepiece to a township that has grown considerably since then. When you pass by on the main road, Dimbaza looks dense and even colourful, and, with an unemployment rate of around 70%, it is always crowded with people. In the 1970s a form of industrialisation came to Dimbaza when the apartheid state built an industrial area next door to the rural slum and provided some incentives to industries wishing to establish there. Main attraction, of course, was plentiful cheap labour.

185

I drove through the industrial estate on tarred roads lined with empty premises. A cow grazed in an overgrown factory yard. Rectangles of discoloured paint showed where the name boards had been. Now there were thousands of broken windows and weeds growing high at the entrances to what had once been quite pompous little reception areas and small office blocks. Plaster was falling off walls that would soon collapse. One roadside building, perhaps an erstwhile security office, had shatterproof glass in the windows through which the bricks had nevertheless penetrated. Street after street revealed only desolation and a sense of waste, the buildings falling into ruin to form this dismal testimonial to the wreckage wrought by separate development.

But one factory had a new sign strapped to the front. China Clothing. A few people dawdled outside. And a moment later, I gave a lift to two well-dressed young women who had bought a bundle of clothing and were now on their way to East London, they said, to sell on the pavements there. One of the young women wanted my telephone number in Johannesburg. 'Jobs are scarce,' they said; 'are you starting a factory here?' I said I wasn't. 'Well, then, you must give us jobs in Johannesburg.' They displayed a bold friendliness towards me, supported by a generosity of easy smiles and a slightly coquettish manner.

There were other follies still evident in that unhappy place. During the decade or so when the Ciskei was an independent state, an international airport with runways capable of handling jumbo jets was built, and two aircraft were purchased. The smaller aircraft, originally built for a Saudi Arabian dignitary, was fitted out with an *en suite* bedroom and other luxury accommodation, and had during its earlier lifetime (according to a newspaper article) been used by Barbra Streisand and the Rolling Stones. A great fanfare accompanied the inaugural flight of Ciskei International Airways. But there were no subsequent flights and after standing idle for years both aircraft were sold, the smaller now doing service as a restaurant and bar in East London. I drove out on the Grahamstown road late one afternoon to look at this infamous Bulembu airport.

I was greeted by friendly armed guards standing outside the main entrance. They showed me a side door where I met an even friendlier black woman who said I was most welcome to look around. In the big lounge area, several hundred bright blue chairs stood in rows on a polished floor. The arched ceiling was clad with aluminium strips, giving the entire space a light, reflective atmosphere. The departures and arrivals board had never been used; neither, presumably, had the scanning machine for hand luggage. Along the back wall were booking kiosks, and a door marked *Airport Management*. The view through the high glass front was of concrete apron and green grass beyond. In the distance, big hangars stood beneath clusters of floodlights mounted on high poles. I had expected considerable deterioration, but this was not the case. Apart from the ironies of baggage trolleys and access steps on wheels becoming entangled in unmown grass, the airport was in reasonable repair, even though it was used only by a few small private aircraft. Perhaps the larger aircraft of VIPs used the runways for visits to Bisho (although East London airport was less than a hundred kilometres away); but there were certainly no scheduled flights to anywhere. There never had been – and no international flight (again according to the newspaper article) had ever landed there.

All the lights in the airport lounge were burning, and it seemed quite festive as the shadows lengthened outside. But there was no sign of life anywhere – except for a radio somewhere playing a repetitive tune in the style of township jive.

THE BLACK consciousness activist, Steve Biko, had been born in King William's Town in 1946. Thirty-one years later, he died in police custody after suffering brain damage caused by the 'application of force to the head'. At some point he was taken from the Eastern Cape (where he had been arrested) to Pretoria, being transported naked and unconscious in the back of a bakkie for over a thousand kilometres. His body was brought back to King William's Town for burial. He was one of many Xhosa-speaking people who had given their lives in the struggle against the apartheid state. To see Biko's unpretentious grave, as I did while visiting King William's Town, was to be reminded how prominently people from and in the Eastern Cape had featured in the struggle. Much of the African National Congress leadership, including Mandela himself, had come from the Eastern Cape as it was now delimited.

Stephen Biko's grave had a simple marble top and a narrow brick-paving surround. It stood in a row of graves in a cemetery lying next to a railway line. The ground was lumpy with the earthworks of moles and scattered with tiny white daisies. Some of the surrounding graves were no more than mounds of earth with simple crosses or stones, and one or two graves were identified with hand-written signs while other signs were made more durably in the manner of vehicle number plates. Outside the graveyard, a wall had been built and ornate gates installed. Words affixed to the wall proclaimed the place as the *Steve Biko Garden of Remembrance*. On a plaque beside the gates were more words: *It is better to die for an idea that will live than to live for an idea that will die.*

I drove into Ginsberg, trying to find Biko's family home. But my directions were faulty and I ended up talking to some people waiting on a corner for a taxi. One of them, a young man named Zweletini, offered to show me where it was. Before we set off, he pointed across the road to a large school probably built in the early 1960s.

'That is Forbes Grant High School,' he said. 'That is my school. It was also Steve Biko's.' He wore a blue Fair Isle pullover, and he had a reserved and gentle face. 'Now go straight down and turn right,' he added.

In front of the modest township house, one of a long row of more or less identical structures, a bust of Biko had been erected. Taken with its plinth it was as high as the top of the front window, seeming too large for the house. The property was obviously occupied – but with the curtains drawn and the doorbell eliciting no response. Biko's father had died when Biko was only four, and it had been left to his mother, who worked at the local hospital, to raise the family on her own. Here, in this cramped place. I noticed a solar water panel on the almost flat roof – obviously a later addition. A neighbour approached us as we lingered momentarily outside the front gate. We shook hands. He, too, he said, had been a black-consciousness activist. We smiled at each other. It struck me as amazing that I was so easily accepted – perhaps simply because I had taken the trouble to visit the house.

As we drove back towards the town, we came across a narrow cemetery below the road. It contained, Zweletini told me, the graves of the victims of the Bisho massacre. I asked if he remembered the event. He shook his head. 'I was only nine years,' he said. 'But we heard afterwards.' We stopped and walked among the graves. An inscription read: *In revolutionary memory of our comrades who fell at Bisho on 7th September 1992.* My cousin Elizabeth had once shown me the place on the Bisho campus of Fort Hare University where the shooting had taken place. I remembered little more than sloping ground and a fence. Ciskei troops under the command of Brigadier Gqozo had opened fire on a protest march. Led by many ANC luminaries, the march was designed to weaken the position of an intransigent Ciskei government in preparation for the establishment of a unitary South Africa. Over two hundred marchers had been wounded, and 29 killed.

Here in the grass before me now were the graves of those who had lost their lives in the process of dismantling a state that had never, like its unnatural capital town, been much more than a grotesque hallucination. Not too long after the protest march, of course, Gqozo had been deposed and the apparatus holding up the Ciskei state dismantled. So the great dance of 1994 had been danced, here, within a unitary Eastern Cape. The Ciskei, and the Transkei as well, had ceased to exist as independent states.

I drove my guide, Zweletini, into the centre of King William's Town. He told me he had passed his matric the previous year, and that now he was doing courses at an hotel school in Durban. Catering and management. 'Yes, I like it a lot. The hotel school is in Smith Street. Do you know where that is in the middle of Durban?' he asked. When I dropped him off he offered his hand which I shook. We wished each other good times and lots of luck. He turned and mingled with the people crowding the pavement.

But my thoughts had lingered with Elizabeth. Showing me the place where all those people had been shot. That had been some years previous to my current visit. She had told me also how oppressed she had often been when she had first come to the Eastern Cape. 'It seemed to me,' she told me, then, 'that there had been too much bloodshed here, too much fighting and suffering. More than anywhere else in the country. Even the landscape, beautiful as it is, seemed to brood. There was for me at first a sense of defeat — a knowledge of defeat — under every bush.'

Now she said to me: 'The Eastern Cape seems so full of cynicism, back-biting, depression, rumours, jealousy, and bringing people down.' Someone else said: 'What is most disturbing is the moral decay.'

AT THE time of my most recent visit to the Eastern Cape, nine years after 1994, there was an undeniable sense sometimes of staggering through a morass, now turned almost surreal, of disarray and corruption. The depth of the morass was indicated by the constant reference to these things in the newspapers.

There was, for example, the case of double payments from the Health Department to a pharmaceutical company to the tune of more than R8-million. Another pharmaceutical company was also under investigation for billing the provincial government for services never rendered. On the same day that this story appeared in national newspapers, six people were arrested in the Flagstaff area for the theft of government cheques totalling hundreds of thousands. Earlier, two high-ranking politicians, both members of the provincial executive council, and both members of the South African Communist Party, were dismissed, and the results of the province's ANC leadership elections annulled. At more or less the same time, four Eastern Cape welfare officials appeared in the East London Regional Court on fraud and theft charges amounting to R4,5 million. An authoritative report on 'chronic administrative problems' in the Eastern Cape listed poor financial management, corruption, failure to maintain discipline, lack of leadership and management, a poor work ethic, the excessive use of consultants and huge service delivery backlogs as lying at the heart of the province's administrative problems. Large numbers of vacancies in the civil service were coupled with an oversupply of staff in 'non-strategic areas'. A black Sunday newspaper accused the government of 'cynically moving to remove political opponents and not tackling the root causes of corruption'. In a single year, the commercial branch of the police service in the Eastern Cape investigated 731 cases involving R247 million of actual and potential losses of government funds. And a survey from Rhodes University suggested that the Eastern Cape government and administration were the most corrupt in the country. The survey was based on interviews with 169 civil servants, 48% of whom believed that they should not be punished for receiving 'gifts' in return for doing something that was clearly a part of their job description, while 14% reported seeing bribes being offered and 12% seeing bribes actually accepted. Nearly 30% of the respondents had witnessed the theft of public resources, and 23% said that all or most of their colleagues were involved in corruption. In addition, over 40% expressed the fear that 'syndicates' would intimidate them if they reported corruption, and nearly 70% were unsure about being protected if they blew the whistle. Naturally enough, the Eastern Cape government scoffed at the survey. It went further. It said through a spokesman that the fact that the respondents had participated in the survey indicated 'the political will to eliminate the scourge'.

Someone told me that considerable anxiety was being expressed, in private, about the seemingly rapid moral decay in the province that had very often occupied centre stage in the struggle against apartheid. Perhaps it was because the people had not given thanks for the 1994 victory. So some big men from the national parliament had came to the province and slaughtered cattle and bathed in a river to appease the ancestors.

A MAN named John told me about his experiences working for the Eastern Cape provincial administration. He had been here for six years, he said, and held a senior position in one of the larger departments. I asked if he worked in Bisho. He nodded. I was therefore able to put his face behind the glass of one of those post-modern edifices standing so self-importantly up there on the open veld.

He said: 'I find the Eastern Cape has virtually defied all my previous managerial experience. The normal orthodoxies of management – things like teamwork, personal incentives and achievement – simply don't apply. Just as one begins to get into one's stride, one discovers in people whole new layers of thought and relationships that have to be taken into account.'

John had told me that his time with me would be limited because of a prior engagement at his church in King William's Town. He said he hoped that I would attend. The event was a public performance of some Easter music. I said that I planned to be there. And then I asked him to elaborate on the layers of thought and relationships that he had mentioned earlier.

He nodded. He was a thoughtful, kindly man, but I saw a depth of will and strength in his eyes as well. He said: 'Let's start at the top layer. The present Eastern Cape administration is a combination of three pre-1994 administrations: the old Transkei, the old Ciskei and the old white Cape administration. Until I started here I had never appreciated the significant differences between the two old homelands, how the administrations developed different characteristics and styles, and how Umtata had felt downgraded by the elevation of Bisho to provincial capital after 1994.'

I remembered the empty offices that Willie had showed me in the old Transkei capital, the sense of having been taken over and therefore also a sense of disorganisation, responsibility for which resided elsewhere.

'It's fascinating,' John went on, 'how the old divisions have come to the fore and also how they've been reversed. Here we're talking about the Red Xhosa in the Transkei and the School Xhosa in British Kaffraria, which ultimately became the Ciskei under apartheid. Obviously the Red Xhosa were the more traditional, the School Xhosa were those who had more easily accepted British rule and were therefore more quickly assimilated. Of course, the real Xhosa status and royalty resided in the more traditional Transkei. But during the homeland era, this seniority was reversed, with the Ciskei being regarded as a cut above the Transkei – because they had been historically better educated. Now all this is re-emerging. In some ways it's a classic tussle between traditionalists and moderns.

'But that's not all,' John continued. 'Underneath everything else is a resurgent consciousness of tribe and clan and family. Even senior civil servants are referring to each other by their clan names now. Old hierarchies are being rediscovered. For those from clans and families lower down in the hierarchies, there's a system of patronage and favour whereby people can find a certain amount of mobility by way of strategic allegiances. To try to manage efficiently, its essential that one knows these networks.

'Of course, during the days of separate development, traditional leadership became blurred and prostituted. But now the whole system is re-emerging. It's a direct blood lineage. The dilemma for democracy in this province is that it operates on the surface of these much more powerful systems and allegiances.

'It's a new tribalism,' John said. 'It's family versus family, clan versus clan, tribe versus tribe, and lastly Ciskei versus Transkei. That's why there is a constant jockeying for position. Without a proven tribal pedigree, a man – whether he be a minister in the cabinet or a director-general in the civil service – is scoffed at. This means: not the best man for the job, but the best tribally connected man. Our western sense of accountability and transparency is simply not equipped to delve this deep.

'And corruption?' He shrugged his shoulders. 'It's happening everywhere. We all know the argument. People say they are simply taking what apartheid has denied them. That's what the struggle was for. Morality is not involved. If they're stopped, it's unfortunate but not in any sense shameful.

'We've made great play of the concept of *ubuntu*. This wonderful ability of Africans to share and shoulder joint responsibility, etcetera. But I am more and more convinced it operates only in the immediate family, and to an extent in the clan. Any other expectation from ubuntu is mere romanticism. And I don't think we should lay too much store by a presumed Christian ethic. Of course there's a long history of Christianity in the Eastern Cape, but it never provided a release from the traditional belief systems. The Christian thing – and I'm a Christian and yet I'm increasingly convinced – has simply been overlaid on top of this thicket of other convictions and imperatives that we call "traditionalism".'

He stood up suddenly. 'Oh dear,' he said, 'look at the time. I'm so sorry. Hopefully we'll see you at church.'

MY COUSIN Elizabeth and I drove to the Holy Trinity Church as darkness fell. We arrived late and hurried up the path, seeing the richness of stained glass like beacons before us. Next door to the church, Elizabeth pointed out, stood the King William's Town mosque.

We waited in the vestibule for a break in the singing. The light came though coloured glass and slanted across Elizabeth's face. She said she thought the music was John Stainer's *Crucifixion*. I remembered the

193

singing at Kei Mouth, those young teachers filling their lungs with power and the air with their effortless musicality. They had danced in the aisles with their twigs and palm fronds falling onto their foreheads or raised powerfully into the air. But Jesus had now entered Jerusalem, and celebration had turned to torment. The crucifixion was upon us. The voices seemed strained and thin, and when they paused, we slipped into the church and sat in an empty pew.

The music alternated with readings from the Bible. Some of the readers and a few members of the choir were Xhosa people, others were midway between black and white. The ceiling arched steeply into shadows above us. I saw John half-hidden by one of the pillars. The readers rose from the congregation and made their way to the lectern. The singing was sometimes plaintive, always disciplined. I saw in a small brochure that the foundation stone of the church had been laid in 1850, and that the first service was held six years later. The stones from which the walls had been built glowed a warm pale ochre; ornate fretwork provided a background for the altar. The soldiers were casting lots for Jesus's clothes. They were deriding Him. The organ played darkly, like a dirge. I read that Nathaniel Merriman, 'probably the greatest of the Border's pioneer Anglicans', had supervised the reburial of a British soldier under the floor of the partially built Holy Trinity. The date was 1848, just two years prior to Merriman confirming Mhlakaza, the first Xhosa to become an Anglican. These were haunting connections and continuities.

After the singing had been concluded and the prayers offered, I looked at the brass plaques adorning the interior walls of the Holy Trinity Church. The most poignant was dated 1857. It commemorated the marriage of a James Londale to a Mary Fuller. Such private happiness, such a hope for the future that marriage always implied, while outside the gates the fevered prophecies of another resurrection (unerringly interpreted by an embittered Mhlakaza) were beginning to take their toll.

So I stood alone in the beautiful church (Elizabeth was talking to some ladies elsewhere) and remembered the birds in the thicket next to the Gxara. So close to my head. Sounding like the starving who had lost their ability for speech and who staggered towards King William's Town and the Holy Trinity Church in their final desperate grab at salvation.

I WENT to see an anthropologist working in King William's Town. He needed little encouragement to talk. He told me immediately that democracy was currently being seen more as majority rule than it was as a system for nurturing individual rights and improved access to the machinery of the state. Such a perception was inevitable considering the size of the ANC majority in the Eastern Cape. So it was not a struggle for political power against political opponents, decided by a well-informed electorate, so much as a struggle for personal or family or clan advantage. The old vigour, from the years of struggle, of grassroots democracy, of consensus decision-making and an inclusive leadership style, had given the hope of something coming out of the struggle for everyone. The ANC-led struggle had undoubtedly raised individual expectations, but now the dragon was unassuaged. Nothing was really working as it should for ordinary people. Many were beginning to see themselves as no better off than before. Why? Because the ANC had in a broad sense abandoned its own electorate. What was the imperative to remain in touch with the grassroots? The popular struggle had been won. The real power struggles were now being played out inside the new black bourgeoisie, the ruling elite, who were driven by those old imperatives of personal gain, or gain for family and clan. The focus had therefore shifted away from the broader problems that the electorate constantly experienced with regard to socio-economic under-development and administrative inefficiency. The electorate, however, needed in some way to be assuaged without being too fully awakened. The fundamental idea behind public policy was therefore to make everything bland, to speak of big schemes for the improvement of all. More and more now, development was being defined in general terms, with little account taken of local perspectives. Local involvement might mean local disagreements with the whole, which in turn might lead to the development of the potential power of civil society and a genuine feel for democracy. And a stronger civil society was hardly the main preoccupation of any ruling elite who seemed to be quite happy to see a perpetuation of the current confusion between democracy and majority rule.

We sat in his overloaded office. Untidy bookshelves lined the walls, and piles of open books and periodicals lay strewn across every level surface. He sat by his computer, but had swivelled away from it to face me as we talked. I should say rather that he talked to me. My questions tended to be answered before they were asked. I thought that he might be a lonely man, and yet he did not ramble. His thoughts were logical, and delivered with a quiet force that bespoke conviction. He did not often smile; and when he did, the muscles seemed to move in a slightly reluctant way, as if he had slipped into a mode with me, this stranger who jotted down his opinions, that he did not altogether trust.

The situation in South Africa, he said, had shifted from the 1994 excitement of a non-racial democracy towards an Africanist majority-rule situation. The root of all that excitement, both national and international, was that race wouldn't matter anymore. But what we were hoping to lose – the obsessive classification of everybody according to race – we haven't lost at all. In fact, there had been a resurgence of ethnicity. The essential spirit of the struggle was democracy, it was the spirit of the Freedom Charter, but this very rapidly has been usurped by all these deeper ethnic urges. But for these urges to achieve full potency, it has been necessary to shuffle the cards of the past in a certain way.

Large majority governments all over the world did this. The Afrikaner had certainly done it during his years in power in South Africa. Now it was happening again: shuffling the cards of the past to suit the ruling elite. The tendency was towards over-simplification. A part of the elitist vision of the ANC was to simplify the population into broad groupings of people and behaviour. Idiosyncratic differences thrived within the democratic model but tended to be suppressed by the majority rule model.

To return to the Eastern Cape, while the imperatives of the ruling elite were based on family, clan and tribal affiliations, their power rested on the assumption that the Xhosa en masse were a general cultural type. Of course, they were nothing of the sort. So that was why the ruling elite weren't all that keen to develop a sense of civil society which might encourage idiosyncrasies to emerge which in turn might begin to erode their power base. And that was why development was being seen in ever-broadening circles and why place names were being changed. The imperative was to bolster a new sense of African nationalism capable of suppressing or at least marginalising the sub-cultural differences among big groups like the Xhosas. Instead of making democratic South

Africans, the ruling elite was intent upon making a pliant and suitably programmed electorate. Push the right buttons, and Africanist rule (like Afrikaner rule before it) is maintained for long periods, but with the great advantage that Africanist rule, however bourgeois and elitist, can be maintained within the basic rules of democracy.

We went outside for a smoke break. He explained with a rueful smile that he was not allowed to indulge his habit inside the institution where he worked. So we stood in a small courtyard while he lit up. He wore jeans and a finely striped shirt. His face struck me then, exposed as it was to sunlight, as being essentially thoughtful and isolated, his forehead horizontally lined, his hair long and curling over his collar, his eyes slightly heavy as if from too much reading.

He said he wanted to stress the method of retaining power by suppressing differences within the main ethnic blocks. The Xhosas were great individualists, he pointed out, with ample allowance made within the old tribal structures for the wide expression of idiosyncratic behaviour. This explained the individual valour of Xhosa warriors. It also explained why Xhosas had been so prominent in the struggle. But once you were in power, the anthropologist said, the preoccupation shifted to its retention. In this context, it was essential that the old emphasis on individuality be suppressed. Indeed, it became desirable that the past itself was ignored – except in broad Africanist terms. If the peasants didn't have a past, it became easier to create their future – and investigative history disappeared.

He walked with me to the street where we said goodbye. He smiled in his slightly reluctant way. He said: I think one of the real glories of the ancient world – the Xhosa world included – was how they were able to build into the civil-society domain a fundamental space for the expression of human individuality.

THANKS TO an initial telephone call made by Elizabeth, I was able to see Paula Batya, the Xhosa educationist I had met at dinner in Umtata. She was the one who had lived abroad for a period and who was keenly aware when her daughter (who had been brought up in England) mispronounced her Xhosa 'just like a European'. She was working and living in East London, so I drove the approximately sixty kilometres down the

highway from King William's Town to the coast. I passed the sprawling Mdantsane on the right of the road. Then the leafy suburbs on the
outskirts of the city began. Paula had given me excellent directions and
I came in good time to the teacher-training facility in an area called
Stirling.

I sat in my car in the shade of some mature trees lining the suburban
street. My thoughts had returned to Umtata, to my first meeting with
the vivacious Paula, and then to my time in Umtata generally. Particularly to the meeting on the open square in front of the building called
Munitata. That strange mixing of road safety with Christianity. The
literature handed out that extolled the successes of the national and
provincial governments. The sense of great comfort and peacefulness of
all those people sitting in the sun and shielding their eyes with Arrive
Alive flags. But now the memory was influenced by more recent events.
The anthropologist had added a caption to this view. I twisted his words
slightly. If the peasants are encouraged to forget their past, or even to
see themselves without much historical accuracy as the 'new wave', it
becomes easier to manipulate their future.

I said to Paula Batya that the connection between the century of
Frontier Wars and the 20th-century struggle against white domination
was unerringly logical. The prominence of Xhosa people in this struggle
could come as no surprise to anyone. But what did not seem logical
was the way in which the ultimate 1994 triumph had yielded so little.
More corruption, in fact, than progress. It was almost like a deliberate
belittlement of the democratic basis for the struggle in the first place.

She looked at me with great seriousness. She spoke slowly when she
replied. She said there was some truth in what I had said. She said, further, that she wanted to respond from her original position of having
been born and bred in a rural area.

'From that perspective,' she went on, 'what comes to me most clearly
is that the apartheid regime – or let me rather say, white rule in general
from its beginnings – was very successful in one respect. It led directly
to the disintegration of my identity. I want to use the scenario of a tree.
It has strong deep roots. But although the trunk and branches are
destroyed, the roots are not dead; they remain alive as part of a recognisable tree. Are you following this?'

'Does the tree represent the Xhosa traditions?'

'Exactly. We know our values, but we don't always practise them. It needs to be said, too, that colonialism brought certain influences that would last. Christianity, for example. There are some positives. But the negatives of colonialism and apartheid are more. And of course there is a conflict between the old traditions and Christianity. For example, if I as a Xhosa woman want to prepare Xhosa beer, why am I criticised? It's brewed at home, using mealies from my own land. It has nothing to do with evil or Satanism. Also when I slaughter. Why is this called Satanism by the Christians who also label themselves as progressive? I can't belittle my own identity. However rich or powerful I become I'll never – in fact, I can't – buy another identity. Christianity has brought enlightenment and education. These things have fed into our resistance to white domination. Had the missionaries not come, this would not have been the case. So to begin with there were the two groups: those who resisted enlightenment, and those who went with enlightenment. Those who remained in the red blanket and said, I will never change, simply had insufficient power to remain as they were. The enlightenment side was a stronger force; it won the battle. But the traditions aren't dead. The roots are still living and they are very strong.'

She regarded me in silence briefly, her eyes seeming troubled. Here was a primary cleavage in Xhosa society being made manifest before me. But could it account, even in part, for the post-1994 failures? It seemed to me that she was tempted then to go to another level of disclosure. Her momentary hesitation was as she succumbed to this temptation. She leaned towards me across the table at which we sat.

'When migrant labour came in,' she went on, 'it was obvious that those on the enlightenment side, those with some education, would fit in best. The economic advantages were obvious, but there were serious cultural and social disadvantages. Do you see what I'm saying?'

I nodded.

She leaned back in her chair and said: 'You are talking to a product of the migrant labour system. My father was a migrant labourer and had little influence on my life. Whose product am I? My mother stood alone, unemployed, looking after five kids. My father had another woman in Cape Town where he worked, and three more kids. Would it be fair for me to say that my father was rubbish? No. You can argue he was forced by circumstances. But let's go back to the tree. The main thing for me – and for everyone – is identity. So my Dad is number one, because he gives me that. Identity is absolutely everything. That's where my pride lies. But the migrant labour system had robbed me of a productive relationship with my father. How am I supposed to react to his illegitimate children? And where do they get their identity from? They have no roots. So there are all sorts of people with identity crises. And the tree has been so badly damaged. Only by going back to the roots will our true identities be discovered. But the people without an identity are always tempted to run away from the search and cling to Jesus. And what a diversity of churches, some of which think they are better than others. My relationship with Jesus is superior to yours, they say. The quarrelling never ends. It goes all the way up to the leaders, this quarrelling about tradition versus progressive, and church versus church. Our whole society is smashed up with quarrelling and insecurity.'

I told her about the distribution of the oil from Israel that I had seen advertised on the front of the Universal Church of the Kingdom of God in Umtata.

'Exactly,' she said, 'casting out devils. Casting out more than the next church. Competing and quarrelling. Which church has the best marketing techniques? Yet it is not what the Xhosa people need. How do we create a new tree from the best of the traditional roots, the best of western influence, the best of Christianity? That's where we should aim. We will have to work hard to recreate our identity. Without a sure understanding of our identity, there can be no sure moral sense, I don't think.'

She gathered up her things abruptly. 'I must go home to my family,' she said. I asked her where she lived. 'Gonubie,' she said. I had an image of her in a modern house in that seaside resort a few kilometres north of East London, chiding her daughter's English pronunciation of various Xhosa words. But more particularly I imagined her in England, perhaps sitting behind her newspaper on the London underground, wrestling with the divisions in Xhosa society, the damage done by colonialism and apartheid to the Xhosa traditions, and the damage done to her own life by the often merciless exigencies of the migrant labour system –

particularly when coupled with the South African refinement of influx control. But above all, I allowed her final words to linger: without identity there can be no morality, she had said.

LATE THAT afternoon I went to see some people living on the Bisho campus of the University of Fort Hare. They lived in a modern face-brick house with double garage and a large lounge. The woman's name was Shume, and she apologised that her husband had been delayed. We sat facing each other in a compact configuration of chairs and settee in the large lounge. From time to time I heard young children playing elsewhere in the house. Shume attended to them briefly. They remained silent after that, their noise replaced by the discontinuities of a television set. She sat on the settee, smiling modestly at me, saying that she could not believe she would have anything of value to say. She was quite wrong in this. Nevertheless, for some time she hedged my questions, perhaps hoping for the arrival of her husband. But he did not appear, and our conversation gradually deepened.

'Could it be a lack of serious commitment, this post-1994 failure?' she asked. 'On a superficial level, might the situation not be exacerbated by the lack of jobs in the general economy? The jobs are predominantly in the state. It's the biggest prize. Everyone is fighting for these limited spoils, so there's a lot of backstabbing and undermining that goes on – and probably not nearly enough sustained work.'

She was in her essence a serene woman, I thought, unconsciously graceful, even as she sat before me, her hands folded in her lap, her face attentive and pleasant – and in no obvious sense restless or dissatisfied. She made, in all our time together, no sudden movements that might have indicated anxiety. Even when what she said began to become disturbing, her poise was in no outward way unsettled.

She said in response to a question: 'I think I might disagree that there's a growing cleavage between traditional and progressive elements in Xhosa society. I don't think the differences are as pronounced as some people like to make out. In fact, since 1994, I've seen a large increase of people who might be called progressive interested in embracing the old traditions. Under apartheid, the emphasis was on ethnic divisions; now the emphasis is on traditional ethnic roots.

'My husband studied for many years in America,' she went on. 'When he returned in 1985, he had difficulty getting a job because he was fond of wearing dreadlocks and traditional Nigerian dress. It simply wasn't done in those days. Now, on the contrary, these fashions are coveted. You have evidence of this every day in the streets. Men and women like wearing something African: it's all the rage now. A few years ago we had to travel to another town to find a traditional Xhosa dressmaker. Now there are thirty to forty in King William's Town alone. There's other evidence as well. At our latest graduation ceremony, red clay Xhosa women danced on the official programme. Whenever you pick up a book, you notice a tendency to quote oral literature. And many more people – we've certainly noticed this trend – are training to be sango-mas these days.'

I heard the roaring of engines and the dee-daa sirens of police cars from the television. She guessed I was listening, and laughed pleasantly.

'Yes,' she said, 'the other side of this back-to-our-roots coin is, of course, the problem of cultural imperialism. The all-pervasive techno-logies ... There are fears that even the Xhosa language is dying. The vast majority of available entertainment is in English. Many children are now going to the previously white schools. They are learning to read and write in English. They're speaking Xhosa, but not reading or writing it. And parents let their children get away with all sorts of nonsense. There's this inbuilt fear of white people because we believe we're not as good as they are. Therefore what happens in the previously white schools must be superior, and must be accepted without serious question.

'But it should not be accepted in this way. There must be a way to protect our uniqueness. Look at the Jews and Indians. They refuse to be assimilated. The strength of the family in those cultures holds things together – even in the West. They're withstanding the onslaught of cultural imperialism. On the other hand, Xhosa people are rapidly becoming westernised, but without any of the Western support systems – which of course have to be bought. The Xhosa clan relationships are now largely nominal. The traditional support systems are disintegrat-ing. Take my own mother. Since my Dad died, she is now living alone – and she doesn't really have the option of buying the care that she needs.

'In fact,' she said, her serenity undisturbed, 'when you think of it, 1994 has left black people worse off in a number of ways. There's much more loneliness and uncertainty, I think. There are fewer jobs, and a high percentage of those that are available are contract positions. Long-term job security is a thing of the past. It's a totally new way of life for us. Does this sound ironic? But I think it's very true that the securities and structures – even if you call them strictures – of apartheid are no more. My older children often say to me: "You guys were lucky. You had a common enemy, a common goal. But what is our legacy from the political freedom that your generation fought for? All we seem to do now is compete, fighting for the top jobs." You can see them struggling for personal security and support systems like medical aids and insurance and pensions and property.'

She smiled a slightly wan smile then.

'I feel a sadness sometimes,' she said quietly. 'I think that maybe people are wearing the cloth and the beads, not so much as a celebration or as a manifestation of pride, but rather with real longing for the old certainties. Perhaps we are all longing for the days of the tribe. But they have gone forever. So we flock to the churches – more often than not with those padded Bibles specially made for clapping. That's something genuinely African, people say, the clapping. So is the singing. We want to bring in these elements so we can call these attempts at worship our own. We crave to belong. We crave to be African, as the Westernisation process sweeps us along. The idea of an African Christianity is gaining popularity. People here are attaching a lot of importance to being lay preachers. Having lived in Johannesburg for some time, we never really perceived this. The urban experience tends to secularise. But here, it's lay preachers and songomas. It's as if we're waiting for those miracles to happen that will save us.'

She looked at me with slight apology. 'I'm sure this isn't what you came to hear. I really do apologise for my husband.'

I assured her that I was fascinated by what she said. I asked her to tell me how the idea of democracy and government fitted into this under-lying longing for security.

'Ah,' she said, as if I had steered the conversation in a direction she was reluctant to pursue. A child came into the large room in the middle of which we sat. She attended to him and then turned her composed face in my direction again.

'I think we need to go back,' she said. 'To understand what is happening now we need to remember the ideas of government then, I mean long ago in the Xhosa tradition.'

I waited.

She said: 'The chiefs and kings of the past were highly respected. But they were discredited by the military and colonial processes, by the wars and the starvation after the cattle-killing, and of course also by apartheid. Naturally enough, there's something of a re-emergence of these figures. It's part of the resurgence of interest in traditional things. But these people look like anachronisms now, of insufficient substance to resurrect the certainties of the past. The focus of power has shifted to the politicians. But it'll take a long time – if it ever happens – for the politicians to take the place of the chiefs and kings. They have no symbolism. The politicians and civil servants seem too unstable. They come and go. They inspire little confidence in a people that so powerfully craves assurance.

'So while the kings and chiefs posture without much conviction – although often their power is not insignificant – the politicians and civil servants are busy creating a powerful ruling class to ensure that the new political status quo remains. It's a definite elite, this ruling class, that seems above all to be preoccupied with amassing wealth and power. Democracy, at best, is of secondary account. The people are given handouts rather than a share in the governing process. Maybe this explains the failure since 1994. What does seem quite obvious to many of us now is that they are creating the classic bourgeois preconditions for revolution. Civil war may yet come to this country.'

She sat on the sofa, hands clasped in her lap, smiling calmly at me.

DRIVING HOME in the darkness I was haunted by something, some sense, that my conversation with Shume had heightened simply because it had not been mentioned directly. It was this sense I had often experienced in the Eastern Cape of some humiliation and disappointment in the Xhosa psyche so profound that not even victory could assuage it. It was a loss of faith in the centre of the very search for faith. It was a wound with a scar of almost unspeakable cynicism and unconcern. The struggle against and victory over the old enemy had been a temporary panacea. The dull pain had returned. Not even the oil of Israel could heal it. This is what I thought as I drove through Bisho, the densely clustered post-modern folly looming vaguely to one side, poorly lit, empty, its dark visage and dense skyline as if scowling at the wounded country upon which it had been built.

But I thought more besides. I remembered Shume's references to the chiefs and kings of the past; and suddenly I found their faces in those heroes that had so inspired Nelson Mandela when he was young. Sandili and Moqoma, fighting valiantly for the survival of their people in the face of the overwhelming influences – including treachery, humiliation and huge cruelty – of the white settlers and their British masters. Moqoma had died a prisoner on Robben Island in 1873, but not before he had succumbed to and extricated himself from a degrading relationship with alcohol. Sandili was killed in battle five years later, and with him had died the century-long resistance of the Xhosa people. Heroes in defeat. The bitterness and humiliation of a defeat that penetrated far beyond the battlefield, far beyond the subservience, far beyond the struggle, far beyond the ultimate victory. This dull and unassuageable pain in the Xhosa heart, overcome either by an astonishing idealism, or by a darker will to power and possession.

Astonishing, certainly, to think of Mandela in this context. At the same time as he acknowledged his heroes, he articulated the result of their inspiration as it had been transmuted through his own experience. *To be free,* he told his audience of tens of thousands at the Union Buildings in 1994, *is not merely to cast off one's chains, but to live in a way that respects and enhances the freedom of others. The true test of our devotion to freedom is just beginning.* Such words are in every respect an impassioned plea for a triumphing of the generosity of the human spirit implicit in democracy. It is the Freedom Charter of 1955 reborn. It is an inspiration to the whole world.

But there is the darker option that also soothes the dull pain of humiliation and defeat. This is the will to power and possession, the drive to build an impervious citadel for some and thereby to create the classic bourgeois preconditions for revolution. This too haunted me as I drove through the darkness of the Eastern Cape evening.

PART FOUR

Victoria West, Tulbagh Valley, West Coast

*We are neither black nor white, and we are losing our identity.
In the past, the comfort was always in our allegiance with the whites,
however they reviled us, because of white power. This is now lost,
and we are being elbowed out.*

11
The merger

IT SEEMED appropriate, as I approached Victoria West one afternoon in high summer, that I encountered a storm. The weather had been overcast for several hours, the clouds alternating between darkly laden and a much lighter fleeciness soon to be blown away. Then, hardly forty kilometres from the town, the sky turned black and lumpy, with light grey wisps scudding at speed beneath the general mass, and then the rain gushed down. Or more accurately, I suppose, I drove straight into the middle of it.

Such turbulence was appropriate because my experience of Victoria West had been largely of a town at serious odds with itself, where racial tensions had hardly diminished since 1994, and where numerous rumours of malpractice in many spheres flourished in a milieu almost entirely devoid of public accountability. When they lost control of the town council, the local constituency branches of one prominent party burned tyres on the main road. Ironically, they had lost control in spite of strong allegations of polling irregularities. Party officials voting twice, and then the baleful stench of burning rubber polluting the clear Karoo air. And the problem of the white Afrikaans school, refusing to merge with the Coloured Afrikaans high school, branded as racist by some, nevertheless widely envied for its results. It was further activity surrounding the school, and the threat of attendant storms, that found me that afternoon on the road back to this unhappy and perpetually smouldering town. Now the merger was supposed to be between the white school and Lillian Noveve, the name of the school provided for children residing in the black township of Masinyusane. In fact, a merger of sorts had already taken place – but without much satisfaction to either side.

The rain flooded the air, and lightning exploded not far above the car. The rain came with a fierce wind from behind, so that when the hail began – jagged stones the size of large marbles – it struck the rear window with unnerving power. I wished to increase my speed, so as to reduce the impact of this battering against the glass, but the scene before me rendered progress impossible, with headlights and windscreen wipers of scant use against the maelstrom of bouncing hail, and the roadway raging and in spate. The noise of ice against metal was too loud for comfort. I inched forward through the darkness of the storm. I felt trapped and insignificant inside it.

Yet within fifteen minutes the worst of it had passed. I could see ahead how the tarmac abruptly changed colour, showing darker where the rain no longer fell. Increasing my speed as the visibility improved, I drove out of the rain. I could see the storm as a dark entity behind me, sweeping across a wide landscape, some parts of which still lay in sunlight. Before me, the only evidence that the downpour had come that way were the stretches of water lying by the roadside, and a high brightness of air bringing clarity to the long view. The low thorn trees and rocky hills of the Karoo stood starkly before my gaze, and the charcoal road had been rolled out like a carpet straight through the middle of the wet but arid countryside.

By the time I got to Victoria West, the clouds had partly cleared and the sky shone like a porcelain dome. The last slanting rays of the afternoon sun glanced in a yellowing glow across the buildings of the town. Masinyusane lay to the right of the road as I entered – the huddled houses, the smoke of kitchen fires already smudging the clear air – and I could see the low rectangular prefabs of Lillian Noveve standing in their bare and treeless yard on the outskirts of the town.

THE PRINCIPAL of Lillian Noveve had been, before the pupils were all enrolled in the old white school and Lillian Noveve closed, a man by the name of Russel van Rooy. I had known him as a casual acquaintance for some time, but a deeper interest in him personally and in the business of the schools had been stimulated when he wrote me a note saying that he wished to discuss with me his thoughts on two important issues. The first was the school 'merger' and how he perceived it. The second was expressed thus: *The in-betweeners – 'coloureds' – their role pre and post apartheid.* The note became a considerable incentive for me to return once again to Victoria West. I tried to imagine on the drive down what his thoughts would be and where they would lead. I had made an appointment, so on the morning after the storm I went to see him as he sat at his desk in the principal's office of the empty school.

The roads in Masinyusane were unpaved and often badly rutted. Fresh damage had been inflicted with the most recent rain. The township, home to approximately two thousand five hundred people, was compactly laid out. Low houses stood close together in small yards. A block of public lavatories occupied a central position in the main street, as did a shop and some government offices. At the top end of the township, infor-mal shack houses had been built on the first slopes of the Victoria West hill, the name of the town spelled out in whitewashed stones. I had read a magazine article by the black writer and poet, Sandile Dikeni, entitled (if I remembered accurately) *Under the Written Mountain,* which described his childhood in Masinyusane. On Friday and Saturday nights Ali's Tavern played loud music with people dancing on the concrete and tiling floor, and there were several shebeens as well in the confines of the cramped little township. The streets were always populated, at night by revellers, during the long and empty days by the unemployed. The main road into town ran along the bottom edge, nearest to a dusty football field, and it was there that the tyres had burned when the election results were announced. Facing the road on the far side of the football field stood a row of small houses with semicircular asbestos roofs – each facade painted a different colour – and beyond these barrel houses stood the pre-fabricated structures of the Lillian Noveve School.

Russel van Rooy said: 'I began to feel that we couldn't take the learners here very much further into the 21st century. Resources were a problem. But as well as this we lacked the know-how to provide the better and constantly improving education that was obviously needed. Also, I per-sonally felt my time here was drawing to a close. I had become involved in sports administration on a provincial level. Perhaps I was looking for a broader engagement than the school could give. But an educationist I had been in contact with advised me at least to see the merger through. It seemed the right thing to do.'

He sat behind his largely empty desk stirring a cup of coffee. He was perhaps 37 or 38 years old and neatly dressed. His eyes were dark and showed some reserve. He gave the impression of weighing his words; and when he smiled, which he did slowly, his expression invariably turned warmer.

He spoke of his daughter whom he had enrolled in a largely white pre-primary school. The child was one of only two Coloured children at the school. I had a sudden sharp consciousness of being surrounded by empty classrooms and barren school yard, there where we sat on the outskirts of Masinyusane. Russel said with a slight smile that some of his friends had not been too happy about the enrolment. 'But my reasoning was that it would be important for her to get to know white children. To meet with black African children is easy. It happens every day. It was the white side I wanted her to explore. I believe that being able to mix with all races is important for her future.'

I got an inkling then of how he perceived himself. He had referred to the 'white side' and he had referred to meeting with black Africans. Clearly he saw himself to be standing between the two. He was in this sense an 'in-betweener', a so-called Coloured. These intimations surprised me because I knew him to be a supporter, perhaps even a member, of the African National Congress. I asked him how many children had been enrolled in Lillian Noveve. The answer was 165, with a teacher complement of eight.

'The merger had been on the cards for some time,' he said. 'Last year, I was approached by the regional education department. They told me that the provincial premier had declared this year to be the year of the merging of schools. It was easy to sell the idea to my staff, to the parents and governing body, and also to the broader Masinyusane community. What were the outcomes that we hoped for? For the department, of course, there were operating savings to be made. For the learners and teachers, there were improved facilities and a broader curriculum to be gained. There was also an obvious political motivation. We were eight or nine years down the line from 1994, and still in Victoria West there were three racially distinct high schools. Only the old white school had a certain amount of racial mixing: some Coloured and one or two black learners from homes that could afford the fees. But there were no programmes for deliberate integration either in or of the schools. Whatever had happened to the idea of a rainbow nation?'

He looked at me across the empty desk with one of his slow smiles. 'But we were stopped before we could really begin to discuss anything like a merger,' he said. 'After the first meeting, people representing the white school came uninvited to Lillian Noveve to inspect the place, and the next meeting we had with them was attended by many of their parents. It was held on Monday morning when a lot of their farming parents were in town and when most black parents were at work. The blacks were outflanked. And the whites were so rude. There was derision and laughter when we tried to speak. One white parent stood up and said: we don't negotiate with you – why should we? They simply pushed their agenda through. We saw no point, then, in trying to arrange a negotiated merger. So with the consent of the department we simply closed Lillian Noveve. And at the beginning of the new school year, we sent all our learners to enrol at the white school.'

Russel explained that the basis, more often tacit than openly expressed, of all the white arguments against the merger was that the presence of black learners and teachers at the white school would result in a lowering of academic and disciplinary standards. His eyes searched my face for my own response.

He said: 'The Coloured parents who use the white school have also been persuaded that this will be the case. Therefore a wedge has been driven between black and Coloured. The provincial politicians promise action, but the wheels are turning too slowly. The chief provincial official has promised us a meeting, but there are constant postponements. The support system from the department isn't working. Is there a problem with their political will? Having made their financial savings, they've dropped us. It's very tempting to come to this conclusion.'

He paused, pushing his empty coffee cup further from his elbow, a slightly irritable gesture. He seemed momentarily to grapple with himself, wishing to re-impose his normal self-control and rationality. His dark eyes had been enlivened by the criticism in what he was saying.

'I can't leave now, and abandon what I've started. I'm responsible. I lie awake at night, thinking about the learners who used to hold school here.' His arm waved in a vague arc meant to include the empty classrooms that I could feel brooding about us. 'But everyone remains silent.'

He walked with me to my car where I had parked it on a strip of concrete between the paint-flaking prefabs. I said that I looked forward with interest to speaking to him again, this time about the second item listed in his note. About being a so-called Coloured caught between black and white. He laughed, as if slightly embarrassed by my sudden allusion to something so close to his consciousness.

'I feel,' he said, 'that I must discover my roots. Not my political affiliations. Underneath that. My real roots.'

'Where are they?' I asked.

'My mother told me that her grandfather, my great-grandfather, came from Java,' he said, and again his eyes expressed a slight embarrassment or reserve – as if he had decided to share with me something he had shared with few others, the source of his innermost conviction about self. Yet he expressed some exasperation also by adding: 'Sometimes I feel that this connection with Java is the deepest thing, and yet I know so little about it.'

It was for me a startling revelation. Java. It clashed too sharply with the context in which it had been evoked. This island in Indonesia – hot tropical climate, wet monsoons, dense vegetation – living in a private place in a man's mind, here, in this harshly arid and equally harshly isolated Karoo town. We shook hands at the car. He had by then covered over his vulnerability with one of his slow and pleasant smiles.

THE EARLIEST manifestations of Victoria West had begun in a narrow valley and then, over the years, had spilled out onto the open ground at the valley's wider end. In the valley itself there was space for only a few streets. The houses were old, dating from the second half of the 19th century, and providing interesting examples in the steep-roofed Cape cottage style. There were as well a few Victorian structures and flat-roofed Karoo vernacular cottages. In the middle of this older part of town, stood the Dutch Reformed Church, its spire dominating all else. The English church was more modest. It had been built in the 1850s under the influence of Sophia Gray, wife of the first Bishop of Cape Town. During their travels around the Cape, Sophia had been instrumental in

214

the erection of not a few churches in the English village style – and all had been established at about the time of the cattle-killing famine on the eastern frontier. The Victoria West church contained a stained-glass window commemorating a young woman who was drowned in a sudden flood that swept through the town in 1871. Upstream dams – ultimately too many of them – had tamed the river that had gouged out the narrow valley in the first place and that now rarely flowed above a temporary trickle.

As the valley broadened, so a semblance of suburbia had begun a modest sprawl. Most of the whites lived in modern bungalows in this part of town, and immediately adjacent and spreading into outlying enclaves that rivalled Masinyusane for dilapidation and poverty, lived the Coloureds. The population of Victoria West had, after a century and a half, reached 14 000, with whites numbering hardly one thousand, blacks 2 500, the balance being Coloured. From almost everywhere in town it was possible to look up and read the name set out in white stones on the steep front face of the written mountain.

In his article, Dikeni described an incident between the local population and a white farmer that led to the poisoning of many dogs in Masinyusane. Dikeni's view of the past tended to be bleak, often drained of any retrospective rosiness by his awareness of racism and those often blatant injuries to the spirit that had inevitably attended apartheid.

Racism had by no means disappeared, and the separation of the races seemed as complete as it had always been. There were white functions and institutions, and functions and institutions for other races, but rarely did they overlap. There seemed sometimes to be an actual repugnance of white for black – which in turn elicited aggression and defiance in the opposite direction – and it struck me that the post-1994 loss of political power had been like an emasculation for many white men in Victoria West. It had deeply embittered them. It had also made covert the articulation of racial antipathy. The belittling of the black and Coloured local authority was delivered largely behind closed doors. White people longed for the failure of the state at any level. It would be like a vindication, an opportunity to jeer; and I could well understand Russel's complaint that some of the white parents at the ill-fated school merger meeting had been derisory and rude.

The old white school, now called somewhat ironically the Combined School, stood on elevated ground against a stony koppie on the southern side of town. The double-storeyed building had been erected, I guessed, in the early 1960s, and it had been carefully maintained, and the grounds were neat and lined with mature trees. The school boasted a swimming pool, extensive sports fields, a library and science laboratory. The learners wore uniforms and their parents paid quarterly fees. The school had catered for just under three hundred children (before the influx of those from Lillian Noveve) spread over all the grades from one to twelve.

The principal, a woman named Christine Spaargaring, spoke to me in her spacious office. Books and lever-arch files were neatly displayed behind her; and on one wall was a detailed representation of the South African coat of arms with its motto spelled out in one of the Khoisan languages. I had asked if she would talk to me about the so-called merger and she had readily agreed. She was a fair-haired woman, perhaps in her late thirties, slight of build but with lively blue eyes and a ready smile.

'Late last year,' she told me, 'Lillian Noveve approached with a delegation to see our management committee and governing body. A meeting was arranged. They expressed their problems: inferior facilities, no laboratory or library, no transport for out-of-town sport and cultural events. With this last problem we were able to help immediately. Lillian Noveve could hire our bus when it was available; it would be far less expensive than the hire of taxis. Then Russel van Rooy gave a presentation of their vision of the future which stopped at nothing short of full educational and social integration.'

I asked her directly what she thought of her Lillian Noveve counterpart. She said: 'Even when we have disagreed, he has never been anything but a gentleman.' Then we returned to the story of the merger.

At the end of that first meeting, she recounted, a task team had been established with members from both schools. The Masinyusane community was also represented by a local social welfare official named Monwabisi Gqagqa. But the representatives of the white school had wondered whether the motive for the meeting, and for the process it had begun, was as straightforward as it seemed. A group of young black people, not necessarily Lillian Noveve learners, had come to the meeting;

and there were suspicions of a deeper political agenda. No mention had been made, for example, of those provisions in the South African Schools Act relating specifically to mergers. Perhaps that would follow as the process developed; or perhaps the desired result, from a black political perspective, was not so much a merger as a full-blooded takeover. Meanwhile, a small group from the governing body of the white school visited Lillian Noveve with a view to assessing what assistance could be given.

'Our people,' Christine recounted, 'found the photocopier, the computer, the books and so on, to be in reasonable repair. The buildings themselves needed paint – and we offered immediate assistance in this regard – but the toilets were in a terrible state.'

But this uninvited visit was sufficient to begin the derailment of the whole process. 'Van Rooy's side was very angry,' Christine said, 'but, really, we were just trying to be helpful.'

It became clear to me, as we discussed the details, that the governing body of Christine's school had hoped that some philanthropy would resolve the situation; while the black school, or at least those people representing it, wanted nothing of the kind.

'The next thing that happened,' she said, 'was that at the beginning of the new school year over a hundred black pupils turned up here, wanting to enrol. We got them all into the hall and began enrolling them. There were some problems relating to children too old for the grades for which they were enrolling. These learners were put temporarily to one side. We also had a problem with overcrowding in grade six. It took a few days, but finally we were able to enrol the whole lot. One morning during the process, Monwabisi Gqagqa turned up, demanding to know why the enrolments were taking so long. It made some of my people believe that the Lillian Noveve side were hoping that we wouldn't enrol everyone, so that they could accuse us of being racist and unconstitutional.'

To have the learner population suddenly increased by nearly thirty per cent posed immediate problems for the Combined School, Christine said. Teacher/pupil ratios were immediately increased. There was overcrowding in grade six. There was also the problem of language. The Combined School had been, and still was, an Afrikaans-medium school.

Lillian Noveve had offered mother-tongue (Xhosa) tuition until grade three, and was thereafter English-medium. Departmental officials arrived from Kimberley and De Aar to solve these problems. The grade six class was split along language lines, which corresponded with the basic division between white and black. And the youngest Xhosa children found themselves being taught in Xhosa by some of their Lillian Noveve teachers, but in prefabs behind the main school building.

The situation was far from ideal – and so a three-pronged demand came from Masinyusane. A dual-medium system should be introduced immediately. A school feeding scheme should be started. And, finally, a bus should be made available to transport the erstwhile Lillian Noveve learners from Masinyusane each morning and to return them there in the afternoons.

'We responded that we could not afford to use our bus for this purpose; that we were quite willing to take over the Lillian Noveve feeding scheme; but that the question of changing from Afrikaans-medium to dual-medium would have to be resolved with the department, and only after the deployment of suitable teachers,' Christine said.

This question of teachers was complicated by the fact that additional staff, to provide advantageous ratios, had long been financed by the white school. Special school fund-raising events were an annual feature of the town. Beneath these special arrangements, teachers were provided by the state strictly on the basis of prescribed teacher/pupil ratios. If the entire Lillian Noveve staff was transferred, the Combined School would be placed in excess, a situation that could lead to job losses. The governing body therefore insisted that it continue to approve all new teaching appointments. A solution would be to apply for parallel-medium status – which in effect would place two separate schools in a common geographical position, rather than attempting to impose dual-medium responsibilities onto the Combined School – but without adequate support. The situation was brought to a head when senior education officials, including the responsible circuit inspector, arrived at the school, ostensibly in response to complaints of racism on the part of the school's several black teachers, and attempted to force Christine and her school management team to accept the dual-medium path. It must be introduced immediately, was the instruction – although it was never put in writing.

The response of the school was a legal one. An urgent interdict was granted preventing the department from forcing dual-medium status onto the Combined School. A court case was pending, Christine told me. Meanwhile, the situation was quiet.

All the merger had meant, in effect, was that more than a hundred black children walked from Masinyusane every morning, many of them being taught by their old teachers in prefabs behind the original Combined School buildings, and then trailing back every afternoon to their cramped little township. In addition, a majority of black parents could not afford the quarterly fees being asked by the Combined School. By law, this inability could not exclude them, but it meant that the school had become poorer and less able to afford the superior ratios and other advantages that had been enjoyed there in the past and that had been so envied by Masinyusane eyes.

Christine sat smiling at me from her side of the desk. 'So,' she said, 'that's the story of our famous merger.'

Impossible, then, not to recall the smothered anger of Russel as he had told me of his sense of disappointment in the politicians and bureaucrats. 'Having made their savings, they've dropped us. It's very tempting to come to this conclusion.' That is what he had said. And his eyes had darkened as he told me of his sense of responsibility that was keeping him awake at night.

Christine said: 'I've tried to give you facts, not opinions.'

'Would you give me your opinions?'

She shook her head. 'Maybe one day when it's all settled.' In spite of this resolve, though, she remarked in a moment that it was impossible not to believe that the original intention behind the merger had been the 'taking over of the white school'.

'I mean the whole thing,' she said. 'Including the principalship. Are you aware there's been huge pressure to get rid of me? I've been offered other jobs out of town. I've declined them. I've also been threatened with disciplinary action. I'm sure the plan was to put in a black principal here.'

'Van Rooy?' I asked, then answered my own question. 'Mind you, perhaps he's not black enough.'

She shrugged her shoulders. 'Some members of the community here – no names – they've let me know that they are perfectly well aware I live alone. Isn't that intimidatory?'

I sat looking at this fair-headed woman with the animated eyes and sprightly expression. She had raised her eyebrows to emphasise her question, and her forehead was horizontally lined for a moment.

I asked if she kept a firearm at home.

She laughed quite gaily; it was almost a small guffaw. 'No, of course not,' she said. 'What on earth would I do with that?'

I ASKED Russel if he could arrange a meeting between us and the social welfare official involved in the school merger, Monwabisi Gqagqa. He did so immediately, and we met that afternoon at the welfare offices that stood at the dusty entrance to Masinyusane – not far in fact from where the tyres had burned on the night that the last municipal election results were announced.

He was a thin man, dark-skinned and hatchet-faced. His eyes moved swiftly from point to point, and he rarely engaged the eyes of his interlocutor when he spoke. We sat in a small office, the three of us, and talked about the merger.

We began at the beginning, during the mid-1990s, when the idea had been to merge the white and Coloured schools, a course of action (we all agreed) that would have obviated the current problems relating to medium of instruction.

Monwabisi said that the white school had resisted the idea of merging on purely racial grounds. 'Mergers were happening in neighbouring towns at the time, so we decided not to press it here in Victoria West.'

I asked who he meant by 'we'.

'The communities here,' he replied. 'We advised the department to allow the other mergers to go through first.'

Monwabisi told me that he had become involved in the Lillian Noveve merger because he had been asked to do so by the school. Russel nodded. Monwabisi said: 'We called a meeting with the community and identified the main reason for the merger as being the lack of adequate resources in the black school. The only solution was for the schools to merge so that the resources in the white school could be shared.'

I remarked that some of those resources had been made possible by the efforts of parents and others raising funds privately for the school. Monwabisi shrugged his shoulders slightly. These contributions from non-state sources hardly diminished what he clearly saw as a fundamental South African injustice.

He provided me with a chronology of the initial approach to the white school. It generally accorded with what I already knew – except that through his eyes the meeting had been much more tense than I had at first understood. Monwabisi said that the governing body of the white school had referred the idea of the merger to their parents immediately. That was when the hostility had begun. 'The atmosphere of the meeting showed just how deep the levels of distrust in our society are,' Monwabisi said.

But it was the visit to Lillian Noveve by members of the white school's governing body that had destroyed whatever co-operation might have existed between the two schools and their respective communities.

'The whites were saying, in effect: we'll help you to fix up Lillian Noveve, so long as you stay there. And the Masinyusane community was saying: we don't want your help; we want a physical merger. Nothing less. So we were deadlocked before we started.'

I asked Monwabisi about the South African Schools Act and the provisions that had been laid down for mergers.

'That was exactly the route we wished to follow,' he replied.

I said that these provisions began with a requirement that the provincial authorities should publish in newspapers circulating in the area the reasons for the proposed merger. Also, the schools in question should be given written notice thereof. Had these things happened?

'We never had the opportunity of getting that far,' Monwabisi said swiftly, and it surprised me how close to the surface an inkling of his aggression seemed to lie. 'We were deadlocked.'

The next steps followed within days. The white school called a parents' meeting at which several Coloured parents were also present. The doors of the hall were locked. When a few of the Coloured parents tried to speak on behalf of Lillian Noveve and the Masinyusane community, they were shouted down. The gist of the white attitude was clear: they wanted nothing to do with a merger. The reaction of the Lillian Noveve

side, led by Monwabisi Gqagqa and Russel van Rooy, was equally deci-
sive. They called in the media and prepared to register the Lillian
Noveve learners en masse.

'The media reports affected the whites very badly,' Monwabisi said,
'and I think that's why they were willing to enrol our children.'

'But what's the next step?' I asked. 'It seems likely that the Combined
School will become a parallel-medium, rather than a dual-medium as you
had hoped. Doesn't this mean a racial differentiation almost as severe as
before? It'll be two schools under one roof. Worse, it'll mean many of
your black pupils being educated in prefabs behind the largely white
fee-paying school.'

'The next step,' Russel said, and it was the first time he had spoken
during the interview, 'is to get some of our parents elected onto the
Combined School's governing body. We'll begin a process of changing
the situation from within.'

Monwabisi said: 'Let the children have a referendum. Let them decide.'

I presented them with the economic arguments surrounding the old
white school: that a merger, however achieved, would drive white
parents, especially the farming community, to remove their children.
The impact of such removals on the economy of the whole town would
be severely detrimental.

Monwabisi's expression showed impatience and mild contempt. 'These
are the arguments of one of the bank managers I spoke to. And the
manager of the Farmers' Cooperative. They accuse us of driving prosperity from the town. I told them: we want prosperity as much as anyone else. But why must we always give way to white racism?'

Russel leaned forward. 'At the heart of this racism, I am convinced, is
the idea that black means a lowering of standards. But is this inevitable?
One of our Lillian Noveve teachers is already part of the Combined
School's management team. She's head of the foundation phase. In fact,
she's training three white teachers in the new outcomes-based education
for the primary grades. She has those qualifications, and they don't.'

Monwabisi stood up. His eyes flickered briefly across my face. He
said he needed to go. We shook hands. As he was putting on his jacket,
Russel spoke again.

He said, looking at me with his clear dark eyes: 'The merger is here to stay. The questions for everyone, black and white, are these. What do we do now? How do we live with it? How do we make it work? We have to accept that integration is inevitable. It should also be an actual goal.'

IN THE late afternoons the last of the sunlight came pouring through a gap in the hills on the western side of town. Masinyusane was on the eastern side, lying in the shadow of the written mountain. Nearly always in the township streets, particularly as evening approached, hovered a sense of impending misery. Inebriated people shouted and slurred and jostled together. Women walked slowly with burdens. Children and young people hung about the shop where a pool table occupied most of the space in front of the counter. Dogs slunk from point to point. I remembered Sandile Dikeni and the dogs that had been poisoned. I had found, in a British magazine, another version of what was probably the same story. A white farmer grazed his sheep on a nearby hill. 'You do not graze sheep in reach of people who are starving,' Sandile was quoted as saying. Poaching took place. The farmer's response was to use a helicopter, flying over the township and dropping pieces of red meat down into the streets. That night many people feasted, as well as the dogs, and then they were doubling up in agony because they too had been poisoned.

I asked Russel if he expected to be made the principal of the Combined School, once the merger had taken place.

He looked at me in surprise. Then he laughed. 'I have already told you that I was looking for a broader engagement than being a principal. I don't think I want to be a principal. In fact, I've contacted the department with the suggestion that I become their merger specialist. I would like to be involved in this way with the integration of people.'

It seemed a noble ambition. In a town where the racial divisions ran so deep, where people went to the trouble of dropping poisoned meat from a helicopter, where confrontation remained the most likely outcome of any contact, the pursuit of integration seemed more than noble, in fact. It seemed, rather, to be hopelessly idealistic. But Russel simply smiled in the face of my cynicism.

'It's time we talked about the in-betweeners,' I said. 'But I want to know more about you first. And about the Java link. You weren't born here in Victoria West, were you?'

'No, no, in Cape Town. Elsiesrivier. But it was only in Victoria West that I became politically active.'

Those words – politically active – brought me back to Sandile Dikeni again. He had been named after that Xhosa chief who had become the hero of the young Nelson Mandela; and he had been politically active, a member of the ANC before that organisation had been unbanned in 1990. He had been imprisoned. He had (according to the British magazine) been beaten. But there was something beyond this that plagued my consciousness, particularly in the streets of Masinyusane. It was the thought of fire.

Dikeni's grandmother had been locked in her township house and burned to death. The date was 1985: turbulent times, heightened political activity. Dikeni himself had been away at university. A crowd had assembled one night, including young people Dikeni had grown up with. The accusations (I had heard whispered in Masinyusane) revolved around the issue of informing. They said she was an *impimpi*, a collaborator. Perhaps that meant no more than that she appeared to be too friendly to white people, white policemen perhaps, or simply that she talked too much. But they had murdered her that night, her own people, howling their revenge as the smoke billowed up towards the stars. Nobody was ever found guilty of the crime; and Dikeni had come home for the funeral.

This too was a part of the flavour of life under the written mountain; and these were the thoughts that brought to me a sense of misery, like the pervasive odour of the communal latrines, leaking into the Masinyusane streets as darkness encroached.

12
In between

TO DRIVE at night in the Karoo is to be constantly conscious of the stars. Through the side window of my car I could see them flooding the sky in their thousands and, by their abrupt cessation, defining the shape of the low black horizon hills. The straight road south went on and on through the darkness. Although I would turn off more than a hundred and fifty kilometres before its end, I knew that the road led ultimately to Cape Town – and to the suburb of Elsiesrivier where Russel van Rooy had been born.

Scores of heavy vehicles travelled on the road. Their headlights blinded me; and even when they were not yet visible, beyond an occasional bend or rise, I could gauge their approach by the way their lights reflected off the clusters of telephone wires strung out along the side of the road, dipping in a shallow arc between each pole. Then this subtle bronzed illumination, like a delicate adornment, would be obliterated as the flaring trucks bore down on me and then roared past, leaving the road ahead momentarily clear.

Road repairs were under way, and the trucks built up into long lines; and several times I stopped at red lights in the middle of nowhere, dust and exhaust fumes filtering through the beam of my headlights. And when the obstacles were passed, we drove on in the night, and then slowly through a sleeping Karoo town. Only the lorries brought life, apart from some small activity on the forecourts of garages. I glimpsed a cat sitting in the middle of a side street, licking its paws in domestic contentment, unchallenged and unthreatened by the vehicles grinding by hardly a hundred metres distant.

Russel van Rooy had said, when at last we spoke about his past: 'My family is Christian, as I am myself. But there is Islam in our background. That's the Java connection. My sister married someone from the Muslim faith. After he had died, she remarried – once again to a Muslim. And when I was growing up, there were Muslims nearby. No, we had no artefacts from Java in the house. It is simply what my mother told me. She made me conscious of my family background. A great grandfather from Java. A father from the German mission station at Wuppertal in the Cederberg mountains.'

Easy to think about these things as the night driving continued. The straight road, and the endlessness of it, brought a twilight to the inner eye. The mind fell back from the present and I could see his dark eyes, his slow smiles, as he pieced together the memories of his own past for me. We were sitting once again in his principal's office with the empty Lillian Noveve classrooms brooding around us. The road was running in a south-westerly direction now, and in the rear-view mirror I caught the first inkling – a hardly perceptible greyness undermining the dark – of the approaching dawn.

'My earliest memories were of living in a two-roomed hut in Elsies,' he had said. 'The hut was in the yard of a small shop. I think the shop was run by Muslims. Cape Malays. I went back not so long ago to see if I could find the shop. But everything's gone. It's all formal housing now.'

I saw him beginning to deal in his spirit with this inevitability: that one reality would be overlaid upon another, again and again. It was a fundamental of the ability to self-contextualise that the earlier realities, though overlaid, were not obliterated. I could see him in his thoughtful way taking this concept and making it his own. I saw also the coming of daylight, beginning at its epicentre behind me and then reaching forward so that soon the vague greyness was before me as well as behind. I was driving away from it and into it, simultaneously.

'It was strange, but I never went to school in Elsies. I don't know why. I went by bus ten kilometres to a school in Uitsig, and then I walked home. I remember running away from bigger boys who wanted for some reason to beat me up. Maybe simply because I was in their territory. Then when I was seven or eight we moved to Bellville South.

'But I suppose the most interesting thing about those early experiences was that I lived through them without ever actually seeing white or black people. I knew blacks only because they were the rubbish removers. Parow was the white shopping area. My aunt said: you can't go to Parow; you're too black. I thought this was unfair. My uncle was blacker than me and he went. My aunt also placed limits on my contact with black Africans. She would always tell me that the blacks would steal me and chop off my head. As a boy I was afraid of them. I was more scared of them than of the gangsterism in our own area, and of the gangsters fighting every weekend. We got used to that.

'Moving to Bellville South was a very positive thing for us. It was a larger suburb. We had a bigger house with electricity and an inside toilet. And we were closer to the town centre. The school was also bigger. Most important, though, was my expanding contact with white and black. I got used to seeing white policemen and officials in the municipal offices. One of our neighbours used to drive a lorry – I think for a government department – and I went with him sometimes, and that was how, for the first time, I went into a black location. I realised immediately that they were friendly. They weren't at all like my aunt had described. But there is that abiding uneasiness that Coloured people have. My mother still speaks about "the natives".

'My aunt was pro-white. At election times, she canvassed for the National Party. I think it was the influence her Jewish employers had on her. Maybe she aspired to being English, copying what she thought were English manners – even down to the brooches clipped at the front of her dresses.'

Now behind me I could see in my mirror that colour had come to the sky: the yellow core, the orange, the vaguely pink slips of cloud floating across. Vehicles going in the opposite direction seemed to rise up against the light, their tail lights diminished, and then they would pass over the horizon as small black silhouettes against the new day's brightening. Later the sun rose, sending the shadow of roadside grasses halfway across the smooth tarred surface; and a thousand ostriches stood tall-legged in camps on a hillside.

'By the time I matriculated, deep trouble had come to the Cape, and I was in the middle of it. In the early 1980s there were the school boycotts. That was largely a Coloured thing. In 1983 the United Democratic Front was formed. In 1984 the final unrest began in Gauteng. In 1986 there was the Crossroads crisis at the Cape. I matriculated in

1985. I was twenty years old. I was on the Students' Representative Council. I had presented as part of my election manifesto the idea of "no politics in schools". We wrote our matric exams under police guard. I walked to the exams in an atmosphere of tear gas and rubber bullets. But I couldn't honestly relate my life to what was happening.'

The mountains of the Western Cape began to loom. The endless plains of the Karoo had given way to lumpy ground, to hills pressing one against the other. The hills were bare, more rocks and shale than vegetation. There was a sudden rainbow. Fine moisture on the windscreen from a remnant of early-morning cloud. The arching rainbow began on one side of the road and ended on the other, with a shadow of itself going into boulders close beside the verge of the road.

'At varsity, as well, I wasn't politically active. I had come to study. My father was the only one in the family working and it would have been too shameful to have lost my bursary, thus compelling my father to pay. So I spent my time in the library with my books. There were quite a few of us who didn't become politically involved. But we were never perceived as sell-outs. People were too busy doing the politics and boycotting to worry about a small minority. I spent four years at varsity, but I never managed a full year's tuition because of the boycotts. I only had seven months during my final year. Nevertheless I passed my degree and my teaching diploma.'

I asked Russel in which subjects he had majored.

'Afrikaans and history,' he replied.

The latter subject did not surprise me. The history student in the midst of tumult, seeing how one reality (even in Elsiesrivier, even in his own experience) would inevitably grow up over the bones of previous realities, again and again and again.

I asked him to tell me about the history he had learned. He listed the topics: the Romans; the rise of Western Europe; Jan van Riebeeck and the Khoisan; modern African history (here, he said, he got exposed to colonialism, and to the African reaction to it: the struggles against domination by European powers or European settlers); and finally he mentioned something known as 'people's history'.

'This was all about finding our own history,' he said. 'We had a radical white Afrikaner lecturer. I wrote a play about my grandmother's life in Cape Town, and then the move to Elsiesrivier. The Afrikaner radical gave me good marks.'

Amusement lurked in his eyes and in his slow smile as he recounted these memories. Yet there was an underlying seriousness also, a puzzlement before his own deepest responses, an unwillingness (as a manifestation of his own composure) to lapse into slogans.

'Through everything I was only a *saamloper*,' he said. I took him to mean that he merely followed the crowd. 'In my heart I was not there. Not really there. While I was making things up about my grandmother's life, students were being whipped with quirts. The students would go to the gates, throwing stones at the police. I was never actively a part of it. I just walked along. Then,' he added, as if announcing something auspicious, 'in 1990, I came to Victoria West. It was very traumatic.'

Not long before my Great Karoo road plunged down towards the Hex River Valley, I turned aside and drove on a narrower road with the beginnings of high mountains to the north and north-west before me. The mountains were near the southernmost end of the 300-kilometre-long Cederberg chain, and I was going high up into these mountains to a place called Kagga Kamma. It was a name I had encountered before on my travels.

But my deepest attention, even then, stayed with Russel as he had told me about leaving the shelter of his family home for the first time. He had also recently married, but the marriage had not survived the move into the Karoo.

'I had become a preacher in the New Apostolic Church, and one of the church bishops asked me to go to Victoria West to help in the congregation there. So I came to Victoria West for a weekend to look. It was terrible. There was nothing there, only dust and heat. Nevertheless, we made the move. I taught at the Coloured school and helped at the New Apostolic church, meanwhile trying to cope with my marriage at home.

'That year, 1990, was really a year that changed a lot for me. I got divorced. And I was living in close proximity to a township where blacks were boycotting and burning tyres in the streets. It was a culture shock for me. Even in this little town, things were happening politically, although my contact with blacks was still extremely limited. On the other hand, simply because the town was so small, my contact with whites had become more intimate. It became patently clear that the Victoria West whites didn't like the blacks or Coloureds. This reality was very in-your-face. Then I joined the teachers' union, and at the beginning of the next year we blocked the main road to protest against the non-delivery of school books. Teachers from the Coloured school were joined by teachers from Lillian Noveve. I began to know them. Also, my church had a small congregation in Masinyusane.'

I asked about the blocking of the main road: had this action achieved the desired results? He glanced at me a trifle sheepishly. 'It was my first really committed political act,' he said with one of his slow smiles.

'But my actual conversion came in 1994,' he went on. 'I became exposed to the various political parties. I had been following the national political news: from CODESA (Convention for a Democratic South Africa, which was the locus for pre-1994 negotiations) right up to the elections. I knew these were big events. I knew the time for protest politics was being replaced by a time for active participation. But I had to make a decision. My teacher colleagues, especially those in the union, simply assumed I was ANC. Another pointer for them was that I played soccer with black people. But I also attended Democratic Party meetings. But when the ANC started coming round to my house, canvassing, I realised I could no longer drift. My experience of the town, the viciousness and the racism of the whites, had radicalised me. I believed I had no future with the whites. I saw myself, really for the first time, as a black person. So I voted for the ANC, wholeheartedly, willingly. Strangely, so did my parents. For myself, it was like a new freedom. I had become politically involved, and I felt comfortable and fully at peace with myself.'

Yet these feelings were not to last. The first seeds of new doubt were sown when in 1996 he applied for the principalship at Lillian Noveve. He got the job. He spent the entire winter holidays preparing what would amount to his inaugural speech to the learners and staff of the small black school.

'The new term arrived and we all gathered in one of the classrooms. Although I had been selected for the job by a panel of black teachers and parents, nobody seemed to be particularly interested in what I was saying. The learners just stared at me because I wasn't black. Some members of the school governing body were suspicious of me, believing that I shouldn't get the privilege (of being principal) because I was a Coloured. There was a lot of confusion and infighting, and town politics began to infiltrate into the school.'

Although the situation at the school gradually improved, it was clear that Russel had tasted at first hand a phenomenon that would increasingly concern him. He told me that the racial makeup of the provincial cabinet – it was significantly black – did not reflect the demographic reality of a province that was predominantly Coloured. He said, also, that through his work in sports development – he served on the provincial sporting transformation committee – he had come to realise that 'transformation' was about increasing opportunities for blacks and the entrenchment of black privilege, to the virtual exclusion of any serious non-racial perception of sports development. Could it be that 1994 had less to do with democracy than it had to do with the installation of majority rule? If this was the case, then belonging to the ruling party meant working for the retention of black African power first, and the socio-economic development and racial integration of a deeply divided country second.

'My honeymoon with the ANC is over,' he told me once.

He seemed disheartened. It struck me as regrettable that a man whose affiliation had taken so long to mature and been so carefully given, had so quickly been damaged. Nevertheless, his commitment to reconciliation remained undiminished. The more I spoke to him the more I realised that the urge to reconciliation was a powerful force in him. I wondered if such an urge was an inevitable characteristic of an in-betweener. Perhaps. But I suspected that the typical in-betweener reaction would more likely be a sullen aggression towards all sides that offered rejection. That so little of such aggression drove his responses marked him, increasingly for me, as an extraordinary man.

AT THE gate to the Kagga Kamma privately owned nature reserve, I saw displayed for sale a row of small stones painted in imitation of San rock art subjects: animals, hunters, dancing figures. I was immediately reminded of that young Bushman named Tjan whom Hennie and I had met during our visit to the Kalahari some months before. Tjan had told us that he and his family had lived at Kagga Kamma for 14 months, returning home to the sand country because they earned insufficient money; and there he was sitting at the roadside crushing terracotta stones to do identical paintings for the tourists passing through the Kalahari.

I asked the guard at the gate, a wizened old man, about the painted stones.

'Yes, meneer, some of the Bushmen are still here to paint the stones.'

'Are you a Bushman?' I asked.

'No, meneer,' he replied. 'I am a Coloured.'

I signed the book and drove through. His reply gave an insight into his own self-perception – and into his understanding of the gradations of a society that had often had ascribed to it an over-simplified homogeneity.

The landscape had for some time been fantastical, and it continued to be so inside the reserve. A cap of sandstone had been severely eroded, leaving large areas of mountain top standing in absolute ruin, as if built structures had been partially smashed, leaving only a wall here, an archway there of eroding rock, grey on the cracked and weathered tops, yellowish and almost pink lower down. That was the first impression. Then I began to see other shapes, reminding me of broken teeth or the backs of dragons. Sometimes the narrow dirt road wound its way through the higher manifestations of these shapes, and sometimes they joined forces to form cliffs differentiating one level of the mountain from another. The country as it spread out beneath the summit road was treeless and hostile, filled with rocks and a sense of massive space and silence. Small flowers flourished at the roadside sometimes – yellow and purple and white – and proteas grew among the ruins.

The Kagga Kamma resort had been built immediately below a long run of ragged cliffs. A few cars were parked on slabs of rock between eroding monoliths. The buildings were of stone and thatch, and seemed to recede into the cliffs behind them. A woman was laying the tables for lunch in the restaurant, while the sound of contented conversations emanated from an adjacent bar called *Doppies*, which is Afrikaans for spent cartridge cases, although it could also be taken to mean small tots of alcohol. Nearby I came across a shop filled with generally disappointing curios and a few books. There was also a board advertising various tourist activities, like night game drives and sundry Bushman events. I wondered if they still paid the participants only R50 a head for doing a trance dance. I bought a slim booklet on rock paintings in the Cederberg and took it outside to peruse. I walked a short distance away from the buildings and sat down on a rock. The silence pulsed against me and the sun was close and hot.

I read that the geology of the mountains had provided an important ingredient for the rock art that had flourished there: strata of clay hardened over millions of years into a substance known as haematite. The San artists had crushed pieces of haematite to a fine powder, mixing it with water or blood or plant juices to provide paint in a variety of warm hues ranging from yellow to maroon. This was exactly what I had seen Tjan doing in the Kalahari. I guessed he had carried some of the raw material back with him from Kagga Kamma.

The little book provided insights into the length of human habitation in the Cederberg. For thousands of years San people had occupied these wild and hostile places, and for all that time they had crushed their haematite and painted their art on the rock walls of caves and overhangs throughout the mountain range. *At the other end of the time scale,* wrote Janette Deacon, *the most recent rock paintings in the western Cape can be dated by their subject matter because they include horses, ox-wagons, people with guns and even a sailing ship – all indicative of contact with Europeans within the last 350 years.*

I looked out over the vista before me. I could see ten kilometres, perhaps twenty, and the mountains went on for three hundred. I felt that I sat in a cradle of great antiquity. Yet how quickly the Bushmen had been usurped. The European bullets, the hunting, the thirst for land – and before long the indigenous people of the Cederberg had joined the slow and painful migration north, a part of that great cycle of retreat that Mario, the leader of the !Xun and Khwe at Schmidtsdrift, had talked about, the big arrow on his map swinging up through sub-equatorial Africa.

Here was Deacon again: *By the early nineteenth century the take-over by Europeans was complete and there is no record of Khoisan living independ-*

ently ... in the mountains of the Cederberg after that time. Their descendants were settled on mission stations such as Wuppertal and were employed on European-owned farms and in the towns and villages.

I read the passage again, engaged to the extent of a sudden discovery. It seemed to lead into a region of darkness and intrigue. A memory of Russel van Rooy came flooding back. A memory of his voice saying: my father from the German mission station at Wuppertal in the Cederberg mountains. I paged through Deacon's book. Here was a map of the Cederberg all the way from Cape Town to Nieuwoudtville. Kagga Kamma was marked, as was Wuppertal. I stood up, searching the most distant haze to the north. It shocked me to realise how close the two places were, although unconnected by a direct road. Hardly more than sixty kilometres of ancient mountains lay between.

Returning to my car, I fetched the region-by-region guide book with which I invariably travelled. I looked up Wuppertal. There on the page I saw two photographs. The first showed a small village of whitewash and dark trees embedded in a huge hostility of mountains. It showed also the road ascending out. Was this the road that Russel's father had one day taken on his way to meet the granddaughter of a man from Java? The second photograph showed a group of smiling Coloured children standing in front of row cottages individually thatched with blackened grass. I read the description, that Wuppertal was the first Rhenish mission farm in South Africa ... that it had been founded in 1830 ... and that in 1838 the number of residents grew considerably when a party of freed slaves arrived ...

I could not understand why these synergies should unease me as they did. I felt acutely, though, that I was in a region of darkness and intrigue, and indeed of ruin. The ruin was like the unrelenting crumbling away of the highest rock of the Cederberg. The darkness was the darkness of loss. I felt that the past was sifting between my fingers in a meaningless stream. There were no rock paintings any longer to chart the spirit of that past. There were few records and only a subservient literary tradition. The delineations and intrigues of the Coloured past had been effectively annulled by external perceptions of inferiority.

The world disintegrates when the past is lost. These words came to me from a source I could not then remember. Could it be that the central travail of the in-betweeners was simply that their various pasts had been so extensively smothered? Those slow smiles on the handsome face of Russel van Rooy lived irrevocably within my consciousness now. And I kept repeating to myself a single sentence as I stared out at the silent hostility of the Cederberg range. No wonder, I repeated, that Java meant so much.

MY BRIEF visit to Kagga Kamma had been a detour. Now it was time to come out of the mountains and descend into the lavish valleys of the Western Cape, as I had originally planned. So down I came on those steep and twisting roads, down to Ceres, and then down again on the final step from the Karoo plateau to Tulbagh. It was a town of mature oak trees and the sensuous curves of Cape Dutch gables, of the bright pavement umbrellas of restaurants and dappled sunlight everywhere against whitewash and dark-framed sash windows. It seemed strange to think that one fine day in September 1969 an earthquake measuring 6.5 on the Richter scale ripped through the town, killing nine people and smashing up many of the fine old buildings.

The town dated originally from the 18th century. The valley which it crowned had been first seen by European eyes a century before that. Gaunt Cape mountains (themselves a part of the Cederberg range) closed in the valley on three sides, and in this shelter the wineries flourished, as did the fruit trees and wheat fields as well. In the dry summers, the shelter of the mountains held in the heat, and often the wind blew, and fires were a constant danger. I stayed on a wine farm during my stay in the Tulbagh valley. My hosts (John and Beverley) were youngish people recently from Johannesburg. They described their first experience of a valley fire approaching at speed, sweeping through vineyards and fruit trees and open veld alike. Beverley was eight months pregnant and she saw the flames leaping across open ground towards their farm. John had gone out with the neighbours to fight the blaze. Beverley put on the sprinklers all around the house and watered the thatched roof. She telephoned her mother and said, 'pray for us', and then ran outside to move the sprinklers once more. Miraculously, their small farm had escaped major damage.

'Of course, we have taken a chance coming to farm here,' John said. Beverley talked about her romantic dream of doing pottery and sitting by big fires on wet winter nights. 'You know how one fantasises,' she said, dandling her baby on her knees. John said: 'You have to take chances and grab opportunities if you're to do what you most want. This is the only way to live your life.'

I had a huge room above their wine cellar. From my balcony I could look out over the vineyards and lands to the mountains beyond. In the evening, after the dust and heat of the day, it seemed a miraculous sight. A small dam surrounded by mature trees lay tranquil just below the house, and the birds were coming home to roost: sacred ibises, hadedas, cormorants and darters; and on the dam were yellow-billed ducks, and scores of weavers' nests hung from branches adjacent to the water. The birds flew in, dark and raucous against the evening sky. And further away, a gang of guineafowl scurried blackly in a golden field.

A visit to a wine farm had always been in my plans. More specifically, the picking of grapes in the cool of darkness had become entrenched within the overall concept of my journey as something I would like to describe. It was a whimsical, almost frivolous, notion; but I had pursued it all the way into the Tulbagh valley. Now, thanks to an introduction via my hosts, I was to witness night harvesting on the estate that had first introduced it.

I DROVE in the dark, arriving just before nine. I stood under large trees near the cellar buildings and watched as the workers assembled. Idling tractors with trailers in tow stood in shadows a little distance away. Men and women clambered into them. They had lights attached to their headgear like miners. A wind blew dry and gusting, and it plucked at the skirts of the women standing in the trailers. Then the tractor drivers arrived, looking as if they were in charge. A siren wailed at nine o'clock exactly, and the tractors moved forward. They drove down the paved roadway, past where I was standing, and out into the darkness beyond. A man accompanied by dogs walked down the driveway after them. His name was Nicky Krone. We had talked on the telephone. He extended his hand with a friendly smile.

We stood talking in the roadway with the leaves of the old trees rustling noisily above us. He explained that the innovations of cold fermentation and night harvesting developed on the estate produced very light, clear and delicate white wines. Night harvesting also helped to retain the ethyl oils in the skins of the grapes. He said the estate, named *Twee Jonge Gezellen*, had been going since 1710 and was the second-oldest in South Africa.

Another tractor churned past on the roadway. The workers on the trailers raised their hands in greeting at the sight of Nicky. He acknowledged them with a cursory wave. I saw the headlights of the tractor, just beyond the main entrance to the estate, channel through rows of vines on their dark timber supports.

Nicky said, following directly on from where he had left off, 'and all that time we've used nothing but local Coloured labour. We've always prided ourselves on being liberal employers. We thought that was one of our strengths. Until recently, that is.'

I looked at him with my eyebrows raised.

He shrugged his shoulders. 'Trade unions,' he said. 'Organisers infil-trating our workforce from the outside. From other parts of the country entirely. The whole process has been very painful and disruptive.'

I wished to pursue the conversation, but at that moment a young man strode purposefully down the roadway to join us. He was Nicky's son. He shook my hand with a steel grip. I saw steel in his eyes as well. He said to his father: 'I don't think you need to talk about our labour problems. We don't have any. What's past is past.' He left us shortly afterwards, but it was clear to me that any talk of trade union infiltra-tion had been terminated.

Nicky took me instead onto the roof of the cellars where we could look out into the night and see the lights of the night pickers bobbing slowly in a group. For some reason, they reminded me of fishing boats. A fitful moon appeared from behind sullen streaks of cloud, and I became aware of the closeness of a huge mass that Nicky said was a mountain called Saron. As we stood gazing out into the windy night, Nicky told me about another problem that had troubled him deeply. It concerned new methodologies that had been adopted by his bottle supplier. Some chemical presence had ruined vast quantities of wine. The losses had been devastating. When his son had agreed to return to the estate, he had devoted himself to researching the problem. Scientists from many parts of the world had become involved. He had 'cracked the case'. Now there were protracted court cases weighing on his mind. 'Thank God for my son,' he said.

His eyes were weary, but his smile was generous, and he was good and informative company as he showed me around the winery, taking me finally to a subterraneous place where tens of thousands of bottles of sparkling wine were going through the ageing process. 'This is the first underground méthode cap classique cellar in the country,' he said. 'And we've retained the old French labour-intensive method of tilting the bottles to get rid of the sediment. It seemed more appropriate in South Africa than elaborate mechanisation.'

We went out into the windy darkness and by the vague light of the moon walked along a road until we came to a scene of night harvesting. The air smelled warm and dusty and laced sometimes with the smell of crushed vine leaves. I could hear women's voices, and also the sound of a radio. The miners' lights seemed to be buried deep inside the vines, illuminating green leaves and gnarled twigs as the pickers searched for bunches to snip off. One of the trailers had already been filled with plastic crates of grapes. A turning tractor illuminated the legs of the pickers as they worked along the rows of vines. I could see the plastic containers titling and awry on the rough tracks between each row of vines. Then all was darkness again, except for the individual lights be-hind the leaves with the unseen faces working in a soothing isolation between them. Nicky said that the workers preferred to operate at night. I could understand why. We stood silent in the wind and the darkness for some time. Then we turned and walked back to the winery.

At midnight, Nicky opened a bottle of Krone Borealis sparkling wine and poured two glasses. We toasted each other. The wine seemed to lift lightly off the palate. I said as much and he smiled with his weary eyes. While we drank, I asked him about his experiences with the trade unions. What actually had happened and how lasting were the disruptions? He worked his way round the questions without answering them. His son's influence was too great. So I let the matter drop.

IN THE early morning I met John, my host, in the kitchen of his house. I had arranged to accompany him to Tulbagh town to pick up labour who would harvest grapes in one of his vineyards before the sun became too hot. He was eating breakfast and turning the pages of a book called *The Art and Science of Wine*. It struck me that it was like reading *The Principles of Sailing* on the eve of one's first around-the-world voyage. He said he had other books on wine making as well. He knew the steps to follow once the grapes were safely picked. This approach was very much in accordance with his overall philosophy. You have to take chances and grab opportunities if you're to do what you most want, he had said. That was exactly how he intended to make his first batch of wine.

After breakfast, we drove in his truck to Tulbagh, turning up from the main street and ending in the heart of the Coloured township. Street lights illuminated empty streets. He parked at a crossroads and we waited. The mountains seemed very close, etched against a whitening pre-dawn sky. A rooster crowed repeatedly from somewhere close. After a few moments a man in brown overalls appeared. John introduced him as Soppies. He was friendly in a deferential sort of way. He told John to drive down the hill to another part of the township. A scrawny dog with a long curving tail loped across the glare of the headlights. We stopped in a suburban street and Soppies went off to bang on doors. We waited. 'You have to go with the flow,' John said.

A few windows along the street began to light up. Women appeared at doorways, the light shining out from behind them. People began to arrive at the truck. They smoked and talked and waited for Soppies to return. Finally the back of the truck was full and we set off, driving at first along the edges of an informal settlement seeming to be full of tin and cardboard structures, and then up out of a gully and back into the gentler streets of Tulbagh proper.

It was already half-light by the time we got to the selected vineyard and the pickers had been deployed along the rows of vines. This was a much smaller operation than the one I had seen the previous night. There were only two tractors, one driven by a young Israeli who three weeks before had married a South African girl and was now paying in labour for his honeymoon holiday being spent in a cottage on John and Beverley's farm.

He was a pleasant young man in shorts and sandals. His hair was dark and curly, and his limbs were deeply tanned. 'I am for seven years in the Israeli army, but I am right now having a rest,' he told me, when I hitched a ride on his tractor. 'The conflict in the Middle East will always go on. It is human nature. There will always be fighting.' We bounced round the top end of the dam I had seen from my balcony. On a tiny island, a few trees had grown to maturity, and then one of them had died. The bleached branches were filled with hundreds of birds not yet risen for the day's excursions. The lower branches were occupied by white sacred ibises, while the cormorants and darters preferred the higher roosting places.

'You see the tree,' the Israeli soldier said over his shoulder to me. 'All the black birds sit on top and all the white birds are underneath. I have told John: this is a tree of the new South Africa.' Then he laughed in delighted amusement at his own joke.

The workers had become spread out and embedded in the vines. The vines were of a smaller variety than those I had seen with Nicky, not much more than chest height. The torsos of all but the shortest pickers thrust above them as they worked their way along the rows. In the east, above the mountains, the light splayed out like spokes from a central hub. Then the sun appeared, a red dazzling presence that touched the vines and the heads of the workers in their caps and doeks. Their faces looked bronzed in the delicacy of the first sunlight. They were Coloured people from Tulbagh, seasonal workers, doing what they had done for several hundreds of years. I watched their hands, the deftness of the work they did among the leaves and branches of the vines. The plastic crates were regularly filled with bunches of grapes, and the tractors hauled them away to the winery for crushing and chilling and fermentation.

I asked a few of them how life was these days in the valley. It was all right, they said. The Lord was helping them, but it was becoming difficult. Too many young people were going to Cape Town. I asked them why. They said: 'The work here is too little.' Slowly it came out of them. In small statements, in response to questions, a picture of competition and potential conflict began to emerge. The Coloureds had been in the valley for generations. But now, since the lifting of influx control and especially since 1994, many black Africans were coming from the east, from the Ciskei and Transkei.

'*Daar's niks wat ons kan doen*,' a toothless woman said, '*die swarte is nou koning* (there's nothing we can do; the black man is now king).'

Her words seemed to break the ice. Several voices began to speak at once, and something like indignation fluttered among the vines. There were too many black people in Tulbagh now. They wanted the jobs but they didn't want to work. They wanted trade unions to protect them. They wanted higher wages and shorter hours. 'They steal our things,' a young woman said. 'They steal our clothes from the washing lines. No, we do not fight them. How can we do that? Tulbagh has always been so *rustig* (peaceful).'

Then it was time for breakfast and, talking among themselves with a sudden resonance that jarred slightly in the freshness of the early air, they drifted away among the leafy sunlit vines.

I HAD coffee in Beverley's kitchen later that morning. I asked her if she knew of any professional Coloured people who might be willing to talk to me. It surprised me, given the brevity of her time there and her commitments to her baby and the farm, that she knew of several. I made a few telephone calls and finally arranged an interview with a Dominee Dreyer who was the director of an institution called the Steinthal Landgoed or, in English, the Steinthal Estate. Beverley said she understood that Steinthal was a kind of reform school and children's home for Coloureds.

So in the windy afternoon I drove back to Tulbagh where the leaves were beginning to be blown off the old oak trees, and turned up once more towards the Coloured township, as John had done that morning to fetch Soppies and the workers. Now in the light the place had lost whatever slight mystique it might have had that morning. The low houses seemed to crouch against the earth, and the fruit trees in the garden were stretched out like ragged bunting in the dust and swirling wind. I asked a man for directions. He pointed towards the mountains. I drove for five kilometres directly towards their base. The trees of Steinthal were clearly visible at the side of the valley, not long before the bald rock of the Witzenberg began its towering ascent. A friendly man at the gate asked me to fill in his book, then directed me to the administration block. I drove on a paved road past sports fields and buildings spread out in spacious grounds. Some boys were playing cricket. A group of laughing girls stepped aside to let me pass.

I sat in a reception area for a few moments, reading a pamphlet that confirmed Beverley's understanding. *Steinthal is an Estate with a Poultry Farm, Dairy, Children's Development Centre and Home for the socially disadvantaged as well as a Secondary School for Learners with Special Educational Needs.* It had been in operation since 1842. The church that ran it, the missionary arm of the Dutch Reformed Church, had come into existence in Tulbagh 25 years earlier, no doubt ministering to the spiritual needs of the precursors of those bronze-faced people who had worked in John's vineyard that morning. But the real impetus for the estate, owned by a Rhenish missionary, was a community of freed slaves who arrived not long after it was established. The similarities with Wuppertal struck me immediately. There was a copy of a Steinthal *Gedenkskrif* (literally, a commemorative memoir) published in 1992 on the table in the reception area. The last quarter of this publication was given over to photographs. I flicked through them. Smiling up at me from one page, but in a slow and dignified way, was a neatly dressed woman with hair that curled gently onto her forehead. The caption said that she had been the *koster* (churchwarden) at Steinthal in 1992. Her name was Mrs A van Rooy.

I was about to ask the receptionist if she was still there when my quest was interrupted by more immediate things. A tall serious-looking man had appeared. He introduced himself as Dominee Dreyer, and I followed him down a short passage and into his office. There I met his assistant, a Mr Visser, who rose to greet me. We sat away from the large desk in chairs that had been arranged more informally for conversation. We conversed. To begin with I frequently found Mr Visser's eyes fixed on my face, only to have them shift quickly away when I met his gaze. Both men seemed stiff with me, reserved, anxious to maintain their dignity.

I tried my best to put them at their ease. I thanked them for seeing me. I told them I had been intrigued to read, while I waited, something of the history and intention of Steinthal. Then I mentioned my scattered communications with the grape pickers that morning, the apparent tensions between Coloured and black.

Dominee Dreyer apologised for keeping me waiting. He presented me with my own copy of the *Gedenkskrif* at which I had just been glancing. Then he said that he had been working at Steinthal for eight years and that his relationship with the black community in Tulbagh had started to evolve not long after he had arrived, taking the form of contact through various community forums.

He spoke in measured tones, his eyes cautiously resting on my face. 'It all started with migrant labour,' he said, 'and then their families joined them. Almost certainly there was also a political motive. I mean I think people were actively encouraged to come and to register as voters in the Western Cape. Very soon there were too many of them here. But the point I want to make at this stage is that the Tulbagh local authority didn't have a sensible plan to cope with this influx.'

'The black children didn't go to school immediately,' Mr Visser added, 'because of the language problem. Do you know what I mean? All our schools are Afrikaans. The black children must be taught first in Xhosa, then they want everything in English.'

Dominee Dreyer described what should have been done in the social sphere to cope with the new situation of black immigration. Infrastructural needs like housing and schools and a clinic should have been a top priority. Then there should have been special public relations processes to increase understanding and acceptance on both sides. But nothing like this had happened. 'The result is there's a lot of distrust building up,' he said. 'Black people have traditionally worked for less. Now they want more. They want unionisation on the farms. They're taking a lot of traditionally Coloured jobs. Blacks and Coloureds are living apart, and there's a lot of tension.'

Mr Visser said: 'Coloured families have been for ages on the waiting lists for RDP housing, but the first houses that were built went to blacks. That was unethical. Many people are now saying that Coloureds are more disadvantaged than they were pre-1994.'

Dominee Dreyer remained more placatory. He spoke about a development organisation formed in Tulbagh by business and community leaders that was drawing up a plan to create more jobs for everyone. In spite of numerous invitations, however, not a single black person had turned up for the first meeting.

'We are very concerned,' he said in his serious way. 'Our young people can't find work. There's very high unemployment, and poverty levels are rising – especially in the winter when the seasonal work dries up.'

The development plan included the upgrading of certain roads using local labour, an upgrade of the caravan park to stimulate tourism, and the establishment of a market gardening project and an African crafts market. 'But there is no co-operation between the races,' the dominee added, his expression perplexed.

Visser, in his more direct manner, said bluntly. 'There has been little regard for the infrastructure and services that we do have. Tulbagh has a water shortage – especially in the dry summer months. But almost overnight the black immigrants moved in. They are living in Chris Hani – that's the local squatter settlement. The population there has exploded from always before about one hundred people to over two thousand. Crime is skyrocketing. The Coloureds are disgruntled. They feel the tension. There is unhappiness, uneasiness, suspicion; and the Coloureds are definitely becoming the targets of the new crime wave.'

'We should talk more to each other,' the dominee said.

'But how?' Mr Visser countered. 'That's what I ask myself.'

To change the subject, I asked about Steinthal and the various projects being undertaken there. Until 1999, came the reply, there had been 600 children from every corner of the Western Cape, all of them in need of the sort of institutional care available at Steinthal. But since 1999, the situation had changed for the worse.

I waited for them to tell me the details of the deterioration.

'The government,' the dominee told me, 'has said they no longer want to subsidise the sort of work we do here. They say the care should be delivered in the community, not in institutions. South Africa is not a welfare state, they say. So our subsidy is cut year by year, until 2005 when there'll probably be nothing. At the moment we have hardly a hundred and fifty children. That's all we can afford.'

'There's forty million rands worth of infrastructure in this institution,' Mr Visser said, his voice tense, 'built up over time by the church and by ordinary individuals. Now it's in the process of being lost to the children who need it most. Orphans, street children, molested children, first offenders. How can special care be delivered to such damaged souls in the community? Shall we send them to Chris Hani where there are umpteen shebeens? As it is, some of our children are stealing for the Chris Hani stolen goods market, and then with the proceeds buying dagga from the same market.'

He laughed a short laugh, looking directly at me for the first time. The dominee sat silent as Mr Visser continued.

'We are being elbowed out,' he said in his tensely controlled anger. 'It is because of who we are. We are Coloureds. We feel such a sense of rejection,' he said.

The dominee said: 'It is true that we sit between the whites and the blacks. We always have sat there. But there are – '

Mr Visser interrupted him, no longer able to restrain himself. 'The old stable Coloured communities are disappearing. They are being broken down. Before 1994, our comfort and stability was in our allegiance with whites. We had the same religion, the same language. However reviled we were – and we were often reviled, make no mistake – we were at least partly in touch with white power. This is now lost. We feel we are disappearing from the stage. We are losing our identity. Material upliftment no longer matters. We have to find a relationship of trust. That's the key. We are neither black nor white, and because of this the present government is not interested in our problems. They do not depend on us – even less than the whites did – for their power. Who can we rely on?' he asked, and now his voice was raised. 'How can we find our place?'

The three of us sat silent for a few seconds. I could hear Mr Visser's breathing, and I glimpsed his pain. I could see that his eyes had reddened as he spoke. Now he turned his face away from me.

The dominee said: 'In spite of the catastrophe of the funding, this institution takes heart in its vision. In the 1840s it played a dominant role in the stabilising of the lives of freed slaves. We have a similar role now. As my colleague says, post-apartheid Coloured communities are breaking down. There is confusion and fear such as must have been in the minds of those people who were no longer enslaved. But we are the torch of the valley! The stabilising light. That is what this school will be – if we trust in the Lord to provide.'

As I was leaving, Mr Visser gripped my hand. 'Sorry for the outburst, hey,' he said, and with a suddenly discovered mutuality we smiled at each other for the first time.

ON MY way back to the farm, I stopped at a vantage point in the Coloured township and looked across a small steep valley at the shacks of Chris Hani. Beyond the abodes and the greyness of the narrow road-ways, a piece of golden wheat country, lying fallow for the winter plant-ing, swept away. And beyond the wheat fields, the stark mountains reared up as backdrop. The gradually sinking afternoon sun slanted across the faces of rock, giving depth to the chasms and ravines that had increasingly deepened over millions of years. The wind blew hard.

A few Coloured women walked chattering on a pathway close to where I stood. How could they find their place? I doubted if it would be in political allegiances that failed to satisfy. How then? I changed the question slightly. How could they find their past? I glimpsed some veracity in this alteration. When the political dream began to disinte-grate, began indeed to manipulate and exclude, then the heart turned back to the problem of an earlier identity. It turned back even to the deepest dreams of an unknown Java and the mysteries of the tiny worlds of Wuppertal and perhaps as well of the Steinthal Estate.

A sudden swirl of grey dust rushed through the shacks and streets of Chris Hani below me. I suddenly envied the black certainty. The fog of doubt was not for them. Black was African: it was past and place enough. Not even the deepest squalor, not even the high-pierced bird sounds of a terrible starvation, could shake the foundations of that. I stood looking across the ravine for a moment longer, then went on my way.

13
No longer fishing

THERE WAS a certain inevitability about my journey culminating at the sea. My other journeys always had. There was also a sense of finality about the sight of that solid blue wall closing off all the vistas of potential advance. I had reached finality. This was the sense I had driving into Lambert's Bay one morning, seeing the blue wall turn to an ocean that stretched away, and seeing smoke from the fish factory leaking into an otherwise unblemished sky.

The factory stood hard against the sea, and the hotel stood immediately behind. The factory chimneys – one brick, the others aluminium-coloured with black tops – smoked sluggishly, and a sudden escape of steam blew out a white cloud. On the seaward side, fishing boats stood on blocks at the top of a slipway. The harbour was protected by rocky breakwaters and an island a few hundred metres offshore. Seagulls wheeled in flight or sat in their thousands on the small island. At sea, a handful of factory boats fished halfway to the horizon. Beyond the picturesque, however, lay a harsher reality: I learned that immediately upon arrival. There were approximately 200 individual fishermen in that fishing town who were no longer fishing. They had no quotas.

'They're being as exploited by black or Coloured fat cats today as they were previously by white fat cats,' a woman told me. 'In fact, it's worse today. That's transformation for you,' she added ironically.

Her name was Maretjie, a pleasant woman in her forties who had recently remarried, this time to a qualified marine diver who for a living sucked up diamond-bearing gravel from the sea bed. She told me she had grown up in Pretoria, and every year the family had holidayed in Lambert's Bay. After her father died, she and her mother had eventually moved down for good. She did some reporting for various west coast newspapers. She had written articles on things like the Lambert's Bay fresh water supply and the smell from the fish factory. It was nice to feel that she was making a difference. Only recently, a young woman's boyfriend had committed suicide when she was nine months pregnant. Maretjie had written about the tragedy and had been able to launch a fund to help the women when she and her baby came out of hospital. And of course she had written articles on the Coloured fishermen.

'The basic problem is the new fishing quotas, and how they had to be applied for,' she explained. We sat drinking tea in the hotel lounge. Maretjie's fingernails were painted a deep blue. 'The old system was corrupt, of course, but at least it also catered to the small fisherman. For most of these men, it's all they know. Some have been fishing for thirty and even forty years. These subsistence fishermen – that's what they're called – were allowed to take out four crayfish every day, Monday to Friday. That was a modest living. Now most of them are sitting in the street or at the harbour, out of work.'

The new system of allocating fishing rights, Maretjie said, was introduced a few years ago to stimulate black economic empowerment. The idea had been to encourage the formation of small and medium enterprises, particularly those owned by ordinary people. Application for quotas had to be made to a newly established Rights Verification Unit. Sizeable fees had to accompany each application. These fees were nonrefundable in the event of an unsuccessful application. For a semi-commercial licence (which roughly coincided with the old subsistence fisherman arrangement) the application fee was R500. All along the west coast, fishermen had begged and borrowed these amounts, but very few had received quotas. Hundreds of thousands of rands had been lost by the very people who could least afford such loss.

'The whole verification business was a scam,' Maretjie said forthrightly. 'Or at least it was incredibly badly administered. To be quite frank, quotas were going to the wrong people. Bribes were flying about like you can't believe. Backhanders to officials, and God knows what else. Talk about nepotism and quotas for pals. And when you look at the lists of those who got quotas, many should not have received them – and that's according to the criteria laid down by the new regulations. Even more worrying is the accumulating evidence that the quota system is being used as a form of favour to people loyal to – to whom? – I suppose the government – or this or that political party.

'But the most awful thing is the damage done to the people at the bottom of the heap. Let me tell you that the old fishing families all along the coast are devastated. The government minister in charge says that people must look elsewhere for their livings. The sea cannot support them all. The only effect of this is that subsistence fishing has been forced underground. Or should we rather say, out of sight.

'What isn't out of sight, is the begging and the crime. The increases are dramatic. The school also suffers. The Coloured principal told me that fees are no longer being paid for many of the children. The school loses this income. The children themselves can't afford the books, the uniforms, let alone any little extras. And the parents wander the streets begging for wine and cigarette money. There's much more degradation now than I've ever seen before. If I look at Lambert's Bay, I find no sign of black empowerment. But white exploitation is thriving. The one significant difference is that they've been joined in their exploitation by hot-shot Coloureds – those with the right political connections.'

I asked Maretjie if she would take me to chat with the affected fishermen.

'Yes, of course I'll take you. Wait for me here.'

I dawdled in the hotel, looking at the artefacts behind the bar and in the various public places. The atmosphere was essentially geared to fishing for sport and as a holiday activity. Outside in the parking I had noticed a few four-wheel-drive vehicles, a few trailers carrying ski-boats. The customers already at the bar wore short trousers out of which thrust substantial sun-brown thighs.

It was difficult, in places like the Lambert's Bay Hotel, to ignore the importance of a kind of frontiersman machismo in the white South African psyche. Activities like fishing, shooting, outdoor living, cooking raw meat over open fires, held a central place in a broad fraternity of men. And this particular way of looking at self and at the group spread into the political sphere as well. Frontiersmen inevitably had human enemies. In one of the smaller lounges that I wandered into while waiting for Maretjie, I found a startling juxtaposition of images to illustrate the thought.

On a glass counter stood a big mounted hammerhead shark, its staring glass eyes occupying the ends of those flat projections jutting from the sides of its head. On the opposite wall, beneath the bronzed propeller of someone's favourite fishing boat, hung detailed illustrations of three of the bloodiest episodes in the history of KwaZulu-Natal, a region that was literally on the other side of the South African world. The first illustration depicted the murder of the Voortrekker leader, Piet Retief, inside Dingaan's royal Zulu homestead. The second showed the massacre of Boer women and children at Weenen. The third illustrated in equally gruesome minutiae the killing of hordes of Zulu warriors at the Battle of Blood River.

Such illustrations seemed less than appropriate for a west coast hotel. Indeed, their presence seemed bizarre. Yet there was an inner and contemporary logic that could not be ignored. Somehow – and the perception was reflected in the glass eyes of the conquered hammerhead – old victories lived on.

WE WALKED down to the small harbour that lay on the northern side of the fish factory. The quay was empty, except for a rubber dinghy that plied back and forth to small ocean-going boats moored some distance away. 'Those are the diamond boats,' Maretjie explained. 'They're getting broken into now, more and more. It never used to happen.' I stood on a concrete step and felt the air from the sea blow into my face. I watched the darters and cormorants fishing, sitting on the water then disappearing beneath the surface for considerable periods and re-emerging in another place entirely. I also saw the sleek body of a seal several times break the surface of the choppy waters of the harbour. The concrete step that we had occupied smelled of kelp. We waited. Gradually the fishermen gathered around us: men of all ages, Coloured men with weathered faces and often shabby clothes. They greeted Maretjie with a familiarity as between more than casual acquaintances. She said we wanted to talk to them about the quotas. Without exception they made disparaging gestures.

I said that the system seemed unfair. One of them said: 'It's not unfair, *dis blote skelmagtigheid*,' it's naked roguery and dishonesty. I sat down on the step to take notes. They settled around me.

Maretjie introduced me to an elderly man wearing a tartan cap from which a few strands of grey hair protruded. He sat beside me and we shook hands. He said he had been a fisherman for forty years. He had three small boats and could employ four people per boat. But he had not been granted a quota. 'My boats lie rotting in my yard,' he said.

I gathered that quotas had been given to local Lambert's Bay fishermen, but preference seemed to have been given to groups rather than to individuals.

'The trouble with that,' someone said, 'is that even though everyone in the group gives money for the application, only one person has signed. Now that person has run away with the quota. The others get nothing. And if you fish for the people with quotas, you have to run after them for your money. Sometimes it never comes.'

Maretjie said to me that too many subsistence fishermen had been left without quotas altogether. That was the fundamental problem. They stood around me, these subsistence fishermen, watching as I wrote in my notebook. A wild-looking man lit one cigarette after the other, sometimes giving his neighbours a puff. The smell of wine wafted from the group. The faces were in a variety of shades from chocolate brown to nearly white. My impression was of weathered skin, beards and stubble, bloodshot eyes, pursed lips emitting smoke into the breeze. These were the excluded ones: jobless, hanging around waiting to fish for those people who had been awarded quotas. Like the Pastoor, someone said. His name kept cropping up. He paid R2,50 to catch a kilo of crayfish worth up to R120. 'I can't work for that amount, not a fuck,' said the man who kept passing his cigarettes around. He seemed slightly drunk. The others laughed at him when he spoke. They pointed out a fenced compound in which rows of small boats lay upturned in the sunlight. 'They're the *roeibakkies* (rowing boats) that the subsistence fishermen used to hire,' Maretjie told me, 'but no longer.' It was a bleak sight, a memorial to a system no longer in use. The system had been prematurely curtailed, according to these men standing around me

I asked what they were doing instead of fishing.

'Washing cars,' a deep voice said.

Someone hawked and spat onto the quay. 'We fish at night,' he said, looking directly and defiantly into my eyes. 'Must I not steal to get bread onto the table?'

The men laughed, looking slyly at me to gauge my response.

'Are you taking undersized crayfish?' Maretjie asked.

Again the men laughed. She remarked that convictions for this offence had at least quadrupled in recent times. The courts were full. But the inspectors were frequently bribed, and illegal fishing was rife. 'It's defeating the whole purpose of quotas,' she said. 'The system is meant to keep the resource sustainable. But look what's happening. And it's happening all along the west coast.'

The men stood poised around me, waiting for me to continue. I looked up at them, squinting in sunlight. 'I've heard,' I said, 'that crayfish are being exchanged for drugs. Is that happening here?'

The man with the cigarettes shook his head. He was stooped forward as he tried to assess my motives. 'That is happening with *perlemoen* (abalone) on the south coast. You know, there by Mosselbaai. Not here.'

'What sort of drugs?' I asked.

'Cocaine, crack, heroine.'

The men were laughing, and the man with the tartan cap was nudging me with his elbow. I turned to him. 'It's here,' he said in a conspiratorial voice; 'it's already here.'

'It's an opportunity for the dealers to establish new markets,' Maretjie commented with a sardonic expression. I asked if she had written about this aspect of the new quota system. 'Not yet,' she said, 'but I'm working on it.'

The men began to speak again about the Pastoor. What outraged them most, it seemed, was that he was not a fisherman. He had never even been to sea. And he was from Cape Town, only recently come to Lambert's Bay.

'If you shake hands with him you must make sure he gives you all your fingers back,' someone wisecracked.

'How can I shake his hand?' another responded.

'He's a number twenty-six, that's all.'

I asked what that meant. The men laughed.

The man in the tartan cap said at my elbow: 'We all voted ANC for a better life. But not one ANC person has come here to help us. All they can say is its bringing black empowerment. What is black empowerment? We want to fish. These white women were the only ones to talk for us. Quotas are going to black people though …'

When the meeting had broken up and we were walking back to the hotel, I asked Maretjie what it meant to call someone a number twenty-six. The breeze from the sea had blown her hair untidily about her face. She raised a blue-nailed hand to control it.

'Oh, it's Cape Town gangland talk,' she said. 'Each sort of criminal has a special number. One number for murder; one for rape, and so on. To be a number twenty-six is to be a lover of money. You'll do anything to get it.'

LATER THAT day I paid the Pastoor a visit. His name was David van Vollenhoven. His church was in the Coloured township on the landward side of Lambert's Bay. The streets were unpaved, the houses low against flat and sandy earth in which little grew without coaxing. The Pastoor was busy with a police officer when I arrived, and he asked me to come back in half an hour. I drove around the dusty little township for a while, then returned. The church was next door to the Pastoor's house, and connected internally so that he could walk directly from his living room to the vestry without venturing outside.

Maretjie had told me that the denomination to which the church adhered was AGS (the *Apostoliese Geloofsending*, a fundamentalist variant of Protestantism) and that the congregation had split in some bitterness over the Pastoor's crayfish quota. He had come from the Cape Town area, apparently, where he had been a deputy mayor in some or other local authority there.

The Pastoor confirmed as much when I saw him. 'Tygerberg,' he said. 'I was mayor there, and for four years the deputy mayor.'

I asked him why he had truncated his political career to come to Lambert's Bay.

'The church called me,' he replied. 'I have a feeling for my people. I've been here for four years now. I'm working with the poorest of the poor – and not only those who are connected to the church.'

He had viewed me with some suspicion, appearing as I had done without warning. Nevertheless, he had made his assessment of me quickly, and after that had been willing enough to talk to me. I guessed him to be in his late thirties or early forties, but with a slightly bloated face as if he was carrying some extra weight. He was neatly dressed in a dull brown suit, almost khaki in colour, but well cut, a bright green shirt and floral tie. We sat in easy chairs in his living room. As we spoke, people intermittently passed through the room: what seemed to be his own children once or twice, and also an assistant of some kind to whom he gave terse instructions. He spoke good English, but with that particular accent characteristic of many Coloured people living in and around Cape Town.

'I think I am having some success, here, with the poorest of the poor,' he told me. 'When I first arrived, I discovered people selling crayfish on the street corners for ridiculously low prices. Then they'd go directly to the bottle stores. How could I, a Christian, stand by and watch them do this? Then I discovered there were about three hundred and fifty of them who had permits to take out four crayfish a day. That was far too many for the local market. So I searched my heart to see whether there was anything I could do.'

What he found to do, although as he said he had no money, was to borrow some in Cape Town and 'start this small factory'.

'I had found a market for crayfish at R120 a kilogram,' he said. 'So I told the local fishermen: stop wasting your resources on the street corners; bring me your crayfish alive; I'll give you R90 a kilogram. I was able to help many families out of poverty in this way.'

The next thing that happened, of course, was that the new fishing quota system was introduced. The Pastoor had personally assisted 44 people to apply for quotas, which meant an amount of R22 000 out of his own pocket, he said. Nearly thirty of these applicants were given quotas, but unfortunately more than a dozen of the people he had tried to help had wasted the money. They had drunk it out before they could make their applications. Drinking was the scourge of these coastal communities, he added.

'This is how I have tried to help my people here in Lambert's Bay. I have also used some of the profits from my small factory to start a soup kitchen at the church. We feed three hundred people here three times a week.'

I asked Pastoor van Vollenhoven if he, obviously a non-fisherman, had been granted a crayfish quota under the new quota system.

He looked at me a second longer than usual. Then he nodded. 'The reason why I applied,' he explained, 'was to attempt to supplement my salary here at the church. I only get one thousand rand a month. There's proof of this that I can show you. Some time ago I bought a big boat and five small boats. Why? Because they were just lying there. I got them cheap. Twenty people have work because of this. The rationale for giving me the quota was this: I had already invested in the industry. That's why I got the quota; and I'm using it, as I'm using everything else, to help my people here in Lambert's Bay.'

I asked if he could tell me how much he paid the fishermen who worked for him.

'Fifteen rand a kilogram,' he said promptly.

I said that a group of fishermen I met at the harbour had told me that he paid only R2,50 per kilogram.

Again he hesitated. 'They would say that,' he said, and a shadow of unpleasantness flickered across his expression. 'Some people are dissatisfied. Of course. But usually they're the ones who waste their money on drink.'

I asked what he thought the average per-kilogram rate was for hired fishermen in Lambert's Bay.

'I know of no one who is paying less than five or six rand a kilogram,' he said with a hint of defiance in the hardness of his voice. 'But I'm the only one who's paying fifteen.'

I nodded, but offered nothing more.

'I love these people and I try to look after them,' he went on in a smoother voice. 'I feed their children here at the church. I personally have lost a lot of money. But some people just don't care. They are wasting all their opportunities. And then of course they look for someone to blame for their lack of opportunity.'

'Do you think the new quota system is a good one? Do you think it's being honestly administered?'

'Oh, definitely,' the Pastoor said. 'But you must remember that you can't satisfy everyone. A lot of fishermen didn't even apply for quotas. That's why they didn't get any. And they have also been judged on their ability to perform. Can they do the job? It's no good blaming the system. But a lot of people blame everyone but themselves. People love to blame the government, of course. But I can say with absolute conviction that the quota system is working well in Lambert's Bay.'

Before I left, the Pastoor showed me his church. We walked along the interconnecting passage and emerged into a large unadorned space filled with wooden pews. Enough for over six hundred people, he informed me; and the knotty-pine ceiling had recently been installed. Leading off the church's spacious foyer (it seemed too large to be called a vestibule) was the church kitchen, equipped with an electric stove and long counter tops. 'This is where we prepare the food for our soup kitchens,' he told me. 'Three times a week.' He stood before me with his hands folded, as if he considered that his point had now been irrefutably made.

Then someone was hovering in the background. It was his assistant again. The Pastoor turned. They spoke in Afrikaans. The Pastoor's boat was approaching the harbour. The Pastoor said that nothing should be sold on the quay. The entire catch should be taken urgently to the factory.

When he turned to me again, it was with an apology and an affable smile of farewell.

I DROVE down the coast towards Elandsbaai. There was no coastal thoroughfare with sweeping views of the sea, but instead a rough privately owned road that travelled in that space behind the dunes where pools of stagnant water lay encircled by sterile white evaporation rings, and where nothing grew. My car threw up a haze of pale dust that drifted sluggishly landward. Elandsbaai had not been in my plans. I had intended to drive towards Cape Town, perhaps diverting to visit a few of the coastal towns that lay around the bulge of land above Saldanha. But someone had given me a name in Elandsbaai, and it was for this reason that I found myself on the stony road behind the dunes.

I knew nothing about this remote coastal village, except that it had been a place where, from time to time and urged to do so by unusually high blooms of oxygen-hungry organisms (the phenomenon being known as red tide), crayfish in large numbers walked out of the sea. According to newspaper reports I had seen, up to a thousand tons of crayfish, in the latest red-tide episode, had ended their rush for oxygen on the Elandsbaai beach. But local residents had been prevented, by contingents of police and finally by the army, from taking any of the high-protein food for their own use. Instead, Marine and Coastal Management officials had tried to get some of the stranded crayfish back into the sea. But most had died. And it had cost the state R130 000 to dispose of the rotting crayfish. Officials said at the time that existing regulations prevented local consumption because most of the crayfish were undersized. It seemed logically preposterous. Someone was quoted in a newspaper as saying that the waste of food was disgraceful. 'And this in front of people who have been denied a legitimate fishing quota.'

The name I had been given in Elandsbaai was that of a town councillor named Johanna Taylor. She would talk to me about this small fishing community's problems. I spoke to her on the telephone and she gave me directions to get to her house. When I arrived, she came out to greet me almost before I was out of my car. She was a middle-aged Coloured woman, neatly dressed, reserved and serious but friendly. I had expected to talk to her, and perhaps a few others, in her home. Yet she looked as if she was about to go out, her handbag already firmly under her arm.

'Ja, meneer,' she said. 'We are going to the police station.'

In a moment we were joined by half a dozen other women. We drove in two cars to a group of prefabricated buildings standing across the road from the narrow beach. I could see, as the bay curved to the south, that the beach became narrower and finally the sea beat against rocks directly above which, on stilts sometimes, stood a row of buildings – and behind the buildings reared the sheer cliffs of Baboon Point.

But my attention was focused on matters closer at hand. I went with the delegation of women into the police station grounds. The flag snapped in a brisk breeze. What followed in one of the prefabricated buildings was a most extraordinary encounter.

WE SAT in a spacious kitchen where chairs were arranged in a loose half-circle around a high counter top that a uniformed policeman, smiling across at the gathering, said would be perfect for use as a spacious rostrum. He certainly had sufficient papers to fill it. A colleague in plain clothes, but with a holstered pistol attached to his belt, sat to one side, reading more documents in a file. Both policemen were white, and they were faced from the semicircle of chairs by Johanna Taylor and the group of Coloured women who had accompanied us. I sat close to the sink with a tap dripping softly behind me. A much-used dartboard hung on one of the prefabricated walls.

The uniformed policeman had pips on his shoulders and I presumed (correctly) that he was the station commander at Elandsbaai. He shuffled his papers. He said: 'I'm trying to get some of the early facts straight. I'm interested in the anchovy quota. And also the R30 000 donation. The *Vroue Vereeniging* had 176 members, and it was the *Vroue Vereeniging* that got the quota. Am I right so far? Who can help me here?'

The women spoke among themselves. They spoke to the commander. He made a few notes, then asked another question. In this way, they held a conversation with the commander. There was some laughter. He seemed a pleasant man, and it was soon clear to me that he had long ago gained the confidence of these women. The plainclothes detective, the one with the pistol at his belt, made no contribution to the meeting, but kept his head bowed over the documents in his files, occasionally turning over the pages. Sometimes the women and the commander referred to a third party named Brenda. She seemed to occupy a central role in the sequence of events they were trying to piece together. How could Brenda have done this or that? Now Brenda is saying that or this? The women shook their heads. The station commander said: 'Don't worry, ladies. We're working on this issue.'

Then, looking my way for the first time, he asked: 'Are you following all this?'

I shook my head. The women laughed. I said to the station commander: 'I need some background. I need to know why this meeting is taking place.'

'It is taking place because you are here,' he replied.

'Good heavens,' I said, and again the women laughed.

'All right. Here's the background. Help me with the detail, ladies.'

So in the prefabricated kitchen in small episodes, and with frequent interruptions, the story emerged. Some of the women's faces had become quite animated. Even the detective several times looked up from his files; and once he suddenly waved a document at me as proof of what had just been said. Then he went to the open door and just beyond the threshold lit a cigarette, taking care to exhale away from the kitchen.

The basic facts seemed to be these. In 1996 the women of Elandsbaai established a non-profit organisation called the *Nood Vroue Vereeniging* (Emergency Women's Association) with 176 members, a constitution and bank account, and a mission to improve the generally impoverished conditions suffered by many in that isolated community. Some funding was raised and various improvements made to the local primary and pre-primary schools. When the new fishing quota system was introduced, the *Vereeniging* applied for and was awarded a quota for 176 tons of anchovies. The next step in the narrative was unclear, but somehow the *Nood Vroue Vereeniging* was taken over or superseded by a much smaller group, including the first chairwoman of the broad-based *Vereeniging*, an ambitious young woman named Brenda. A new organisation, registered as a close corporation with around ten members and named Boundary Road 82, came into being. And it was the latter business entity, led by Brenda, that began to exploit the quota. The *Nood Vroue Vereeniging* engaged the services of a lawyer. He took the women's money but did little to resolve an entirely unsatisfactory situation.

'The community has been ripped off,' the station commander told me. 'Their quota has been hijacked by a small group, most of them not even residents of Elandsbaai, and the community sits again with nothing.'

'Boundary Road 82 is thriving. They are making a lot of money.' The voice was Johanna Taylor's. 'So now we are getting ready to lay a charge.'

'A criminal charge,' the commander said. 'Fraud.'

I asked him if the woman concerned – this Brenda Pieterson – had any political affiliations.

He shook his head. 'Anyway,' he said, 'she has every right – a constitutional right – to affiliate with whoever she wants.'

One or two of the women snorted.

The detective suddenly spoke. 'Mandrax, cocaine, crack,' he said in a harsh voice. 'It's all here. There's increasing crime. Unemployment is rife. If this project hadn't been hijacked, conditions here would not have been as bad.'

He got up suddenly and made for the door to light another cigarette. This time he stood inside the door, puffing almost savagely in his sudden anger which he tried to control with an overlay of fierce solemnity. 'But this quota business, ninety per cent of it, is all about backhanders. The whole system stinks. It's abused. It's not looking after the poor. It's robbing from the poor to assist the rich. And the favoured.'

'When you think,' the station commander said, joining in. 'The total quota of crayfish for Elandsbaai is eight hundred tons. That's approximately eight million rand. But where's that money going? Out of town!'

'Boundary Road has got more quotas now, not just the anchovies,' a woman said. 'You must see the cars they drive.'

'I can't understand those clowns in Cape Town,' the station commander said. 'Take the red-tide crayfish. Guard the crayfish, they said to me. With what? I said. Reinforcements were sent from headquarters. While they were getting here, I went to the community and said: you've got two hours to take the crayfish away. The whole community came to the beach. They were singing. They took away thousands. But you couldn't notice. There were millions of crayfish crawling on the beach. Then the reinforcements came and they started to guard the beach. But we had no problems with the community.'

Some of the women clapped.

'This is our community,' the detective said in his fierce way, blowing smoke in a rush towards the kitchen ceiling.

It was a spectacle that should have astonished me – this allegiance and camaraderie between these doughty Coloured women and the white Afrikaner policemen – but it did not. It seemed for the most part logical, so much a part of the quality of the country, its new freedoms and potentialities, since it had begun its dancing with the freedoms inherent in the democratic idea.

After the meeting, I shook hands with the policemen. The detective had withdrawn once more underneath his carapace of gruffness. The station commander, on the other hand, grinned quite enthusiastically at me. He said: 'We should not talk politics. But privately I can tell you. Yes, of course there's political affiliations. This is South Africa. Everything is still political. There's no change.'

DRIVING DOWN the coast towards Cape Town, now with the signs of an early winter coming on, I thought again of Maputo where my travels had begun. I kept remembering the two-dimensional rats I had seen in a filthy side street on my way to talk to the Mozambican economist, Dr Maria Tumbi. The rats had been squashed flat by passing tyres, but still with their eyes staring as they must have stared in their last instant of life, and with their long tails intact. Caricatures of rats. Caricatures. The word remained, running as a constant from one context in my memory to the next. Grandiose caricature and chaos. So here it was, I had thought then on the eastern coast of southern Africa, and it came to me forcefully now as I drove through the ins and outs of the south-western coast. Here it was: the post-colonial African pattern. First the struggle, then the euphoria of success and freedom, then the collapse into grandiose caricature and chaos; and only after that, the pale new dawn, the promise and sometimes the reality of ascent.

I thought of these things nearly constantly now, and particularly one evening as darkness fell and I was driving on the road towards Velddrif and Port Owen. The memory of my Maputo perceptions now chilled me. Perhaps it was no more than the sight of the darkening sky above the sea that brought to me my sense of chill. But I kept thinking of the flat caricatures of rats and those other caricatures that grew less or more grotesque and grandiose in direct proportion to their propensity for chaos. Caricatures of freedom; caricatures of democracy; caricatures of justice; caricatures even of responsibility and concern – all bobbing like flotsam upon the dark torrents of an indomitable will to power and profit. And only after that, only after the storms had blown themselves out and the torrents had subsided, came the pale new dawn.

Velddrif in the darkness presented a dreary sight with its wide empty streets and the occasional brightness of take-away neon. I stood on the balcony of the small apartment I had hired for a few days at the Port Owen Marina. Below me (I was on the second floor) black water glinted with reflected light, and the masts of yachts swayed in a ghostly assortment of cross-rhythms. From nearly every balcony in my block, smoke and the smell of cooking meat billowed out. At one point it looked as if the building was on fire in several places. But all was peaceful, with children playing on the grass below, and young men with large stomachs and short hair drinking beers from the bottle. It was inevitable, then, to recall the hammerhead shark and the pictures of KwaZulu disasters displayed in such an unconscious and sinister proximity.

In the morning, as I was descending the stairs, an elderly man with a wizened face held up an ash-filled bucket and broom. 'Meneer,' he said. 'I can clean your braai.' I said there was no need. He looked at me in scepticism and disbelief.

In a tearoom in Velddrif I saw a copy of a west coast newspaper with a report on attacks on Western Cape farms, one near Porterville hardly a hundred kilometres inland, in which three had died, a man and his wife in one incident, and an 80-year-old woman who was found 'dead in a pool of blood in the TV room of her home after attackers stabbed her repeatedly'. Such reports always brought a sense of unease. The hazards of the frontier. I was reminded of a police notice I had picked up somewhere on my travels. It bore the photographs of six white men, the majority in their twenties and all with Afrikaner names. *These individuals*, the notice said, *can assist the police with their investigation into the recent bombings in our country.*

A rugged-looking old man in the Port Owen Marina office gave me his views on the steel works that had been built down the coast at Saldanha. He said he had learned to speak English by talking to visitors like myself. He told me that the steel works had brought some jobs to the west coast, but had also brought a large influx of black workers. For every black worker, there were fifty black dependents, he said, and this had upset the balance of west coast society. This society for a long time had comprised God-fearing platteland Afrikaners and seafaring Coloureds. Now this third element was being introduced, and with it had come new tensions. To make matters worse, the new fishing quota system had brought widespread unemployment to the Coloureds. Now everyone was worse off than before Saldanha Steel had been built.

I went to the St Helena Hotel for lunch. The shiny over-decorated bar was filled with white Afrikaners – and three Coloured men drinking in a group to one side. The place was run by a retired attorney from Johannesburg who was very enthusiastic about what he called his 'new stimulus – probably my last'. Crayfish, he said, had rapidly become the hotel speciality. As a result, people travelled for miles around to eat there. His wife was gushingly friendly in the gift shop in the hotel foyer. She told me she had stocked it with the work of local arts and crafts groups. I noticed on the table at which she sat, waiting for customers, a half-empty bottle of white wine.

Below the hotel, between the coastal road and the sea, I came upon a row of derelict cottages and a few old sheds. Rickety wood and iron walls; crumbling masonry, graffiti on once whitewashed walls, and a few cormorants on one roof, fresh from fishing, in poses of wing-drying crucifixion. The blackened earth between the buildings was now used for crude panel beating and mounds of diesel-engine debris. Wild and emaciated children collected twigs for a fire somewhere. The sense was of a human purpose passed on. The fishing cottages had turned to slums. I stood among the waste material of progress and inevitable change. I noticed collapsed tombstones in the grass and weeds growing among the rubbish, and thought of the fishermen beneath them, their remains seeping down into the sea. The hotel seemed very white and bright up there on the slope above the coastal road.

A storm lashed the windows of my apartment that night. To begin with, the electricity supply failed, and it was only then that I noticed the lightning, white sheets of it cutting across the lagoon. The water turned dark with the rain and a buffeting wind. Thunder ruptured the roaring of the sea. I went to a restaurant on the beach, running in from the rain. The sea was invisible beyond a concrete wall, although sometimes the spray of crashing swells flew high into the air. The restaurant was nearly empty. 'Are we going to be washed away?' I asked the waiter, a young man with long blonde hair. 'I don't think so,' he replied cheerfully, 'not tonight.'

In the morning the storm had subsided, but the sky remained low and grey. I drove to Saldanha and watched boats unloading crates of fish onto the wharf. Seagulls circled screaming above, and I could see hundreds more, resembling rows of spikes along the apexes of pitched asbestos roofs across the harbour. Two young white men threw the crates up out of the boat. I wondered if they had been granted a quota. A slight drizzle sifted down. Then they started the motor and the vessel curved across the harbour.

I drove to the top of a high hill and looked at the town as it lay in the greyness of the morning. I could see the black shapes and chimneys of the steel works in the distance. But most of all I could see the long curve of Saldanha Bay, and vessels with undisturbed wakes going about their business on those calm broad waters lying open beneath me. I stood in the drizzle, staring down. Then I descended and drove inland to the main road where I turned in the direction of Cape Town.

The sight of the mountain came unexpectedly upon me. I had been thinking once more about the question of caricature and chaos, and then the pale new dawn. This African pattern that I had pondered during my stay in Maputo. How could I say where South Africa lay on that switch-back line? Then my attention was drawn away. I had driven over another undulation in the country, and suddenly there it was. The grey mountain, standing at a distance of 15 kilometres but clearly visible in the grey day; the supporting sentinels of Devil's Peak and Signal Hill in place; the pale structures of the city visible as tiny rectangles against the mountain's base. And on my right-hand side, the grey Atlantic stretched towards its invisible marriage with the sky.

For a few seconds the sun threatened to break through. The light improved. The view was unimpeded. It rained harder then, and by the time the city had enveloped me – the streaming traffic, the wet signs, the lights in the gloom – I was swallowed also in spray from the surrounding tyres and a steadily thickening mist.

EPILOGUE

Cape Town

The fact is that in black society after 1994 there was a collapse of social purpose. The bogey man disappeared, and in his absence we lost the plot. Now the understanding is that civil society is a critical counterbalance to raw political power-mongering.

14
Ending in mist

THE FIRST thing I did when I got to Cape Town was to telephone Russel van Rooy's aunt to ask if I could pay her a visit. Russel had paved the way by telephoning her himself. Nevertheless, she was reserved with me. She gave me careful instructions on how to get to her house in Elsiesrivier. When I said I was looking forward to meeting her, she said she was also looking forward to meeting me. Then she laughed; it was as if she could no longer sustain her reserve. 'Ag, I've also asked Elizabeth to come.' I inquired who this was, and she said: 'Another of Russel's aunties.'

While I waited for the day of the interview to arrive, I wandered somewhat aimlessly around Cape Town, seeking a conclusion to my travels. Yet I knew well enough that the conclusion lay simply in the cessation of movement. I was now at the end as surely as I had known, standing on the balcony of my Maputo hotel at the other end of this long summer, that I was at the beginning. What lay between the beginning and the end were some of the places and faces that helped to describe the quality of South Africa in the first years of the 21st century. More subtly, perhaps, these places and faces were portraying the new inner landscape – as if the dance had been earthquake – that had in raw and jagged form been configured in 1994. The streets of Cape Town, as had the streets of Maputo, shone wet sometimes with a vague drizzle.

I walked in the Company's Garden that had been established by the Dutch East India Company 350 years ago, when Europeans first set their feet permanently on the southern tip of Africa. For more than half of those years the garden would have been tended by slaves. Here was a replica of a bell that had called the slaves to work. When they were finally manumitted, in the 1830s, not a few of them found their way to mission stations like the ones at Wuppertal in the Cederberg mountains and Steinthal near Tulbagh.

Just south of the Company's Garden stood the Parliament building with its large colonnaded portico and white-and-terracotta walls. By the time it was built in 1885, the Frontier Wars were over, diamonds had been discovered, and gold was already being mined in places like Barberton and Pilgrim's Rest. In 1948 the National Party came to power here, and in 1966 Dr Hendrik Verwoerd, one of the early architects of apartheid, was stabbed to death inside the House of Assembly. Nevertheless, the design and execution of apartheid's more sophisticated but equally degrading offspring, separate development, was made manifest in this building. The result was the rise of places like Transkei and Ciskei into largely ludicrous caricatures of independent states. But it was only in 1994 that black politicians walked the corridors of power for the first time. There was then such a rejoicing in the country, and also plans for the removal of a century of historic portraits – Eurocentric, every one – from those venerable parliamentary walls.

I began to talk to people, both inside this handsome building and in the city beyond, about what I called 'the African pattern', that process I had pondered when visiting Maputo at the start of my journey, and that occupied my thoughts quite often now at journey's end.

I sat at people's desks, or in coffee bars, sketching in my notebook the idea of the post-Uhuru African pattern. Here was the period of struggle against colonialism and oppression, I would explain, running my pen in a horizontal line; and here was the point at which freedom was finally achieved. Thereafter, the post-colonial history of Africa had all too often shown, the line plunged in a series of descents before finally levelling out and then beginning a slow climb out. The descent had tended to be characterised by coups d'état, collapsing administrations, economic failures, large-scale corruption and power-mongering; and the depth of the trough was determined by the severity, or the complexity, of these things. The gradual ascent seemed to be motivated, in those countries where it was discernible, by new attitudes to democracy (as distinct from majority rule) and a gradual balancing of political power with that of an increasingly intricate civil society. Was it realistic to think – I put the question to many – that such a pattern had any relevance to South Africa as it edged its way into the 21st century?

'Yes, I think so,' one man replied. He was an ageing academic in an open-necked shirt and baggy pullover. 'There are two significant elements to consider. The first is the growing corruption of the ruling elite. The second is the disaffection of the poor. Those in power have openly set out to enrich themselves. But the new black bourgeoisie is not large. Only about ninety thousand have gained significantly out of the new regime. Probably about fifty thousand of them have taken top jobs in the public sector and forty thousand in the private sector. In other developing countries – in Malaysia or Taiwan, for example – the poor found a way into the economic game. The result was huge growth rates in those countries. This has not happened to any significant extent here. There's a definite ceiling that separates the elite above from the masses below. The masses are merely a political constituency receiving handouts that help to maintain the power-base of the ruling elite. The masses definitely aren't in the main economic game. In fact, the poor as a sector of the population has grown from forty-one to forty-nine per cent in recent years – that's an increase in that sector of approximately three million people. So,' he concluded, 'my view is that we are definitely talking about a post-freedom descent. Or something like it.'

Another person, a political analyst, said: 'Let's go back to 1994 and all the hype about a rainbow miracle, about transformation without revolution. The point is that most people in the country were geared for revolution. For them, 1994 was like a sleight of hand. The results were undecided, and white people continued to hold the economic power. This is a classic case of expectations unfulfilled. Then there's the nature of the struggle itself. The biggest strength of the opposition to apartheid and minority rule was also its biggest weakness. The diversity within the ranks of the struggle was immense. Xhosa intellectuals, urban Zulus, white and Indian communists, Coloured activists, trade unionists, churches, black nationalists – unified by a common enemy, but inevitably beginning to splinter now that the struggle has been won.

'The broadest divisions within the ruling elite now are between the cream of those groupings which went into exile or prison, and those rough-and-ready troopers who remained on the ground, carrying the struggle forward through the streets and on the frontline barricades.

'To find fault is a fruitless exercise. The corruption and tendency to misrule is entirely predictable. So is the crime in the country. So is the misfiring of development. As a nation we are poorly educated and most people have extremely limited access to capital. What else did you expect but imperfect progress? Hopefully not this fatuous rainbow-nation nonsense.'

The words tumbled over me in a frenzy of analysis and prediction. The complexities of the country's mother city (if that is still what people were calling Cape Town) formed an appropriate backdrop. There was architecture preserved from the four centuries of its life; there were acres of glass soaring into the sky; and there was the rugged mountain, when occasionally the drizzle lifted, standing immovable behind. The sense, overwhelmingly for me, was of mist, of darkened glass, of visibility reduced. I did my best to pay attention to the words, but I kept thinking of the faces and the places of my journey which seemed to occupy a space beneath the words.

'I think the struggle was essentially about the forces of right triumphing over the forces of might. The Freedom Charter was the guide. Then Mandela set South Africa on its democratic way with a Freedom Charter face. But we have deviated from this straight and narrow. There has been a shift from Freedom-Charter democracy at all costs to power at all costs. But I don't think this necessarily represents the end of the line.'

A finger prodded the point in my diagram where the struggle phase ended and the line changed direction for the descent. Fingers kept prodding my diagram, showing how this or that opinion might have redrawn it to show a more gradual decline perhaps, a shallower trough perhaps, a steeper post-trough ascent, and so on. The faces passed in a bewildering procession on the other side of desks strewn with documents I would never read, or in more intimate surroundings, eyes narrowed above coffee cups or beer glasses in the talkative places in the crannies of the city.

'The fact is that in black society since 1994 there has been a collapse of social purpose. The apartheid bogey man has disappeared, and in his absence we lost the plot. Now the understanding is growing that civil society is a critical counterbalance to raw political power-mongering. Take the public hearings of the various parliamentary committees. At first, not many people attended. Now, they're packed. These meetings are helping to balance the two powers.'

'Some form of collapse or descent is inevitable,' a voice intoned. 'Corporate business may want to rescue the ruling party. I think they'd have to withdraw their support entirely for the descent to be complete. The other probability – it's closer to a certainty – will be a renewed hammering of whites, blaming them for apartheid, of course, and blaming them for current failures. It'll be the same old story. Nothing new. But what else will the ruling elite be able to do to maintain their power base and hence their power?

'What are the imperatives for South Africa right now? Good administration, definitely. And a system whereby the poor can legitimately enter the mainstream economy. But the winner-take-all system is providing neither. The obsession is with the retention of power. Did you know that in a study conducted about eighteen months ago, it emerged that most South Africans still considered the country to comprise various racial groups, and that they thought it was best that way. In fact, forty per cent – and that included millions of black people – said that these divisions should be acknowledged in the way the country was constituted. Don't we live in an interesting society?' the voice said.

'Yes,' another voice put in, 'the classic African pattern has been to ignore the under-class and bolster the ruling elite. Yes, it's happening here. But it's much more dangerous here. There's the question of the divisions within the ruling party. It is interesting that the Black Africanist view thrived in exile while the concept of a more pragmatic non-racial democratic model stayed alive in the hurly-burly of the actual struggle. But of course there's the question of white economic power, as well as the white role in the history of the country, to add into the mix. I think the country is living on a knife edge.'

I stopped listening to the voices after a while. The pundits and the players marched along the corridors of power. The drizzle descended onto wet cobblestones. Sometimes I walked in the fine rain to cool down. And it was that sensation, the cold moisture on my face, that returned me once again, and after many months, to my memory of the poet of the crash.

That young man, Mpumelelo, standing with me up there at the monument to Samora Machel on the green hillside at the beginning of my quest. His jacket and tie had flapped a little in the breeze of that remote and sorrowful place. We had listened to the wailing of the pipes. We had looked down into the pit at the pieces of the smashed aircraft. We had read the words that Mandela, still in prison, had written to Machel's widow whom he later married. Mpumelelo's eyes had been so clear. He had not been swayed by rumour. He had thought for himself.

His memory came to me in my car in the darkness one night. I drove on De Waal Drive, returning to my lodgings with friends. The road was wet, and as it curved along the first slopes of Table Mountain, a huge area of lights could be seen sweeping away into the north-eastern distance. One of my companions suggested in a melancholy way that each individual light in that galaxy probably represented one small point of human unhappiness. It was then that Mpumelelo returned, standing before me in my mind's eye while the drops of rain descended into our faces. I remembered his spirit exactly, that essential tenor of his presence. The compassion, the thoughtfulness. 'Everything is so difficult and it is also easy,' he had said. 'There is this tragedy, and then there is this love. There is always tragedy and love. And yet there are also enemies. And I think: why is it so easy to have enemies? I cannot find the answer. But I hear the pipes, and I think the answer must be in there, if I can one day understand.' He stood within me that night as I drove along De Waal Drive as a potent counter-argument to the thunder of the new, the pending, the dangerous. He seemed to me to speak of a layer of human experience beneath the seeming, and hence as the bearer of a deeper set of verities.

ELSIESRIVIER WAS a conglomeration of small houses packed together in narrow streets directly south of Parow, which itself was some fifteen kilometres from central Cape Town in the eastern suburban sprawl. When I saw this relationship between the two areas, I immediately remembered Russel van Rooy telling me about his early childhood spent in Elsiesrivier. 'Parow was the white shopping area,' he had recalled with one of his slow smiles. 'My aunt said: you can't go to Parow; you're too black. I thought this was unfair. My uncle was blacker than me and he went.'

I drove into Elsiesrivier with his aunt's directions firmly in my mind. Turn left into Owen Street and then left again into 47th, Connie Esau had told me over the telephone. I turned as instructed. In Owen Street stood grey tenement buildings, four storeys high, flat roofed, with dipping lines of washing crammed into the balconies. The lower walls were filled with graffiti, the yards blew with rubbish, children played, young people hovered about, leaning against walls, waiting for something to happen. Perhaps, I thought, it was where the tenements now stood that the Muslim shop with the two-roomed hut behind had been. So the tenements would have been the 'formal housing' that Russel found when he had gone in search of his earliest remembered home.

Connie Esau's house, from the street, looked modest but very neat. At the sound of my car she emerged from the front door to greet me, a short dumpy woman wearing a white T-shirt and dark tracksuit pants. We met in the front garden where she shook my hand. Her eyes were watchful, and filled with that initial reserve I had heard on the telephone. She invited me inside and we sat in the front room, a space made elaborate with doilies and ornaments and photographs in frames. In one of them I saw Russel, debonair and much younger, perhaps in his early twenties, looking over his shoulder at the camera while he did something in a kitchen. I remarked on the photograph, and Connie said: 'He's a lovely boy. I'm just cross that he never comes to see me any more.'

She looked at me expectantly, as if waiting for me to give an explanation for my visit. So I told her of my interest in Russel's Javanese connection, and in particular in the importance that Russel himself had seemed to attach to it.

'He's a proud boy,' Connie responded.

I wondered then, in the company of this reserved Coloured woman, whether perhaps the Coloured identity had not been too closely linked to the responses of white society. It was as if they had all lived for far too long vicariously through white eyes. Where was the conviction or validity in that? Almost certainly Russel had asked such questions. He had

273

reached a point, in Victoria West, where he believed he had no future with the whites. He saw himself, really for the first time, as a black person. But that too had brought disillusion. What was he to do? Return to the white side of the chasm in which he (and many others) perceived too many Coloureds to be living? That had seemed impossible. Therefore he went back, moving out of the in-betweener role to seek a deeper identity for himself, and this is where Java fitted into the picture. But perhaps Russel was not yet conscious of his own motives.

These thoughts flashed in upon me as I regarded his Aunt Connie with her tracksuit-clad legs stretched out before her.

'Tell me about the family's Java connection,' I said.

Connie said in her reserved voice: 'I know very little about Java.'

I asked her to tell me instead about herself.

'I was born in Bo-Kaap, you know, there at the top end of Cape Town. But we moved away when I was still young. Six or seven. We came to Elsiesrivier.'

She looked at me with a slightly pained expression. 'I'm sorry I can't help you. Elizabeth is coming soon.'

I tried to reassure her by saying that it was interesting for me to be in Elsiesrivier. It must have been even more interesting to have grown up here.

'People called it *"buite"*. That means it was outside Cape Town. We were eleven children, eight sisters and three brothers. But in the last three years, I have lost so many. First it was my son of 21 years; then a grandson; then two months ago I lost a sister to cancer; and now I've just lost a brother.'

An aircraft flew so low over the house that I paused in my response. 'All day and all night,' she said with a sudden laugh. 'The airport is just over there.' Yet the noise seemed to break the ice between us, and she spoke more easily after that – although from time to time she paused, wondering aloud where Elizabeth could be.

She told me that her mother (Russel's grandmother) had been a woman named Doreen who, having produced the eleven children, had died at the age of 39 years. They had moved from Cape Town in a so-called slum clearance programme, but it was actually, she said, the beginning of apartheid. She, Connie, had gone out to work at 15, so she had not been close to the family for long. Doreen had talked a lot about Java, she said, but she, Connie, had not been there to hear it. 'I have a photograph of my mother,' she said, 'wait, I will show you.'

She left the room momentarily. I remembered Russel as a university student, writing a play about his grandmother, this woman named Doreen who had lived in the Bo-Kaap streets, producing babies and communicating with her own father who had come from Java (or was it her grandfather who had come?), listening to memories from the old country, that green island somewhere far away across the sea. Now the woman's face was before me in a slightly blurred photograph: thin-lipped and determined, a handsome woman with both strength and patience in the quality of her expression.

I looked up at Connie and said: 'She really is rather beautiful.'

Connie said: 'That's the only photograph. It's enlarged from her ID picture.'

At this point Elizabeth arrived. She was immediately jovial with me, and she released Connie into a more relaxed joviality as well. Elizabeth was, I felt certain, the aunt who had said to Russel as a small child that he was too black to go to the white shops in Parow. Her sense of humour seemed slightly outlandish, and she enjoyed its effect on others. She had thin orange-coloured hair, and immediately mischievous eyes, dark and lively in a face creased with wrinkles. She had a bandage on one of her ankles, and she wore lace-up shoes on her tiny feet.

She told me that her son was a policeman who had just been promoted. 'I'm so proud,' she said. Then she related a story about two sisters, one almost black, the other almost white. 'I used to call them black and white scotch whisky,' she said. Connie went out to make some tea and Elizabeth chatted easily to me.

'Equal rights,' she said, somewhat dismissively. 'Whites and Coloureds working for freedom and all that, but they've got nothing out of it. I was locked up myself once. Let me tell you how it happened. The madam next door and my madam were Black Sash, and they took me to a meeting. I liked what I heard. I joined. A girl called Katie and me were good at reading and writing, so we did the notes. I had the notes in the house. Then the police came. They found the notes in my room. For two days me and Katie had to stand on our feet in the police station.

You should have seen my feet – swollen out like balloons. Then they let me go. But now? Now the South African rainbow is only black. They are now the only ones who ever did anything for freedom.'

She laughed quite cheerfully, stirring the tea that Connie had brought.

We began to speak about the family again. So there was Doreen and her husband, a man from Swellendam, Elizabeth remembered; and Doreen's father (Russel's great-grandfather) was this man from Java.

'His name,' Elizabeth said, 'was Suliman. Later he changed it to Solomons. He was the first from Java, I think. He came with some other people. They were artisans come to do building at the Cape.'

'About one hundred and fifty years ago,' Connie added.

Elizabeth nodded. 'I suppose he was an adventurous person looking for greener pastures.'

'He was a Muslim,' Connie said.

'Yes, but he married a Christian from Genadendal,' Elizabeth responded. 'The woman's religion always wins. Mind you, at the end of his life, he went to live at the mosque, probably in penance for becoming a Christian. But I think they lived a good life. Our mother – yes Doreen, Russel's grandmother – used to talk about a piano and a grandfather clock and a big sideboard. So they couldn't have been poor, living up there in Bo-Kaap.'

'Poor old mother,' Connie put in. 'She said you could always tell a Java. The slightly slanting eyes, the straight hair, the yellowish complexion. And then she goes and has all those children and dies so young. We're better off today.'

They sat together, these two sisters, and recited all the names of Doreen's children. Jacob, Adelaide, Frederick, Elizabeth, Peter, Constance, Caroline (Russel's mother who had married Jonty, the man from Wuppertal), and Enid and Avril and 'we've left out two but I just can't think who they are right now ...'

They accompanied me to the front gate when it was time to go. An aircraft flew in, seeming to aim directly at where we stood. It sailed low over the house, its wheels already lowered for landing.

When the noise had subsided, Elizabeth said: 'Sometimes I feel quite guilty. I pray every day that I'm still alive when the ANC becomes a minority. Maybe we are all traitors. But that's what I pray for.'

Connie laughed. They both laughed. They told me to come back soon and have more tea with them. 'If you see Russel,' Connie Esau called, 'tell him to visit.'

I drove off with the image of Russel firmly in my mind. I had an inkling of the complexity of his transformation. Had he not already found a way out of the valley of the in-betweeners? The Coloured past – in all its manifold variations – had itself been subsumed by this great need for external acceptance. Now he could follow the markers laid down by an acknowledgement of his personal past, thus emerging from the valley and standing upright, looking for confirmation neither to the left nor right, and thereby changing his position from acolyte to disentangled man. Perhaps one day soon he would rewrite the play about his grandmother. And perhaps this time it would come in the form of something that might serve as guide for his fellow dwellers in the in-betweener valley.

I WALKED up the steepening gradient of Wale Street to the Bo-Kaap Museum. Beyond the cross-cutting Buitengracht with its charging traffic, the architecture changed from city-centre monoliths to houses with front walls that extended into simply-adorned pediments concealing the front edge of the flat roofs. Bo-Kaap, literally translated, means above-Cape. It was certainly true that the city stood on lower ground beneath this tiny district where Connie Esau and Elizabeth had spent their earliest years, where their mother, Doreen, had been born, and where Doreen's father, Suliman the immigrant from Java, had first settled when he came as an artisan to the Cape. Or was it Suliman's father who had first settled there, after his slaving days were over? There seemed to be some doubt, but it hardly mattered. Some of the houses had been gentrified and painted in bright colours, but the essential flavour seemed to have remained, the narrow verandas, the small lanes between the houses giving access to the next street, young boys in Muslim clothes, a few women in saris talking on a corner.

The house in which the Bo-Kaap Museum was housed had been built in the 1760s. Other houses in the area were of a later vintage, representing a mixture of the Cape Dutch and English Georgian styles. I knew these things because I had bought a photocopied pamphlet from a friendly young black man at the entrance. The museum comprised five rooms furnished as if the house was still in use. In the sitting room, on a V-shaped wooden stand, had been set a large copy of the Koran; and on the walls two mirrors both decorated in Arabic calligraphy with texts from the Koran. In the pamphlet I had bought I read that the term Cape Malay (now replaced by Cape Muslims) had been used for all slaves imported to the Cape from the east because they shared a common language (Malayu or Malay-Portuguese) and not because they were from areas in modern-day Malaysia. In fact, none of them had come from there.

My attention was captured by the narrative unfolding on boards hung on the walls of the various rooms. Enlarged photographs brought an added atmosphere to the story. Slavery was finally abolished at the Cape in the 1830s. Thereafter the descendants of the slaves did much of the menial work in Cape Town, from construction labouring to domestic cleaning, and lived close to the city centre. By the late 1930s, however, the city council began to move people to specially built townships on the outskirts of the city, like Elsiesrivier. The process was completed by the apartheid government after 1950. There were photographs of men in fezzes, and of fezzes with black tassels which meant that the wearer had made the journey to Mecca; of children playing in the steep Bo-Kaap streets; of a fishmonger blowing his copper fish horn on the corner of Chiappini Street; of women and children gossiping on the front veranda of a Bo-Kaap cottage; of young men playing guitars; and of a joyful wedding in Upper Dorp Street in 1953. The sense of joy was in the movement of the procession through the dingy street, with the shadow of apartheid, the shadow of Elsiesrivier, approaching. It was in the lavish dresses and corsages, and in the flower girls and small boys in suits and shiny shoes and bow-ties, all coming down the narrow cobbled street with bystanders smiling and the bridegroom looking at his bride. I read in my pamphlet that the Cape Muslims played an important role in the economy of the early Cape, as tailors, fishermen, cobblers, carpenters and builders. In another place in the pamphlet I read that the slave ancestors of the inhabitants of the Bo-Kaap had come from many places in the world, but particularly from the area known today as Indonesia, from places like the Celebes and Sumatra – and also from Java.

I stood looking at the photograph of the 1953 wedding procession, and I could hardly understand why it should render me so vulnerable, so moved, so grateful that my past had never been obliterated or denounced. In a new volume of history I had glanced at in a Cape Town bookshop was this quotation from a Jewish novelist whose central obsession had been to record the destruction of European Jewish communities during World War II: *To live without a past is worse than to live without a future.* It was somehow for that reason that the wedding procession, as prelude to an uprooting, came to me so powerfully then. Connie and Elizabeth, and Doreen and her father Suliman, and the man from Wuppertal, and finally the slow-smiling Russel van Rooy, all of them markers in a personal past that had almost disappeared.

I drove up a steep road behind the crowded houses of Bo-Kaap. A row of dilapidated council flats occupied a ledge in the steeply rising terrain. Coloured youths with beanies pulled onto their heads looked at me without smiling. At the bottom of the hill, the flat roofs of Bo-Kaap spread out in their tight huddle, and in the middle of it I saw what I thought to be a pale green minaret. Beyond that stood the harsh skyline of the city and the steel grey waters of the bay. The rain descended in a steady stream. A group of young boys with curly hair and embroidered white skullcaps hurried past, one or two of them with newspapers held over their heads for protection.

I thought of the dance, then, those astonishing days when South Africans had rejoiced and stood in the queues to vote, when the taste of the idea of a universal franchise, of equality before the law, of new individual freedoms, of democracy and peace had lightly brushed the national palate, and nothing could ever be the same again. Now, in the rain, not much seemed to have changed. Yet the taste of democracy, once encountered, could not be eradicated. Was it simply this that my journey had taught me?

The changes that democracy had brought lay beneath politics, beneath power, beneath fear even. They were small changes in the heart, in the perception of self. They were like a renewed flow of oxygen after the constrictions of ideology and ruthlessness. Democracy had come to South Africa not so much through the Constitution, essential as the process of writing it had been, but through a million small messages straight into the individual heart. Here was the source of a new creativity, of new commitments and of a new ability to question. Here too was the possibility of claiming the right to individual idiosyncrasy, the right to an individual and collective past, the right to a similar future, the right to break the power of ideological cliché and demand, and to make those small secret victories against whatever mould imprisoned. I was certain that this is what had brought to so much of my journey a sense of lightness and buoyancy however bleak the foreground might have often appeared. Whatever was happening in the political arena, this is what unconsciously was being prepared in the earth beneath. Seeds were being planted there that would ultimately crack any new monolith of repression, or any power that celebrated its own continuance above a celebration of the human spirit. This, most essentially, was what the struggle and the celebratory dancing with democracy seemed destined to achieve.

At the Waterfront an encirclement of gulls screamed above a vessel going out to sea. A few irrepressible tourists stood outside a slate-clad building with the words *Nelson Mandela Gateway to Robben Island* emblazoned on its facade. The rain swept across the cobblestones; and the dark green water of the harbour, disturbed by the passing vessel, heaved against the stonework of the wharf. A ship's hooter sounded from a distant part of the docks. The sky was a deep grey. The buildings of the city centre seemed as if sunk backwards into the mists of distance. The mountain had disappeared. The gloom of the afternoon clung cold and wet and discomforting, and no lights anywhere had yet been turned on. Nevertheless, an essential vision and potential had been kindled and would now remain.